Linguistic Labor and
Literary Doulas

Linguistic Labor and Literary Doulas

Spanglish, Portuñol, and Judeo-Spanish Languages and Literatures

Remy Attig

BLOOMSBURY ACADEMIC
NEW YORK • LONDON • OXFORD • NEW DELHI • SYDNEY

BLOOMSBURY ACADEMIC
Bloomsbury Publishing Inc
1385 Broadway, New York, NY 10018, USA
50 Bedford Square, London, WC1B 3DP, UK
29 Earlsfort Terrace, Dublin 2, Ireland

BLOOMSBURY, BLOOMSBURY ACADEMIC and the Diana logo
are trademarks of Bloomsbury Publishing Plc

First published in the United States of America 2024

Copyright © Remy Attig, 2024

For legal purposes the Acknowledgments on p. xi constitute an
extension of this copyright page.

Cover design by Eleanor Rose
Cover image © Olga Shumytskaya / Moment / Getty Images

All rights reserved. No part of this publication may be reproduced or transmitted in any form or by any means, electronic or mechanical, including photocopying, recording, or any information storage or retrieval system, without prior permission in writing from the publishers.

Bloomsbury Publishing Inc does not have any control over, or responsibility for, any third-party websites referred to or in this book. All internet addresses given in this book were correct at the time of going to press. The author and publisher regret any inconvenience caused if addresses have changed or sites have ceased to exist, but can accept no responsibility for any such changes.

Library of Congress Cataloging-in-Publication Data
Names: Attig, Remy, author.
Title: Linguistic labor and literary doulas : Spanglish, Portuñol, and
Judeo-Spanish languages and literatures / Remy Attig.
Description: New York : Bloomsbury Academic, 2024. | Includes
bibliographical references and index.
Identifiers: LCCN 2024006456 (print) | LCCN 2024006457 (ebook) |
ISBN 9798765111000 (hardback) | ISBN 9798765110997 (paperback) |
ISBN 9798765111017 (ebook) | ISBN 9798765111024 (pdf)
Subjects: LCSH: Literature–Translations–History and criticism. | Spanglish
literature–Translations–History and criticism. | Portuñol literature–Translations –History
and criticism. | Ladino literature–Translations–History and criticism. |
Languages, Mixed–Translating. | Queer theory.
Classification: LCC PN241 .A885 2024 (print) | LCC PN241 (ebook) |
DDC 468/.02–dc23/eng/20240422
LC record available at https://lccn.loc.gov/2024006456
LC ebook record available at https://lccn.loc.gov/2024006457

ISBN: HB: 979-8-7651-1100-0
ePDF: 979-8-7651-1102-4
eBook: 979-8-7651-1101-7

Typeset by Integra Software Services Pvt. Ltd.

To find out more about our authors and books visit www.bloomsbury.com
and sign up for our newsletters.

Contents

Preface		vi
Acknowledgments		xi
1	Introduction to *Literary Doulas* and *Linguistic Labor*	1

Part I The Languages

2	Spanglish	23
3	Portuñol	45
4	Judeo-Spanish	61

Part II Queerness, Translation, and Translanguage

5	The Queerness of Linguistic Labor	77
6	Translating Linguistic Labor	89
7	Spanglish, Portuñol, Judeo-Spanish, and the Translingual	105
8	Conclusion	117
Bibliography		125
Index		160

Preface

Subject Position

The book that follows is born out of a personal quest to understand myself. As with most of us, I grew up believing that languages were fixed things and that informal ways of speaking were uneducated or wrong. As a child, I learned this belief by watching how adults reacted to people who spoke with different accents, categorizing both accents and speakers alike as elegant, crude, exotic, dangerous, patriotic, or treasonous. I learned that in America one is supposed to speak English, but not all Englishes carry the same weight. Likewise, I learned that when I spoke Spanish, I was supposed to resist the urge to mix in any English at all regardless of what others around me did when they weren't busy correcting me. Despite learning these ideologies, the way I actually spoke varied highly depending on the context, sometimes following the rules I had been taught and sometimes not.

As a child, I grew up speaking English and Spanish in Florida and traveling to Latin America frequently. Speaking English with teachers and Spanish in social contexts was a regular practice for me. Even though both of my parents spoke only English, I privileged social interactions with peers in Spanish, an atypical experience in the United States. Since only my peers were bilingual, not my parents or teachers, keeping Spanish and English separate with adults was essential and effortless, or so it would have appeared to an onlooker. But there was an unexpected comfort—one that perhaps monolinguals experience every day without knowing it, or perhaps one they'll never know—that came when I didn't have to keep my languages separate; in other words, when I spoke Spanglish.

Speaking Spanglish among friends was relaxing. I didn't have to find the "correct" word for a thought; I could just say whichever word seemed to fit, even if it wasn't in the "right" language. I knew that those who understood that, and who replied in kind, understood a piece of me that others didn't. It didn't feel like there was a barrier between me and those who didn't speak Spanglish, but rather an extra spark with those who did.

As an adult I moved to Canada where I learned French and spent a decade in the language contact zones of Ottawa—specifically the fully bilingual

French/English University of Ottawa—and Montreal. There I saw the same strict divisions between languages at some levels of society, but I also saw a constant renegotiation of linguistic boundaries as a shared experience between all of us. There, language was a playground, especially with others who spoke Spanish, French, and English. Word games and multilingual jokes (for example, why Marie-Maïs is a fantastic name for a drag queen) established strong in-group and out-group relationships that undermined the prescriptivist—indeed politicized—linguistic norms which often felt antagonistic coming from both sides.

After all, for many of us who grow up bilingual or live multilingual lives, the most comfortable option is to speak without constraints, using all the linguistic tools available to us. Sometimes this is at an individual communicative level, for example, translanguaging in educational settings (Otheguy, García, and Reid 2015). At other times, this can be highly public and performative, such as when a speaker seeks to demonstrate cosmopolitanism or a certain socioeconomic class (Attig 2019a). But this can also be a community-wide phenomenon (McClure and Mir 1995). The present study explores the latter situation.

Given my upbringing and personal life experience as a multilingual queer person, I was curious as to how shared this translingual experience actually is. So, I decided to use the tools from my disciplines of translation studies, sociolinguistics, and literary studies to explore further.

This Book

The resulting book was born from a very different question than the one that lies at the heart of the final project. My original question centered on how to translate the literature written in Spanglish, Portuñol, and Judeo-Spanish given the explicit choice of the authors to privilege writing the way that their communities speak rather than following the language conventions of the dominant society where they live. This was to see in part how we can be equitable in our translation practices, but also to understand how monolingual speakers of dominant language varieties understand the experience of multilinguals. To achieve that goal first required me to identify the extant literature in these three languages, and only later to consider how it has been translated. It was in that first step that I decided to shift directions when I noticed three major gaps in the field that I thought should be addressed before returning to the question of translation. Those three gaps form the core of this book.

First, in embarking on this project to understand Spanglish, Portuñol, and Judeo-Spanish literature in parallel, I noticed that there is no published research that considers these three language varieties together in a sustained way. While some sociolinguistics works consider Spanglish, Portuñol, and Judeo-Spanish in tandem, they're often mentioned only briefly as contact or diaspora varieties of Spanish—or, in the case of Judeo-Spanish, the bizarre claim is made that it is a living version of medieval Spanish. Given the geographic and cultural distance between Spanglish, Portuñol, and Judeo-Spanish, it's not surprising that few have looked at them side-by-side. At the same time, the many parallels that I've observed between these cultures, which will be explored at length in the pages that follow, have shown me that there is much to be gained by considering them collectively.

Second, relatively little scholarship has been dedicated to the way that literature is born to previously oral languages or the role that literature can play in language death. In the case of Spanglish, the emergence of a substantial body of Latinx literature, some of which is published in Spanglish, has been widely discussed, but in isolation from the other languages discussed here. Often extant studies consider such samples as written depictions of the oral registers of specific characters and are studied as idiolects. However, here I argue that these depictions are part of a larger community-wide and theoretically broad phenomenon. Similarly, linguistic anthropologists and anthropological linguists have said much about language revitalization, but often view language death or decline as a very different phenomenon to the shift from orality toward literary production. I argue that these two very different points in the linguistic lifecycle are intimately intertwined and require similar effort on the part of authors who choose to write in languages at both ends of their literary lifecycles. To that end, this book introduces two concepts: *linguistic labor*, as the term given to the emotionally charged work that such a transition from orality into writing demands or the mourning required as a language slowly declines, and the figure of the *literary doula*, the individuals who take it upon themselves to shoulder *linguistic labor*.

Finally, this book seeks to destabilize the concept of "hybrid" languages or cultures, not by discussing the term at length, though I do address it in the introduction and the conclusion, but rather by focusing on the stories of three languages that have often been considered to be "hybrid" and painting a picture of the separation they have from the influencing languages. The notion of "hybridity" was valuable when it was introduced, as the overwhelming epistemologies of the time had focused on perpetuating essentialist categorizations of language and culture; centers of power had languages and cultures, while the rest of the world had dialects and crafts. "Hybridity" was then indicative of that which lies between those centers of power and mixes them to varying degrees. In certain postcolonial contexts this may make sense, as a society may be stuck with relics of a colonial age that has imposed external systems and beliefs on a people. In such cases those systems or beliefs may be unevenly adopted by different segments of the population based on socioeconomic or educational divisions. It also may accurately describe the life experience of individuals such as recent immigrants, so-called third-culture kids, a term that is often applied to expat children who grow up with very different cultures at home and in the public sphere, and the like. However, the term "hybrid" has since been stretched and applied to large swaths of people who do not have these experiences. When applied to entire cultures or languages, the theoretical framework of "hybridity" perpetuates the idea that "hybrid" cultures and languages lie in between "real" languages and cultures that are sufficiently powerful so as not to be "hybrid." This is not necessarily intentional, and may be, in fact, at odds with the values and beliefs of many scholars of such communities. Nevertheless, the implications of this term can lead us to no other conclusion than that "hybrid" cultures are incomplete on their own and are but a mere mid-point on a colonial spectrum defined by national languages and cultures.

Similarly, the term translanguaging or translinguistics has been misinterpreted by many scholars who equate it with linguistic "hybridity." In Chapter 7 and in the conclusion, I will explore the distinctions between notions of hybridity and translanguaging and suggest some disciplinary shifts that need to take place for us to understand languages such as Spanglish, Portuñol, and Judeo-Spanish more accurately.

Concretely, this book demonstrates that Spanglish, Portuñol, and Judeo-Spanish should not be conceived of as poor facsimiles of languages and cultures but recognized as full languages and cultures that were influenced by different forces than those that have so far gained widespread prestige on the world stage. These languages and cultures are minoritized, but they are not inferior, nor do they strive to mimic the norms of these colonial paradigms and fail. Instead, they succeed at representing themselves against all odds.

Drawing from sociolinguistics, literary studies, translation studies, and other adjacent disciplines, this book provides a critical framework to allow us to recalibrate our understanding of linguistic lifecycles regardless of the languages or cultures in question. My hope is that this book will serve as a go-to overview for Hispanists interested in the literatures and peoples that the field often forgets.

Acknowledgments

I owe much of the success of this project to my colleagues in the Department of World Languages, the College of Arts and Sciences, as well as the Jerome Library at Bowling Green State University. Their support, both economic and personal, helped keep this project alive through a pandemic that prevented its progress for far too long. I'm also thankful to my friends and family members who have endured long and excited diatribes about my wild ideas and insatiable curiosity; they made a space where I was comfortable being me, and from that space has grown this book.

On a more personal level, quiero agradecerles a Cindy Ducar y a Pedro Porbén por su apoyo como mentores en mis primeros años en BGSU, no es poca cosa cruzar una frontera cerrada durante una pandemia para empezar un puesto nuevo. Ellos me recibieron y gracias en parte a sus consejos, I'm thriving.

También quisiera agradecerle a mi amigo y primer jefe (en la esfera académica), Wojciech Tokarz, que siempre ha creído en mi capacidad y que me ha apoyado tanto personalmente como profesionalmente. Le debo un montón por su fe en mí y por su esfuerzo por ayudarme a tener éxito en esta carrera.

Peter MacDonald, my closest friend, must of course be thanked directly. His emotional support through the tumultuous and stressful job search, the pandemic, and some major life overhauls has kept me from going completely crazy. I would not have had the strength that I had to make the decisions I needed if I had felt alone. Thanks to Peter, even in my roughest moments, I never did.

I also want to thank the love of my life, Miles. We met in the oddest of times and when neither of us was looking. But the Universe knew you were exactly what I needed. You kept me from working too hard but supported me when I did. Tusen takk!

1
Introduction to *Literary Doulas* and *Linguistic Labor*

In childhood we are told that our language is wrong. Repeated attacks on our native tongue diminish our sense of self. The attacks continue throughout our lives ... Until I can take pride in my language, I cannot take pride in myself ... Until I am free to write bilingually and to switch codes without having always to translate, while I still have to speak English or Spanish when I would rather speak Spanglish, and as long as I have to accommodate the English speakers rather than having them accommodate me, my tongue will be illegitimate.

(Anzaldúa 1999, 80–1)

Linguistic communities that reside at the geopolitical or metaphoric borders, described by Anzaldúa as "a vague and undetermined place created by the emotional residue of an unnatural boundary" and populated by "those who go through the confines of the normal," live in a space that is understood by some as between cultures (Anzaldúa 1999, 25). Postcolonial scholars have theorized these as "hybrid" in nature (Papastergiadis 2015, 274). But the notion of hybridity is still predicated on an understanding of culture that privileges dominant languages and defines as "hybrid" something that combines two or more dominant languages or cultures into a new one. This concept, however, often fails to recognize that the individual cultures that it attempts to describe have existed for generations and strive to define themselves as something greater than the sum of their multilingual and constantly evolving parts.

In these contexts, speakers of minoritized languages that are unrecognized by the larger societies in which they live—such languages are often viewed at best as vulgar or uneducated and at worst are actively repressed—must live their lives constantly translating their experience into the dominant language(s) of the societies in which they live. In these situations, public life and access to government services must be conducted in the official, be it de jure or de facto, language of the state and socioeconomic mobility depends on the ability to perform convincingly in the prestige varieties of those languages.

However, since the 1980s this established order has been challenged by some speakers of three minoritized language varieties in the Hispanic world: (1) Spanglish, conventionally defined as a language contact variety that blends elements of English and Spanish spoken mostly by Latinx communities in the United States; (2) Portuñol, a Spanish-Portuguese contact variety spoken in regions near the southern borders of Brazil; and (3) Judeo-Spanish, the romance language of the Sephardic Jewish diaspora in the Eastern Mediterranean. Speakers of these three languages have begun resisting the dominant monolingual publishing conventions of the countries in which they reside to battle for recognition of their own tongues and to advocate for the experience of their communities to be included as part of the collective imaginary of the places they call home. This *linguistic labor* and the authors who push such work forward, whom I have deemed *literary doulas*, are the topic of this book. In this introduction, we will consider the nature of this *linguistic labor* before turning our attention to the *literary doulas*. Literary doulas are, in short, the people whose activist writing serves to give birth to literatures for languages that had previously been oral, or who accompany a community as their language dies. We will go on to explore, in Part I, the specific case studies of Spanglish, Portuñol, and Judeo-Spanish and discuss examples of different ways the concepts of *linguistic labor* and the role of the *literary doula* are manifest in diverse contexts. Part II of this book focuses on approaching *linguistic labor* as outsiders and will address how *linguistic labor* and *literary doulas* are inherently queer, how such literature may—or may not—be translated for international audiences, and its relationship to the emerging body of translingual scholarship. In the conclusion, I discuss the challenges of presenting poststructural scholarship when the ideas are at odds with the available vocabulary. I close by raising some questions as to future applications of these theories in a transnational and poststructural world.

Linguistic Labor

This book introduces two terms that are theoretically and metaphorically intertwined: *linguistic labor* and *literary doulas*. The term *linguistic labor* describes the emotional work of writing, publishing, and conducting other language advocacy work (ethnography, language revitalization, etc.) for minoritized languages with which one identifies. Minoritized languages should not be confused with minority languages; minoritized languages may be spoken by a minority or majority in their geographies, what sets them apart is a history of being outlawed, stigmatized, or otherwise marginalized by colonial, governmental, class-based, or race-based structures of power. *Linguistic labor* is so named because it works against those powers that have dictated how language "should" be used if its speakers are to be worthy of respect and considered as full members of the imagined community that makes up an often linguistically determined nation (Anderson 2006, 44–5). Furthermore, this labor is restricted to members of the communities who speak these languages because, as we saw in the epigraph by Gloria Anzaldúa, their very identities are intertwined with the effort and outcome of their work in a way that cannot be true of work conducted by outsiders. Being recognized as an author or scholar who works to "save" or otherwise depict a minoritized language for their own advancement is quite different from being stigmatized for speaking the same language as a native tongue (Young, Barrett, and Young-Rivera 2014, 15–17).

Before considering the *literary doulas*, there are two principal characteristics of *linguistic labor* that are manifest through the languages and literatures studied in this volume which I'd like to discuss: (1) this work is a gendered form of emotional and unrecognized labor and (2) the literature consulted demonstrates a *surconscience linguistique* that clarifies that the choice to write in these languages rather than more dominant languages is an intentional rejection of the need to translate these communities' experiences for the dominant linguistic groups of the nations in which the authors reside (Gauvin 2000, 182).

Emotional Labor and Gendered Work

Linguistic labor is so named because, from an equity point of view, it mimics the emotional and unpaid labor that are typically associated with domesticity and are therefore gendered in nature. Emotional labor is defined as "[t]he work of trying to feel the appropriate feeling for a job either by evoking or suppressing feelings—a task we accomplish through bodily or mental acts" (Hochschild 2013, 25). This term is often applied to the so-called caring professions of nursing, childcare, respite care, and the like and is dominated by a female workforce (Nixon 2009, 307). While emotional labor can be well compensated—clinical psychology is one such example—Hochschild demonstrates that it's often devalued work that exploits the emotional connection of workers to the people or communities they are serving (Hochschild 2013, 27–31). It is often also a colonial and class-based form of work that outsources tasks that were traditionally performed in the home to lower paid workers so that members of higher socioeconomic classes can pursue more lucrative careers outside the home. Migrant female workers from Eastern Europe, Latin America, North Africa, South Asia, and the Philippines, for example, often must leave their own children behind to care for children or the elderly in other countries, sending money home, but requiring an even higher degree of emotional labor to regulate not only their emotions at work, but also the reality that they are not present to care for their own families (Hochschild 2013, 135–8).

In addition to being undervalued economically, emotional labor can be undervalued in prestige, as are other forms of gendered labor such as the service and hospitality industries where docility and deference to clients are highly valued (Nixon 2009, 302–5, Hochschild 2013, 77). Nevertheless, this gendered work is no less difficult. In fact, it is easy to see that the broad gamut of gendered work, and more specifically *linguistic labor*, is essential if a community is to remain healthy and vibrant (Glenn 2002, 70–1). The perpetuation of language use is so foundational to a community that should members decide not to engage in it the very existence of the linguistic community would be in danger. To promote that community language, which may not yet be viewed as being of great prestige—probably initially with no guarantee of remuneration or recognition—is, therefore, a form of gendered emotional work.

Though *linguistic labor* is gendered, I am not suggesting that all *literary doulas* are women; that is not the case. Nevertheless, this is gendered work since it promotes a recognition of the mother tongue that is traditionally viewed as belonging to the sphere of domesticity, rather than the prestige language of the public and professional sectors. In this case, domesticity is feminine and undervalued, while professionalism is masculine and held in higher esteem. Whereas teachers and authors of the dominant language are often praised and compensated for their work, teaching and writing of a minoritized language are rarely afforded the same recognition; instead, it is an essential practice seen by many as unworthy of a second thought. At best it is a labor of love that may result in some form of compensation through book royalties, for example, but to a much lesser degree than does work in the prestige language.

The parallel to emotional labor in the form of respite care is clear when we consider how *linguistic labor* manifests toward the end of a language's lifecycle.

As a language dies, *linguistic labor* takes the form of the heart-crushing work that prepares the community for that eventuality by creating post-vernacular cultural references such as songs, recipes, folktales, or other forms that preserve elements of the language for its descendants, but that do not require or foster fluency (Shandler 2004, 21).

On the other end of the linguistic lifecycle, at birth, this work is a different type of labor. When we consider the metaphor from a reproductive angle, *linguistic labor* struggles to give birth to a new literature for a language that was previously oral and, by extension, seeks to foster new prestige through the recognition of these art forms. That this is a form of labor rather than simply a creative endeavor is predicated on an understanding of language prestige that is founded on Bourdieu's assertions of symbolic power. He asserts that there are no power-neutral language exchanges and that language itself is inseparable from the power dynamics present between the speakers (Bourdieu and Thompson 2001, 37–40). In some cases, this is a power dynamic of equals and language can be used to signal common understandings as a type of in-group speech. Examples of this include: how Orthodox Jews may use English in ways that differ from a more standardized variety of English as a litmus test for belonging (Benor 2009) or how secrets may be told in code at once to obscure their subversive ideas from the authorities while communicating important messages to like-minded people (Lucas 1997, Barrett 2017, 4–6, Agence France-Presse 2020). On the other end of the spectrum, any linguistic exchange may demonstrate a power differential. Such cases would include how members of one socioeconomic class may speak down to or deferentially to another (Fanon 2008, 14), or the tendency of members of the privileged ethno-linguistic group to speak differently to other native speakers of the same language who look differently or whose names lead the former to imagine them to be immigrants, even when this is not the case (Flores and Rosa 2015, 159–62). The symbolic power inherent in any language exchange further exacerbates gender, class, and racial power distinctions because it has traditionally been the privilege of the wealthy learned men in positions of power who have been able to speak in whatever way strikes their fancy without the risk of being seen as uneducated; after all, they are the ones who set the standard. Often this perpetuates existing prestige or standardized language norms, which already reflect their peers' use of the language; but at times they are more liberal with their language use. In the latter case those members of the elite are not viewed as using language poorly, as would be the case if the speaker were from outside those structures of power, but rather they are praised for their creativity (Bourdieu and Thompson 2001, 69, Young, Barrett, and Young-Rivera 2014, 15–21). If we consider the language varieties discussed in this book, the histories of Spanglish, Portuñol, and Judeo-Spanish demonstrate that the power dynamics surrounding these languages have created a linguistic ecosystem which has prevented the speakers of these varieties from populating the halls of erudition. Instead, their language use has been seen as impoverished or ignorant forms of more prestigious languages. For them, the ability to be creative with the language is not a given; it must be fought for. In the context of the often linguistically determined national identity of the societies in which they live, speakers of these three languages, as we shall see, have a history of being seen as linguistic and cultural Others who distract from the establishment of an imagined ethnolinguistic nation.

A *Surconscience Linguistique* and the Rejection of Translation

Across the three linguistic communities studied in this book there is a recurring *surconscience linguistique*, a term coined by Lise Gauvin to describe a heightened awareness, on the part of the authors, of the language and the sociolinguistic positionality of their varieties relative to the dominant society (Gauvin 2000, 8–9). This notion will be further discussed in Chapter 7. Gauvin identified this tendency as a central element in Québécois literature over the centuries, stating that Québécois authors commonly speak openly about their decision to write in French in the larger Canadian context in which English was the language of the majority and of prestige (Gauvin 2000, 17–32). By extension, even when authors were not writing about a political matter, the choice to write in French in Canada was, nevertheless, a political act. Similarly, authors writing in Spanglish, Portuñol, or Judeo-Spanish frequently discuss the language itself. Sometimes this *surconcience linguistique* manifests in textual interventions, such as when Fabián Severo discusses his role as a language broker between his teacher and his mother (Severo 2017, 58). At other times the *surconscience linguistic* is paratextual in nature, with forwards or prefaces discussing the language use, but without significant reflection in the body of the text itself. An example of this is in Paul Allatson's foreword to Susana Chávez-Silverman's *Killer Crónicas* and her own preface entitled "Glossary Crónica," both of which discuss her use of Spanglish (Chávez-Silverman 2004, ix–xii, xix–xxi). Metatextual examples of the *surconscience linguistique* can be seen when textual or paratextual examples would be out of place. Matilda Koén-Sarano likely couldn't include textual references to Judeo-Spanish since most of her work consists of publications of folktales collected from the oral tradition, but she discusses her language use at length in her Judeo-Spanish-language memoir *Por el plazer de kontar* (Koén-Sarano 2006).

This heightened awareness across the board solidifies the notion that their writing is not merely creative, as it might be for authors writing in more central languages, but that it is iterative and political. It creates a tradition while reflecting on its position of minoritization both implicitly and explicitly through thematic choices and meta-commentary of both textual and paratextual nature.

Also central to this type of labor is a rejection on the part of the authors of translation. The term "translation" in this sense can refer to a few different concepts which are explored in more depth in Chapter 6: On the one hand, there is the idea of an interlingual exchange of information from a source text into a target text, which is what most people associate with translation. On the other hand, the term translation can also be understood to mean the breaking down of a concept and its reiteration for a different audience.

Some authors have, *a priori*, rejected this first idea of translation. When I first approached Susana Chávez-Silverman about translating some of her works, she hesitated, citing Gloria Anzaldúa's missive:

> Until I am free to write bilingually and to switch codes without having always to translate, while I still have to speak English or Spanish when I would rather speak Spanglish, and as long as I have to accommodate the English speakers rather than having them accommodate me, my tongue will be illegitimate
> (Anzaldúa 1999, 81)

Chávez-Silverman consented after understanding the theoretical underpinnings of my research. Rather than just being undesirable, some theorists have suggested that translating some of this literature is in fact impossible. Of Portuñol, María Jesús Fernández says, "Can this register be translated? Or better yet, can this identity be translated? We certainly cannot translate these fragments into one of the implicated languages, be it Spanish or Portuguese, without erasing the desired effect" (Fernández 2009, 88).[1] Despite this theoretical rejection of interlingual translation, the majority of authors of Spanglish, Portuñol, and Judeo-Spanish that I've worked with or studied have allowed their work to be translated.

On the other hand, Fernández's deeper question, whether the identity can be translated, is more fruitful in this instance. Considering the question from this

---

[1] Translation is mine.

angle and contextualizing Anzaldúa's previous quote, we can see that the larger question facing the authors and communities considered in this work is not whether a translator somewhere in the world can make their ideas accessible for a new audience; after all, there are a great many reasons translation may further the ideals of the authors themselves (Attig 2019c, 25–6). Instead, this rejection centers on the issue of the degree to which speakers of minoritized languages must work to render their identity and daily life accessible to those in positions of power in the absence of reciprocal effort in return. How much these various communities must struggle, and the limits placed on them if they refuse to do so, varies greatly. There are no blanket assumptions that can be made, though some tendencies will be explored in the following chapters. What is uniform in the literature and communities represented in this study is that authors have rejected this second understanding of translation. Rather than attempt to write minor literature in the Deleuzian sense—that is to say literature about a minority or minoritized group written in the language of the majority so that the latter can pretend to understand them—these authors have decided to write their experience in their own words (Deleuze and Guattari 1986, 16–17). To do this is no easy feat. It requires strong *literary doulas* who are willing to conduct the type of *linguistic labor* needed to dismantle the primacy of the dominant languages in their geographies, potentially with little to no recognition.[2]

Literary Doulas

Literary doulas is the term that I'm coining here to describe the people who conduct the work of *linguistic labor*. This term is inspired by the role of the doula as a support worker who aids in childbirth or, in the case of death, the death doula who provides support for a dying person and their family. *Literary doulas* either facilitate the birth of literature to what was formerly an oral language and/ or use literature as a form of linguistic palliative care for a community whose traditional language is dying. But who are these people?

Since we began this discussion by referencing Bourdieu, it is pertinent to return to him and debunk some myths about who he suggests might lead this

---

[2] On several occasions I mention the idea that these authors may receive little to no recognition for their labor. The risk of that is real, but the outcome for the authors considered here is that their work has "made it" on an international level or else I would likely not have come across it, but that is not true of all *literary doulas*. Some may never receive this level of renown through no fault of their own.

charge. He asserts in the early 1980s that "as sociolinguists have often observed, women are more disposed to adopt the legitimate language (or the legitimate pronunciation): since they are inclined towards docility with regard to the dominant usages" (Bourdieu and Thompson 2001, 50). The problem with this assertion, which may have appeared to be supported if not for the blatant sex-based stereotypes that have long since been discarded, is that sociolinguists have found the opposite to be true since the 1990s. Labov problematizes Bourdieu's view by demonstrating that gender is, after all, a social construct and that there is nothing inherently biological about how language is used—nevertheless, at the time, many of the linguistic corpora classified language use based on a binary understanding of gender. However, even if we were hypothetically to accept the gender binary, men only appear to use a higher frequency of nonstandard language forms than women where there is a stable sociolinguistic stratification, meaning power dynamics are clearly established in the language and that said language is not undergoing significant change (Labov 1990, 205). Where that stability is not the norm, such as with language varieties that are dynamic and do not have clear prestige varieties or established literary norms, he concluded that women are more inventive with their language use and tend to be agents of language change far more than men (206). After all, women traditionally had roles much more restricted to domestic spaces where their language prestige was under less scrutiny than in the public sphere which was dominated by men. Consequently, mothers could pass their linguistic creativity on to their children who could then spread that change more widely across society.

More recently, we have also come to understand that queer folk are also agents of language change (Livia and Hall 1997, Leap and Boellstorff 2004, Tagliamonte and D'Arcy 2009, Epstein and Gillett 2017, Robinson 2019). While causation is not widely addressed in the research, it can be assumed that a similar dynamic to the one discussed above would also apply to queer people. We know that professionalism and prestige are dictated by cis-hetero-masculine norms. Femininity and visible queerness, then, must often be minimized by women and queer people who aspire to access professional spaces or those of high prestige; this is often true even in progressive societies. Consequently, it should come as no surprise that women and queer folks are often denied access to the positions of power that inform and perpetuate prestige language varieties.

In the case of Spanglish, Portuñol, and Judeo-Spanish there is significant variation in the demographics of the *literary doulas*. In Spanglish and Judeo-Spanish, for example, women and queer folks make up the vast majority of the authors. In Portuñol, most are cis-men. Nevertheless, they are all taking a language that had been traditionally relegated to the domestic sphere and forcing it into public spaces. In so doing, they are seeking not to conform to the patriarchal systems of language prestige, but to redefine the notion of language itself outside that paradigm.

In Part I of this book each language will be explored in turn with a focus on the language's history, the struggle for recognition, and with a brief discussion of one or two *literary doulas* working in the language. Part II is dedicated to theoretical and practical implications that the theories of *literary doulas* and *linguistic labor* have on the fields of queer theory, translation, and linguistics and vice versa.

But Are They Languages?

Throughout the book, I work from the translinguistics-informed assumption that Spanglish, Portuñol, and Judeo-Spanish are languages in the same way that Spanish, Portuguese, and English are languages.[3] Still, despite my convictions, it seems pertinent that I discuss this terminology from the outset, particularly since terms like language, dialect, language mixing, or linguistic hybridity are often used without a full discussion of the implications of these terms. To address this terminological quandary, there are three problems we must consider that touch on the linguistic and ideological implications: (1) what is a language and what is a dialect, (2) what do native speakers have to say about the matter, and (3) what does it mean to associate a community's linguistic production with the notion of "mixing" and "contact"?

Language vs. Dialect

What is a language and what is a dialect? This seemingly innocuous question is usually a follow-up question asked by those with an interest in disciplines such as literature or cultural studies which are often defined by the languages they study. However, for a sociolinguist this is a difficult question to answer.

---

[3] Some linguists who study translinguistics might assert that none of these are languages. Regardless of the approach, we would agree that there is no empirical difference that would indicate that some of these are languages and others are not.

This question can imply one of two separate lines of inquiry. First, some ask because they are inclined to associate the term "language" with a variety that has reached a plateau and is in a place of slower or more stable evolution. Of course, all languages continue to change even after they've been standardized, but the asker who seeks an answer to this first line of questioning is usually wondering if the language varieties that I study have reached some pivotal point in linguistic evolution that objectively sets them apart as a language rather than as a dialect. Unfortunately, such a clear line simply doesn't exist.

On the other hand, there is a more conservative line of inquiry that this question may imply, one of standardization or prestige. When this is the line of thinking that the asker is hoping to have answered, we are dealing with definitions of the terms "language" and "dialect" that are not used by linguists. A "language" is often misunderstood as being a standardized way of speaking and writing that is official to a state or jurisdiction—though there are many languages that are neither standardized nor official. On the other hand, a dialect is often erroneously believed to be an incorrect, ignorant, uneducated, regional, or lower-class attempt at speaking a language. In reality, standardized varieties of languages are only standardized because they are spoken by those in positions of power who took the trouble to codify them (Penny 2003, 10–12). Once codified, the social classes who established the newly canonized form use it to measure the legitimacy of other speakers against it; those who speak differently are said to speak in dialect. By extension, those who do not speak like those in positions of power were judged as lesser; to aspire to power was to learn to mimic the speech patterns, among other things, of powerful people (Fanon 2008, 2–9). In other words, the distinction between language and dialect is largely ideological.

That this distinction is ideological rather than empirically defined, however, does not mean that it is easily overturned. Consciously and unconsciously, linguistic ideologies serve a great many functions in our daily lives. They are part of the collective imaginary that defines who belongs in a nation (Anderson 2006, 44–5). Such ideologies inform our opinion as to the veracity or trustworthiness of our interlocutor. They allow us to identify people with whom we may share a bond and dismiss those with whom we likely do not. In some instances, these ideologies may seem harmless enough, but they can also exclude, ostracize, and perpetuate racist or ableist views (Lippi-Green 2012, 101–29). In extreme cases, we see examples of raciolinguistic ideologies that promote the view that some people are languageless, theoretically unable to communicate complex ideas, despite evidence to the contrary. Often the targets of these ideologies are those who in fact command two or more languages. Rather than seeing their bilingualism/multilingualism as an asset, the ideology of languagelessness suggests that because one language may influence the other, resulting in the speaker having a perceived accent in one or many languages, that they do not command any. In some cases, the so-called languageless person has completed advanced study or held positions of certain prestige and responsibility. Despite these accomplishments, in the minds of those who espouse these beliefs, their bilingualism subtracts rather than adds to their linguistic competency (Rosa 2019, 125–43). In the US context, this argument is most often applied against Latinx people, regardless of their citizenship or country of birth, but it has also often been levied against Deaf people by those who believe signed languages to be inferior forms of communication and against African Americans whose language use—known as African American Vernacular English (AAVE)—has been stigmatized. Other linguistic ideologies have occasionally promoted quite harmful nationalist ethno-linguistic unification initiatives that we'll explore in the case studies of Spanglish, Portuñol, and Judeo-Spanish later in this book.

Despite these ideologies, however, there is nothing intrinsically superior about a language or inferior about a dialect. In fact, linguists refer to both as "varieties." Consequently, a prestige variety of the language—that variety that has been standardized and is spoken by those in positions of power—is only one of many varieties in use at any time, and all of them have the same capacity to express complex ideas. Potowski and Shin illustrate the idea of language varieties by likening them to flavors of ice cream: one may prefer one flavor to another, but there is no intrinsic superiority of any (Potowski and Shin 2019, 2–3). All varieties are ice cream, they assert, they are simply different types.

This raises the question, if there is no difference between language and dialect, where are the limits? Language lies on a spectrum; some varieties are closer to the standardized form and others are more remote. If we take the ice cream metaphor one step further, we can consider that there are seemingly endless possible flavors of ice cream, each representing a variety of one language. Similarly, there are seemingly endless varieties of soup, each representing a variety of a different language. At first glance the distinctions between ice cream and soup seem clear, one is cold, sweet, and served on a cone; the other is hot, savory, and served in a bowl. But what of cold gazpacho or a bowl of artisanal garlic flavored ice cream? What if the former is frozen or the later melts? There is a line, but sometimes it's quite hard to find and is not always as useful as it may initially appear to be. From a purely theoretical perspective, how far one variety must be from another to be considered its own language is complicated and is debated on a case-by-case basis, but there are certainly no universal lines in the sand (Penny 2003, 10–20). This brings us to the second point we must consider when responding to this question: social factors may also determine what is or is not a language.

Language and Self-Identification

The importance of self-identification is central to this study, and we'll consider it from a variety of angles. As a first step, let's explore how sociolinguistics approaches the matter of linguistic self-identification and why I rely on these views to support my assertion that Spanglish, Portuñol, and Judeo-Spanish are their own languages.

Self-identification and the role it plays in classifying languages are another linguistic ideology that can't be overlooked. How one identifies can be as big a factor in determining the language one speaks as are grammatical differences. Some examples of this type of ideology can be seen in a variety of contexts. For example, why do Brazilian and Portuguese people both say they speak Portuguese but Galicians, whose language demonstrates more overlap with northern varieties of Portuguese than do some varieties of Brazilian Portuguese, say they speak Galician? Why are Valencian and Catalan considered by some to be separate languages while others view them as varieties of the same language? What about the many varieties of Arabic, the Slavic Balkan languages, or the diverse varieties of Chinese? In some cases, like Arabic, a common religious heritage and scripture may be enough to unite disparate language varieties, many of which are not mutually intelligible. On the other hand, separate religious and ethnic identities and related historical tensions may suffice to determine that language varieties with significant overlap go by different names. A good example of this are the languages of the former Yugoslavia: Serbian, Bosnian, Croatian, or Montenegrin. National unity ideologies, such as those of the People's Republic of China, promote the belief there is one Chinese language with many dialects, never mind that Chinese citizens would be unable to speak to each other if it were not for the mandatory teaching of Mandarin across the country. National linguistic-unity ideologies, such as those in China, or independence ideologies, such as those of the Balkans, can be assimilated into the collective imaginary by the populace who may then self-identify with the promoted ideology.

Here again we see that the division between what is and what isn't a language is messy business with no clear and defined answers. To ask, then, if Spanglish, Portuñol, and Judeo-Spanish are languages is, from a sociolinguistic point of view, to ask if the speakers believe they are, and as we will see in more detail one by one, it would seem that to varying degrees they do.

Language Mixing/Contact Varieties

Finally, what are the implications of suggesting that Spanglish and Portuñol are merely "language mixing" or, in linguistic terms "contact varieties"?[4] A more bizarre assessment is often made of Judeo-Spanish, which some view as a living relic of medieval Spanish, nevermind that it has also evolved for hundreds of years since the end of the Middle Ages. Similar to the first question addressed, the idea that one thing is a language and another is a dialect is a rather arbitrary distinction. Consequently, to decide that these are not languages is an equally arbitrary declaration. But what we tend to mean when we suggest that something is "language mixing" or a "contact variety" is that it has emerged as the product of close interaction between two languages that each have some degree of standardization and international recognition. "Language mixing" and "contact varieties" are understood to not have that degree of linguistic stability. The result of a close interaction between languages is similar in some ways to pidgins, which may become more stable as they evolve into creoles. A major difference, however, is that pidgins tend to evolve when people who speak different languages need to communicate. They bring forms of their various languages together and create a new form that they can all understand. Pidgins emerge to fill a void. This situation does not apply to Spanglish or Portuñol; instead, speakers of these two languages consistently display high levels of fluency in Spanish and either English or Portuguese. Spanglish and Portuñol, then, evolved not from a void, but rather from a surplus of language. That is to say that everyone can understand both influencing languages and thus one is able to move fluidly between them to some degree or another.

---

[4] "Language mixing" and "contact varieties" are nearly synonymous terms. The former tends to be used in informal settings or by those with more prescriptivist approaches to language use; the latter term is a linguistics term that is more common in descriptivist contexts. Nevertheless, both terms, when viewed through a postcolonial lens, present similar problems, so they are discussed together.

If we were to isolate the question of linguistic evolution and consider it from a purely theoretical perspective, I can see why Spanglish and Portuñol would be classified as "contact varieties." But we cannot isolate languages from their cultural context. When we look at the language evolution in its social context, we see that both Spanglish and Portuñol have evolved in diglossic communities over the course of several generations.[5] Furthermore, while isolationist disciplinary-specific approaches have an important place, the most fruitful new scholarship comes by considering how multiple different disciplines can inform a topic. In this instance, a purely linguistic definition can obscure the larger implications of the terms "language mixing" or "contact variety." A more holistic understanding comes to light when viewed through a postcolonial lens. Scientists like to believe that the research they conduct and the empirical findings they observe are objective; however, we know that the questions they ask, and therefore the answers they find to those questions, are culture-bound. The discipline of linguistics is no exception. When we categorize languages as "contact" or "mixing," the implications clearly suggest that they are "hybrid" in nature and lie somewhere between real languages. We'll consider hybridity more holistically later in this chapter, again in Chapter 7, and in the conclusion, but, for the purposes of the question at hand, an excessive focus on how a language evolved can risk delegitimizing the language as merely derivative or impure. After all, contact and mixing have played a significant role in the evolution of a great many languages. Similarly, referring to a language as a list of lexical, grammatical, or other linguistic elements (i.e., "Spanglish is code-switching" or "Judeo-Spanish is a living relic of medieval Spanish") is reductionist and doesn't consider the previously mentioned social elements or the identities of its speakers.

Furthermore, such a focus on evolution or linguistic features perpetuates harmful ideologies that promote European or Anglo-American varieties of language as pure while others—often languages that were colonized or are the product of the colonial process—are contaminated. We saw an example of this moments ago: African American Vernacular English (AAVE) uses three adjectives to set it apart from what might be described, but is not, as White

---

[5] Diglossia is a linguistic situation in which more than one language is circulating in a society, but where there are clear differences as to where the languages are used. One may be used, for example, in education, government, and business transactions while another language may be reserved for home or more relaxed environments. This contrasts with bilingualism in which both languages are understood to be on similar footing and available for use in a wide range of settings.

American vernacular English.[6] Instead, the name English, unmodified by racial or situational adjectives, is understood to be the form of speech that whites use and that which deviates from it is marked as Other. AAVE isn't the only example of this; due to racist hierarchies that are fundamental to the organization of the Americas, these so-called impure varieties of the language are often associated with racialized others, be they the descendants of Africans who arrived on slave ships or the survivors of indigenous genocides. Consequently, the fear of language mixing and of the perceived contamination of normative European or Anglo-American varieties of languages is intimately intertwined with racial purity ideologies. It is not a stretch to say that arguments that promote language purity, which are still entertained in many circles, have become the successor for racist and anti-miscegenation rhetoric that is now taboo. Instead of perpetuating these outdated beliefs, I would suggest that we reflect on the great number of borrowings from French in English or the presence of Arabic vocabulary in Spanish and ask ourselves why we have such little trouble accepting English, Spanish, and Portuguese as languages but tend to qualify Spanglish and Portuñol as merely "contact varieties."

In short, my answer to the question of whether or not Spanglish, Portuñol, or Judeo-Spanish are languages or dialects is twofold. First, for the purposes of this study, it doesn't matter. Whether theoretical linguists would categorize Spanglish, Portuñol, and Judeo-Spanish as independent languages, by their linguistic features, or as contact varieties is a separate issue to how speakers see themselves. No pronouncement one way or the other on these matters can diminish the fact that these varieties are being written and spoken despite the societal prejudice against them. Instead of categorizations, descriptive adjectives, or reductionist arguments, what matters is that the speakers, as we shall see, determined that their own linguistic identities were not represented in the literature that they saw around them. Consequently, they decided to write the way they spoke. Second, from a sociolinguistics perspective, given the several-centuries-long history of each of the communities studied, the collective self-identification with these languages, and the emerging literature, perhaps it is time that we considered them as languages. After all, the boom in publication of literature in Spanglish, Portuñol, and Judeo-Spanish is not that different from when, in the Middle Ages,

---

[6] Some are moving away from using the adjective "vernacular" when discussing African American English.

people in Castile, Île-de-France, Florence, and Lisbon got tired of writing Latin and decided to write in what we now understand and accept without question as the languages of Spanish, French, Italian, and Portuguese.

Part I: Case Studies

Part I of this book considers Spanglish, Portuñol, and Judeo-Spanish as individual case studies. These chapters each address the history and evolution of one language as well as the sociolinguistic positionality of that language relative to the national prestige varieties of the larger societies in which the speakers live in order to illustrate how minoritization materializes in each instance. Starting from that understanding, we can come to see how the work of the *literary doulas* of these languages is the type of *linguistic labor* that has previously been defined. To arrive at this goal, I describe the following three key points for each of the language varieties discussed:

First, I consider the sociolinguistic status and positionality of these languages. To achieve this goal, I discuss the evolution of each language, describe some linguistic features that set it apart, and consider where and by whom it is used.

Second, I turn my attention to how the notion of *linguistic labor*, as described in this introduction, applies to each specific case study. In every instance I present the history of writing in the language variety and explore how literature has emerged and evolved over the years. To contextualize the minoritized nature of these languages, we'll also consider government and societal actions that have actively suppressed these communities or persecuted the use of these languages over time.

Finally, I consider select *literary doulas* who personify the theories discussed in this book. In some cases, these linguistic activists have written themselves quite explicitly into their work, in other cases, less so. To the degree possible, we'll see how their lives, their motivations, and their beliefs about their own communities intertwine to inform their work. While some languages studied, such as Judeo-Spanish, have clear *literary doulas* who take center stage, others like Spanglish have a great deal of such figures. These case studies are not exhaustive but provide enough context to exemplify and illustrate the role of the *literary doula* as it exists in society and beyond merely the theoretical. My hope is that others will expand upon my ideas and apply them to a wider range of doulas and languages in the future.

Part II: Linguistic Labor and Interdisciplinarity

Following the case studies, the book takes a more interdisciplinary turn to consider the role of *linguistic labor* and *literary doulas* more broadly. Chapter 5 builds from the concrete observed examples to consider *linguistic labor* as an inherently queer art form, as alluded to briefly above. It is an approach to literature that seeks to break with prestige, public, or official manifestations of language and thrust real-world language use into the public eye. This chapter connects *linguistic labor* to Tim Dean's *Beyond Sexuality*, Jack Halberstam's *Queer Art of Failure* and Paul Preciado's *Countersexual Manifesto*.

Chapter 6 considers the relationship of such activist writing to translation. While Anzaldúa suggested that her language and identity should not be translated, but rather that those in positions of power should do the work to access her ideas on her own terms, there are a great many reasons that literature such as this might be translated which go beyond market-based motivations. Some examples would include south-to-south translation or transnational solidarity work. This chapter will discuss those possible motivations and consider how translators can work in solidarity to ensure a respectful rendering of this work in other linguistic contexts.

Chapter 7 situates these languages within the emerging work on translinguistics. Translinguistics is an orientation that opposes, in many ways, the traditional understanding of code-switching. Code-switching is predicated on an understanding that languages exist as discrete codes that speakers can then switch between as they speak. Translanguaging, however, understands linguistics differently. From a translingual perspective, we understand that language exists in the mind of speakers as a single complete system, regardless of how many languages one might speak. Speakers then choose the features of language that best fit the situation in which they find themselves, mixing and matching to fit the context. In this chapter I dive into the implications that translinguistics has on the study of Spanglish, Portuñol, and Judeo-Spanish and consider how these languages further illustrate the points raised by translinguistics as a disciplinary orientation.

In the conclusion chapter, I explore the challenges that emerge when conducting scholarship in the absence of compatible vocabulary. I also suggest that while the experiences and contexts may vary greatly across the linguistic communities studied in this book, I suspect that there is a certain universality to the notions of *linguistic labor* and *literary doulas* that can be applied to language communities well beyond the Hispanic communities I've considered. As we look to the dominant languages in today's global marketplace, it's evident that *linguistic labor* and *literary doulas* have left their marks. Looking forward, I am excited to observe and speculate on the effects of the *literary doulas* working today and learn about those working in languages with which I am unfamiliar.

Part I

The Languages

2

Spanglish

In the collective imagination of many Anglo-Americans the establishment of large communities of Hispanic peoples in the United States dates to the post–Second World War period. The emergence of Spanglish as a colloquial contact variety of Spanish/English mixing, many assume, was the result of this immigration. But the story of Spanglish is more nuanced than this. Hispanic communities have lived in what is now the United States for hundreds of years; in many cases they predate the incorporation of their respective lands into the current borders of the country. Prolonged contact between Spanish and English has profoundly impacted language use since at least the 1800s in some communities. In others, immigration from Latin America or circular migration between Latin America and the United States has created a different type of language-contact situation—one with a shorter history.

In this chapter I begin by providing a linguistic overview of what I mean when I speak about Spanglish, as the term is used differently by different people and some people prefer a different term all together. I then look at how a plurality of Spanglishes evolved into predominantly oral registers, and later into a written language. As the chapter continues, we will look at the *linguistic labor* which prompted the emergence of the first published examples of Spanglish in poetry and fictional dialogue (in theatre and prose). More recent examples of the language in music, prose (rather than dialogue), and TV/film will be discussed. The chapter closes by considering the *linguistic labor* and lives of two notable *literary doulas* who have been influential on the post-1980s boom in Spanglish publication.

The Linguistics of Spanglish

Spanglish is the name given to a group of language varieties that transcend, redefine, and resist the linguistic borders of English and Spanish. Some have referred to this as radical bilingualism and others understand it as translanguaging or code-switching. These terms all bring with them a certain posture and a particular set of linguistic tools which are considered in more depth in Chapter 7 and in the conclusion; at this point in the conversation, however, we'll accept that for many those terms reference a similar linguistic reality. In addition to these criteria, and since all the media and cultural context considered in this book are from the United States, we will further define Spanglish as being the product of US-based Latinx communities.[1]

While myriad varieties of Spanglish exist, they do have some elements in common that allow us to discuss them together. Most importantly, all mix elements from English and Spanish as a result of centuries-long use of both of these colonial, and later national, languages in geographic and social proximity to each other (Stavans 2000b, 29). Spanglish can be, but is not only, the result of postwar immigration from Latin America to the United States. Similarly, it is not typically an auxiliary language that serves as a stepping stone that new immigrants use while they are learning English. Furthermore, it is anything but a monolith or a standardized language variety nor do its speakers aspire for it to become one. Spanglish is spoken differently by different populations and in different regions of the country—each speaker brings to it influences from the varieties of English and Spanish that they navigate in their own lives. Of her own language use Susana Chávez-Silverman remarked the following:

> My idioma, 'tis of thee. Bueno, mi lengua … is a hybrid? Nah! Demasiado PoMo, trendy, too Latino Studies (even if it's true). Been there, done that. A verrrrr, mi lengua …. Es un palimpsesto? Sí, eso está mejor. It's a sedimentation of … hmm. […] it circles back, flashes patrás, wildly inappropriate, really, to the last port en el cual eché ancla.
>
> (Chávez-Silverman 2004, xix)

That individuals navigate language differently is far from novel; we are all shaped differently by the linguistic borders that we cross and the paths by which we do so.

The linguistic borders between Spanish and English in a North American context, however, should not be conflated with the 3,200 km geopolitical boundary that marks the division between the United States and Mexico, but

---

[1] There is a variety of Spanglish known as Llanito which is spoken in the British Overseas Territory of Gibraltar, but the history of this context is quite different to that of US-based Spanglish, so it won't be discussed here. It's also important to note that Spanglish in Canada and other English-dominant societies does not seem to have the same uptake as in the United States.

rather to a larger Anzaldúan concept of borderland—that of a porous division that is in constant flux. According to this definition, Chicago, Miami, New York, Los Angeles, and even the very capital of the country, Washington, DC, are all linguistic borderlands with large populations of Spanish speakers living amid a larger Anglophone majority. Spanglish is the unofficial language of these borderlands and speaking it is a way of saying, "I belong to two worlds and can function in either, but I am most at ease when I can shift back and forth from one to the other" (Zentella 1982, 54).

For the sake of establishing a common understanding, we can describe Spanglish as containing elements such as code-switching, calques, homophonic translations, and relexification of terms that deviate from the standardized uses of English and Spanish. At first glance, Spanglish may seem to be haphazard, random, or disorganized, but linguists have observed that it has an internally consistent grammar that requires a high degree of fluency in both influencing languages, rather than a deficiency in one or the other, for speakers to be able to code-switch fluently (Toribio and Rubin 1996, Becker 1997). This is because code-switching must take place between utterances in a way that preserves the phonetic and syntactic integrity of both the Spanish and English parts of the phrase (Poplack 1981, Budzhak-Jones and Poplack 1997). Despite the role that code-switching has in Spanglish, this language is more than just that.

Another aspect of Spanglish that stretches its definition beyond merely code-switching is Inverted Spanglish. Jonathan Rosa coined this term to refer to the use of homophonic or calque translations from Spanish into English as a source of in-group humor (Rosa 2015, 43). One such example is "pink cheese, green ghosts, cool arrows" (for "pinches gringos culeros"). In this example we see that the speaker has used homophonic translation to replicate the sound of the Spanish utterance "pinches gringos culeros" using English words. The resulting "pink cheese, green ghosts, cool arrows" requires fluency in English to create and Spanish to decipher. Without this bilingual fluency, a listener would be unable to link the English words to their homophones in Spanish. However, for fluent bilinguals, jokes like these create a liminal space of creative transgression against the linguistic standards that are often imposed from both sides, from the Anglo world and the Hispanosphere.

Calques can serve a similar role to homophonic translations. Calques are literal translations between languages that may obscure the sense of the word to outsiders. For example, the Cuban expression comer mierda (noun: comemierda) and the English expression "eat shit" do not mean the same thing; despite that, a calque translation between the two would suggest they do. Comer mierda is more accurately understood as goofing off or, in its noun form, as a dumbass. Still, in a Miami Spanglish context, it's not uncommon to hear people using the English term "eating shit" to mean goofing off. These calque translations depend on bilingual fluency, but also on the ability to navigate between mid-points that are neither English nor Spanish, but something else entirely.

These strategies which rely on bilingualism (and more accurately, Spanglish) to convey meaning can often shelter speakers from the opinions of outsiders who may only be able to access fragments of the message. This was likely the case in Rosa's observation, as he was studying language use in a high school context where students may risk running afoul of their teachers or other classmates should their insults be too direct.

Another aspect of Inverted Spanglish, according to Rosa, is the appropriation of an intentional English accent in Spanish—known as mock Spanish when employed by Anglos to stigmatize Spanish speakers—as a way of "performing particular identities that are unique to the US context" (Rosa 2019, 145).[2] When Latinx speakers use Spanish expressions but with a forced English phonology, they highlight the pan-ethnic and transnational nature of US Latinx identities— that is to say that Latinx people come in all phenotypes and with many linguistic backgrounds—while simultaneously indicating that the speaker can speak English without an accent but is instead choosing to speak Spanish (Rosa 2015, 43–4).

Given everything that Spanglish is, why am I arguing that it's not a register that English-second-language learners use while they achieve mastery in their new tongue? There is certainly some space for this in a mutable and highly idiolectal language like Spanglish. But, as we've seen, a high degree of fluency is required in both English and Spanish for a speaker to code-switch fluently and to be able to play the standardized languages off each other through relexification, calques, and homophonic translation. This bilingual reality is commonplace in US Latinx communities in a way that is uncommon in the Spanish-speaking world.

In Latin America Spanish and English mixing occurs in different ways and for different purposes. In Puerto Rico, for example, Englañol—a name given by Rose Nash to the English of Puerto Rico—is dominated by direct syntactical and phonetic carry-over from Spanish into English and shows frequent use of false cognates in English. Englañol does not demonstrate significant lexical

---

[2] On mock Spanish, see Callahan (2014).

borrowings or code-switching, perhaps because the use of English in Puerto Rico is an attempt to access certain professional contexts where such linguistic practices would be more of a barrier than an entry point (Nash 1971). Similarly, in other Spanish countries bilingualism does not emerge as a community-wide phenomenon as tends to happen in US Latinx communities, but rather as an individual effort that is the product of a controlled classroom experience where normative standardized American English is highly encouraged (McClure and Mir 1995, 34, 46). In Spanish-dominant societies there are certainly borrowings from English, but these practices are quite different from the Spanglish we see in US contexts.

Spanglish has clearly evolved beyond a mere auxiliary language; it now includes such innovative uses of language as Jonathan Rosa has shown us to be the case with Inverted Spanglish, but where did it come from, how has it evolved, and how common is it?

The History and Evolution of Spanglish in the US Linguistic Borderlands

Contact between Spanish and English, which would later result in the emergence of Spanglish, has a long history and involves multiple people groups, each with their own unique stories. While it's impossible to consider every group who has added to this evolution in depth here, in the following pages we will consider some of the most influential groups and events that contributed to this development through both historic and sociolinguistic lenses.

The early history of the Spanish-speaking population in the United States begins long before the constitution of the country and predates the presence of English in the Americas. The first permanent settlement in what is now the mainland United States was Saint Augustine, founded in 1565 as the capital of the Spanish colony of La Florida (Elliott 1984, 327). In the 1600s the Spanish established settlements in Texas which would later be annexed into the United States. In 1682 the first Spanish-speaking Sephardic synagogue was founded in New Netherland (New York City). Even later, in the 1770s while American Colonists along the Eastern Seaboard were considering revolt against the British crown, the Spanish were establishing missions in California. All these examples predate the independence of the United States and the later amalgamation of these territories into the nation. But how these territories, and more interestingly their inhabitants, were brought into the union and the resulting cultural contact is at the heart of our story.

Manifest Destiny

Since the focus of this chapter is on the emergence of Spanglish and the language contact situations that lead to this, let's pick up our story in Los Angeles in the 1830s. At this time, in what was then the Mexican territory of Alta California, there were communities of "Mexicanized" Anglos who spoke Spanish with Spanish speakers and engaged in highly translingual language contact practices with other Spanish-English bilinguals with whom they resided. Such is the case with Hugo Reid and Abel Stearns. These two men were immigrants to Mexico and adopted a native-like fluency in Spanish, as demonstrated in their letters to Mexican officials. Reid employed fluent translingual practices in his correspondence with Stearns (Train 2013). Robert Train suggests that these were among the earliest written examples of Spanglish—though the term Spanglish, as "espanglish," only appeared in 1948 (Zentella 2017, 209). These texts, Train argues, may be indicative of a rather common practice among Anglo immigrants to Mexico during that period. This should come as no surprise; immigrants in most contexts adopt the dominant or prestige language of their new home in order to access new opportunities, the promise of which motivated their immigration in the first place. However, Spanish in these areas, as well as in the Spanish colony of La Florida, would not remain the prestige language for long.

In the early 1800s Anglos from the relatively newly independent United States started moving in droves to Florida and Texas, both controlled by Spain at the time (Gonzalez 2011, 36). Following the Napoleonic Wars in Europe and the Mexican War of Independence, neither Spain nor Mexico was poised to control this flow of immigrants. Consequently, Florida was ceded to the United States in the Adams-Onís Treaty of 1821. However, by this point, Florida, having previously been passed from Spanish to British hands and back again, had few Spanish speakers left and the transfer did not result in the same type of language contact situation that we see in other areas of the United States.

Meanwhile, Texas was still a part of Mexico, but by the late 1820s Anglos far outnumbered Mexicans in the region and they revolted in the Texas War of Independence in 1836 (Gonzalez 2011, 42). In 1845 the Republic of Texas was annexed to the United States. Shortly thereafter, motivated by the doctrine of

Manifest Destiny, the United States invaded Mexico. This doctrine of Manifest Destiny suggested that the US government was ordained by God to extend its control and spread the ideologies of capitalism and democracy across the entirety of North America. Rather than compromise the white racial dominance of the country, the United States annexed only the least populated sections of Mexico in the hopes that those who remained would assimilate into mainstream Anglo society in the years that followed (Gonzalez 2011, 44).

Gloria Anzaldúa summarizes the conclusion of the war and its symbolic and concrete ramifications. She says:

> With the victory of the U.S. forces over the Mexican in the US-Mexican War ... The border fence that divides the Mexican people was born on February 2, 1848 with the signing of the Treaty of Guadalupe-Hidalgo. It left 100,000 Mexican citizens on [the American] side, annexed by conquest along with the land.
> (Anzaldúa 1999, 29)

Half of the land mass of prewar Mexico was transferred to the United States, inhabitants and all. Five years later, in 1853, the Gadsden Purchase further dismembered Mexico and fused parts of it to the United States. These actions created a significant Spanish-speaking diaspora in the United States overnight and redefined Mexicanness from a national to a transnational identity. The Mexican Americans who remained after the war lived in the same language contact zone as we previously saw to be the case with Hugo Reid and Abel Stearns, but with the prestige language now being English as government institutions adopted it for widespread use. Despite the change in prestige, English was adopted much more slowly in the US Southwest than politicians had hoped. Furthermore, in contrast to the predominantly protestant population of other regions of the United States, Mexican Americans generally retained their Catholic faith. This resistance to assimilation, both by Mexican Americans in their practices, and by Anglos in their acceptance of the new Mexican American population, meant that, despite being considered white in the (post)civil-war era conceptualizations of race, Mexican Americans were still Othered by the Anglos in power.

The United States and its doctrine of Manifest Destiny did not stop at Mexico. Following the independence movements that swept Latin America in the early 1800s only Cuba and Puerto Rico remained under Spanish sovereignty. Cuba declared its independence from Spain in 1895 and the United States intervened in support in 1898. After the three-month-long Spanish American War, the Treaty of Paris (1898) was signed granting Cuba its independence. For their efforts, the

United States was given Puerto Rico, the Philippines, Guam, and the Northern Marianas Islands as spoils of war (Gutiérrez 2004, 11–12). Nearly two decades later Puerto Ricans were granted US citizenship by the Jones-Shafroth Act in 1917, which afforded them freedom of movement between Puerto Rico, where Spanish was and remains the majority language, and Spanish-minority areas in the mainland (Gutiérrez 2004, Meléndez 2017, 25–9). Though Puerto Ricans began moving to New York in the 1800s, while Puerto Rico was still a Spanish possession, this new freedom of movement and the economic dependence of the island on the US mainland set the stage for mass migration of Puerto Ricans to the mainland that culminated in the Great Migration boom of the 1950s.

Postwar and Cold War (Im)migration

Two major developments in the postwar years, the Bracero Program and the Great Migration, resulted in the mass arrival of Spanish speakers to the mainland United States. The former brought Mexican workers north, while the later encouraged Puerto Ricans to move from the island to the mainland. This movement of people further bolstered the Spanish-speaking community in the mainland United States and perpetuated the language-contact situation that had begun many generations previous. A third mass arrival, this time of Cubans fleeing political ideologies and war, began a bit later, but these three communities—Mexican, Puerto Rican, and Cuban—would go on to establish national organizations, cultural institutions, and literary icons that would ensure the survival of Spanish and indirectly encourage the move of Spanglish from the oral to the literary sphere.

An in-depth historical summary of the Bracero Program, the so-called Great Migration, and the arrival of large numbers of Cuban political and economic refugees to the mainland United States is well beyond the scope of this chapter.[3] However, it bears mentioning that these three developments were fueled by US policies which were established to further advance US interests, be they for cheap labor on the one hand or from a cold-war anti-socialist orientation on the other.

In the late 1960s the vast majority of Latinxs in the United States were either Mexican Americans, Puerto Ricans, or Cubans, concentrated respectively in the Southwest, New York City, and Miami. Each of these communities used

---

[3] For more information about the Bracero program consult, see Craig (1971). For an overview of the Great Migration, see Meléndez (2017). To learn more about Cuban communities in the US consult, see García (2004).

Spanish and English slightly differently in accordance with the cultural norms with which they were in contact. Consequently, different varieties of Spanglish emerged in parallel. The terms *Pachuco*, *Caló*, or *Tex-Mex* are some of the terms used to refer to Mexican American Spanglish, while *Nuyorican* and *Cubonics*, as the names imply, are some terms given to the Spanglish that emerged in the Puerto Rican or Cuban diasporas (Anzaldúa 1999, Stavans 2008b, 77, Moreno Fernández 2009, 415).

These communities, the politicians who represented them, and the media and marketing agencies who catered to them considered them to have little in common. After all, demographically, ethnically, and economically there was little overlap between them, and the notion of a common Hispanic identity that united Latinx people from diverse backgrounds had yet to emerge. Such a panethnic label would emerge slowly across government, advocacy organizations, and the media beginning in the 1970s and reaching its full saturation by 1990.[4]

The emergence of a shared concept of panethnic latinidad was cemented by the emergence of Univision, a broadcaster that brought together content and news of interest to a wide range of Spanish-speaking communities across the country (Mora 2014, 145–6). While Univision originally formed to unite the larger Spanish-speaking communities in the Southwest, New York, and Miami, it set the stage for later immigrants to the United States to begin to view themselves as part of a larger multi-ethnic Hispanic community. This shared identity is still a common theme in Spanglish literature.

Though some Latin American immigrants of all nationalities had been arriving to the United States for quite some time, the late 1960s through 1980s marked a notable boom in immigration from a wide cross-section of Latin America. Dominicans, motivated by political and economic instability at home and following decades of US involvement in their domestic policy, began to immigrate in large numbers to the United States (most notably to New York) in the late 1960s. This trend increased for the next two decades only slowing in the 1990s (Levitt 2004, 237). Central Americans, for their part, arrived in large part in the 1980s but immigration has continued, spurred in large part by refugee-seekers fleeing the wars and ongoing violence in El Salvador, Guatemala, Honduras, and Nicaragua (Stoltz Chinchilla and Hamilton 2004, 187–8). Finally, a wave of South American immigration reached its peak in the 1990s, increasing in large part due to political and economic instability in various countries. This

---

[4] The emergence of a pan-hispanic identity is covered in depth in both Mora (2014) and Oboler (2005).

wave came on the heels of an earlier wave in the 1980s by those of a certain socioeconomic and educational background who were viewed as "professional" upon their arrival in the States. Some of this immigration, such as that of Argentines and Chileans who fled the dictatorships of the 1970s and 1980s, was motivated by a desire for political or ideological freedom that was not available at home. Others, such as Colombians, came fleeing an upsurge in military and paramilitary armed conflict (Espitia 2004, 264–8). These more recent arrivals settled across the country, often times in large cities, but many made their homes in small towns far from the border in areas which had previously had no Spanish-speaking communities at all.

English-Spanish Tension and the Growth of Spanglish

These new language contact zones, influenced by every variety of Spanish from across the Hispanic world, further cemented Spanglish as an element of the US national identity that could be heard in even the most remote of locations. Anglo-Americans had, since the Treaty of Guadalupe-Hidalgo, considered Latinxs to belong to the white side of the white-Black racial binary, which has defined the US cultural divisions for centuries. Consequently, this afforded them the opportunity to gain full citizenship, hold property, and access the courts—all rights that had been available only to whites (Oboler 2005, 32). In exchange, they hoped Latinxs would abandon their Spanish and Catholic-dominant identities and assimilate into an Anglo-Protestant society. Anglo-American society, however, has never fully believed this expectation and has called into question Latinxs' place in American society in a way that white Anglos and African Americans do not experience (Flores-González 2017, 91–2).

Due to the contradictory discourse that suggests that Latinxs people are white and as such should have a high degree of social mobility, while simultaneously questioning their place in the Nation, Latinxs people often feel excluded from the social fabric of the country.[5] This conflation of language with race, and consequently both with belonging to the nation, resulted in the migration of Spanglish from a private oral language variety into a new public consciousness beginning in the 1980s.

As Gloria Anzaldúa said in her seminal work on the experience of the cultural borderlands:

---

[5] Nilda Flores-González shows that this racialization of Latinx people is independent of their perceived (phenotypical) racial makeup, their fluency—or lack thereof—in Spanish, and the ethnic make-up of their family. See Flores-González (2017, 1–30).

Until I can take pride in my language, I cannot take pride in myself ... Until I am free to write bilingually and to switch codes without having always to translate, while I still have to speak English or Spanish when I would rather speak Spanglish, and as long as I have to accommodate the English speakers rather than having them accommodate me, my tongue will be illegitimate.

(Anzaldúa 1999, 81)

For their part, Latinx authors, poets, playwrights, musicians, and bloggers have begun to take pride in Spanglish in a variety of different ways. Some have sought to be true to themselves while still "accommodating" the English speaker; others have rejected the need to do so.

Toward a Spanglish Literature

Spanglish's voyage from the oral sphere into the literary sphere involved a wide breadth of literary genres and countless creators who have used the language in myriad contexts. The volume of works that contributed to Spanglish's journey deserves proper consideration. Consequently, in this section I'll take a moment to explore how the language emerged through theater, poetry, and music before emerging as the dominant language of some prose beginning in the 1980s.

Early Spanglish in Literature

There is an important distinction to consider as we discuss the evolution of a body of literature in Spanglish, broadly defined as any media aimed at a public (rather than private) audience: the difference between Spanglish literature and Spanglish embedded into English (and in a few examples Spanish) literature.[6] These two types of writing are intimately intertwined but are not the same.

Where Spanglish is the dominant language of the text it requires the reader to have knowledge of Spanglish—in some instances being bilingual in English and Spanish is not sufficient—in order to fully grasp all of the nuances of the text. While we've seen that Spanglish is a language that uses elements of English and Spanish, we've also seen that there are elements of translingual wordplay that can bewilder even fluently bilingual speakers of English and Spanish who have not been exposed to Spanglish. On the other hand, where Spanglish snippets appear

---

[6] For the purpose of this book, only works published through traditional publishing houses are considered.

in a text otherwise written in English or Spanish, it serves as a marker of identity for a readership who may not navigate Spanglish at all. Despite a lack of access to the language on the part of readers, the Spanglish in these texts may be minimally distracting from the larger narrative as they are only occasional departures from the dominant language. In other words, whereas the latter imagines a broad readership and is to some degree written to ensure wide access to the texts, in the former the primary preoccupation is to render Spanglish visible presumably for a Spanglish reader. This binary is shifting in more recent works, but historically the shift from Spanglish-as-embedded to Spanglish-as-dominant was a milestone.

Latinx authors have for decades embedded some Spanish or Spanglish in their writing, and much scholarship has considered these works. Consequently, I won't focus too much on the English-dominant works of authors such as Junot Díaz, Sandra Cisneros, or others. However, a brief discussion is important for context.

In earlier examples of Spanglish in literature, the dominant feature is embedding through its appearance in dialogue (Torres 2007). This way of using vernacular to separate the characters from the narrator is not atypical of such new manifestations of previously oral registers; Lise Gauvin observes a similar trend in some Québécois literature from the 1940s (Gauvin 2000, 101). This embedding never disappeared; it is still an important option available to Latinx writers. But, from the 1960s to late 1980s it was the dominant linguistic departure from monolingual English or Spanish texts. This departure paved the way for the emergence of a truly Spanglish-dominant literature and, for this, it deserves some discussion.

1960s: Spanglish in Theater

Luis Valdez, who would later gain fame for his 1979 Broadway play *Zoot Suit* which followed the story of the Zoot Suit Riots of Southern California and his movie *La Bamba* (1987), which was a biographical film about the life of musician Ritchie Valens, has a grassroots origin story. In 1965 he founded the Teatro Campesino as the cultural arm of César Chávez's United Farm Workers (Valdez 1994, 3). In this role Valdez wrote plays that sought to portray on stage the struggles and shared experience of Chicanxs[7] as a galvanizing and

---

[7] Chicanx is a gender-inclusive adaptation of the term Chicano or Chicana. This term was reclaimed between the 1940s and 1960s by Mexican Americans who wanted to distance themselves from their relationship to the United States that is evident in the term "Mexican American." For more information, see Contreras (2017).

solidarity-building art form. In an attempt to distinguish between Chicanx workers and Anglo bosses, Valdez uses Spanish and Spanglish elements as a form of in-group speech for the proud and united Chicanx workers. The Anglo and Anglicized Mexican American characters in his plays use only English, even occasionally using English pronunciation of Spanish names—one example comes to mind of a shopkeeper who pronounces her own last name, Jiménez, with Anglo pronunciation as "JIM-enez" (Valdez 1994, 41).

Valdez was one of the first authors to make extensive use of Spanglish in his work, which was clearly written for a Chicanx public who would understand this language use with no barriers. Also, we should note that dialogue in theater in many cases, though certainly not all, attempts to reproduce a vernacular that would be true to form for the characters that the playwright is trying to recreate. As such, using Spanglish in theater is a logical first step in the evolution of Spanglish literature and in the cultivation of a reading/viewing public. This is, I suggest, because the orality of theater makes it a lower barrier literary form that more easily accommodates registers that would be considered undesirable for other types of media. As a performance, Valdez's Teatro Campesino works were written to promote a labor movement of farm workers who may have been less inclined to read experimental literature, which is certainly what Spanglish literature was then and remains in most cases today, but for whom these plays represented a satirical reflection of their own lives.

Spanglish Poetry

Poetry is another genre that, like theater and music, is more malleable and accepts linguistic innovation—known colloquially in this context as "artistic license"—more easily than prose. Consequently, it should come as no surprise that Spanglish poetry emerged just slightly before prose. Lesbian philosopher Gloria Anzaldúa, herself a Chicana from the borderlands, was one of the earliest poets in Spanglish. A significant portion of her seminal 1987 book *Borderlands/ La Frontera: The New Mestiza* is dedicated to her Spanglish poetry. While this book also contains significant amounts of Spanish embedding in English works—a topic I'll return to momentarily—her poetry is far more translingual with various works in English, Spanish, and Spanglish. And, in 1987, her work was some of the first Spanglish literature that was not presented as dialogue to be performed, but rather meant to be read as a textual literary art form. The following is a short fragment from her poem "Sus plumas el viento":

> She pulls ahead
> kicking *terremotes*,
> *el viento sur secándole el sudor*
> *un ruido de alas* humming songs in her head.
> *Que le de sus plumas el viento.*
> The sound of hummingbird wings
> In her ears, *pico de chuparrosas.*

(Anzaldúa 1999, 138)

In this poem, dedicated to Anzaldúa's mother, we can see that, while the text of her poem is clearly Spanglish, shifting back and forth between English and Spanish elements, she nevertheless continues to mark the Spanish elements, highlighting its otherness in italics. Only a few years later did another Spanglish-language poet first resist marking either the Spanish or English elements in his work.

In 1995, Cuban-American academic Gustavo Pérez Firmat published his collection of poetry entitled *Bilingual Blues*. This collection, along with several other works of his poetry published over the years, deploys Spanglish as the dominant language of the texts. What makes this poetry so distinct from that which precedes it is that no global language, whether English or Spanish, seems to dominate. Similarly, Pérez Firmat does not mark either his English or Spanish as separate through quotation marks or italics, further confirming to us that there is no process of departure, as there is no identified singular dominant language. This is clear in this fragment from his book's namesake poem, "Bilingual Blues":

> Soy un ajiaco de contradicciones.
> I have mixed feelings about everything.
> Name your tema, I'll hedge;
> name your cerca, I'll straddle it
> like a Cubano
> …
> Soy un ajiaco de contradicciones,
> un puré de impurezas:
> a little square from Rubik's Cuba
> que nadie nunca acoplará.
> (Cha-cha-chá.)

(Pérez Firmat 1995, 28)

As we can see, in this short fragment of the first and last stanzas of the poem there are utterances in English and in Spanish, as well as translingual wordplay ("puré de impurezas" or "Rubik's Cuba") but at no point is any word or phrase marked as Other through the use of quotation marks or italics, nor are any translated for the reader. This distinction is among the first examples that announce the emergence of a body of poetry whose linguistic identity goes beyond embedding of one language into a different clearly dominant language. Instead, this is a fully Spanglish work.

Spanglish and Cross-Over Music

Like poetry, music was another genre that set the stage for the later emergence of Spanglish prose. Ritchie Valens was the Chicano rock-n-roll star who brought the world *La Bamba* in 1958. Though his career was short-lived due to his tragic death in a plane crash at the age of seventeen, his musical contribution brought Spanish lyrics into the American rock-"n"-roll sphere perhaps for the first time. This hit song foreshadowed a mix of Latinx sounds in American music that wouldn't explode onto the scene until two decades later.

Cuban American Gloria Estefan was the lead singer of the Miami Sound Machine from 1975 and started a solo career in 1989. In both contexts she mixed Spanish and English lyrics and included Cuban sounds targeted at a US audience (Mendizabal 2015). Estefan went on to become one of the most successful female artists of all time. Mexican-American artist Selena Quintanilla's career spanned from the late 1980s to the mid-1990s and brought Tejano music to new international audiences, including to the US Anglo market in her posthumously released album in English.

This so-called crossover music reached its pinnacle following Ricky Martin's 1998 performance of *La Copa de la Vida* at the World Cup in France. Mindful of his international audience he adapted his lyrics to include English, Spanish, and French elements. His Grammy performance early in 1999 followed quickly by the release of his first English-dominant, but nevertheless translingual, album *Livin' la vida loca*, which initiated a wave of crossover music that blended Spanglish lyrics and Latinx sounds but was marketed to US Anglos. Artists such as Enrique Iglesias, Shakira, and Jennifer Lopez also dominated the scene. Some Anglo artists like Madonna, Will Smith, and others recorded some numbers following their lead but were generally less successful. Even German singer Lou Bega released his own version of the Cuban song *Mambo No 5* in 1999. Crossover music raised awareness among many Anglo-Americans of the cultural mixing that was already commonplace among many US Latinx communities. That the Anglos were in the dark, though, didn't mean that this translingual and trans-genre artistry was new, as some artists like salsa singer Rubén Blades have criticized (Cepeda 2010, 58–9). Instead, it was an emergence into the popular conscious of the type of translingual innovation that had previously been mostly reserved to the oral sphere. In short, Spanglish's success on the global music scene gave it a level of prestige that it had never seen before.

While the late 1990s and early 2000s wave of crossover music has waned, it would seem that its influence is here to stay in some genres, as we can see in recent releases by Pitbull, Luis Fonsi, Romeo Santos, and others. Though not without its critics, we cannot underestimate the importance of the crossover boom in raising visibility of Spanglish and so-called hybrid US Latinx identities that would pave the way for its emergence in other art forms later on.

The Emergence of Prose

Published prose in Spanglish, as we've seen with other genres, emerged with the help of a tradition of embedding Spanish into English-dominant texts. Lourdes Torres describes a few ways that authors have attempted to replicate the nature of Spanglish when writing for a predominantly English readership.[8] One common technique is to use Spanish words only when the meaning can be deduced from the context including "culturally recognizable items like food (mango, taco, tortilla, etc.), places (casa, rancho, playa, etc.), familiar common nouns (mamá, hermano, hijo), and so forth" (Torres 2007, 77–8). Another commonly used approach includes the use of Spanish followed by an English translation. These two approaches ensure a minimum degree of discomfort for the monolingual English reader while at the same time marking the text as not belonging to the ethnic majority. However, Torres goes on to criticize this by saying that they:

> … may serve to perpetuate mainstream expectations of the Latino/a text in that they can make the text exotic and allow the reader to believe that s/he is interacting with and appropriating the linguistic Other, while in reality a reader does not have to leave the comfortable realm of his/her own complacent monolingualism.
>
> (Torres 2007, 78)

[8] It should be noted that Torres wrote this before translinguistics and translanguaging were being widely applied to literary analysis. Nevertheless, a great deal of what she discusses can be applied to the evolution of a Spanglish prose. However, I do not want to put translingual ideologies into Torres' writing and have opted to reflect the terms she uses in her analysis here, despite the fact that those are not the terms I would choose to describe this and may, or may not, be the terms she would use again if she were to publish this paper today.

A contrasting approach to including Spanish within an English-dominant text would be to prioritize the bilingual reader, albeit at the potential discomfort of the monolingual reader. Examples of this would include leaving Spanish words untranslated and unmarked (not in italics, for example) or including calque translations of words in English that may look bizarre to the monolingual Anglophone but would resonate with the bilingual reader much as we have seen above with Inverted Spanglish. One such example of this in literature is Sandra Cisnero's novel *Caramelo* (2003) where one character is referred to both as "Aunty White-Skin" and later "Titi Blanca" (Torres 2007, 78). For the bilingual reader this is no doubt the same character, but the monolingual English speaker may not arrive at that same conclusion. Torres says that many of the works that she studied include a plurality of these elements; however, as prioritizing the bilingual reader is more subversive to the larger English publishing market, techniques that prioritize the monolingual English speaker tend to prevail. The choice of authors to include Spanish within English texts dates back decades but has gained much more attention in recent years with the commercial success of authors such as Sandra Cisneros, Junot Díaz, Esmeralda Santiago, and others. It is clear, however, that while they draw inspiration from Spanglish for their writing, these elements, even when used in tandem, don't truly replicate Spanglish. Torres has one further approach that some authors have chosen; albeit far less frequently, she calls it "radical bilingualism." This is the attempt by authors to produce highly bilingual texts, sometimes employing all of the elements of Spanglish that we have previously discussed. Giannini Braschi and Susana Chávez-Silverman are two such authors. In their texts Spanglish forms the core of the prose, which stands in contrast to, for example, Junot Díaz's work in which roughly 90 percent of the text is in English with only 10 percent showing some kind of Spanglish or "hybrid" elements (Derrick 2015, 100–3). Chávez-Silverman and Braschi have had a profound impact on the Spanglish cultural sphere by being among the first authors to publish prose in which Spanglish is the dominant linguistic variety of the text. Nevertheless, perhaps because it is not in a language that is accessible to most of the North American market, their works have not been picked up by mainstream publishers; rather, they have been published in smaller runs by academic presses (Torres 2007, 86). This "radical bilingual" writing is what we are discussing when we talk about a body of prose in Spanglish.

Since Spanglish has been predominantly an oral variety for much of its history, the orality in the work of both Braschi and Chávez-Silverman almost requires a performative reading of the text, an element it shares with the Judeo-Spanish folktales we'll consider later, and indeed a common element in many early written texts from previously oral communities. Braschi and Chávez-Silverman have provided significant contributions to the literary corpus of Spanglish and have done so through the subversion of mainstream North American publication norms. The mere act of publishing this work has given Spanglish a never-before-seen degree of prestige and has allowed the Spanglish-speaking community to see themselves in prose for the first time. Still, we must not fool ourselves into believing that any prose is truly representative of a vernacular. Whereas a vernacular can be understood as a variety in which the least amount of attention is paid to style and form, writing—short of a written transcription from oral ethnographic sources—requires far more thought and editing. Still, the publication of Spanglish prose after two centuries is important to recognize. And, just as written English (or Spanish) varies from its spoken mode, sometimes substantially; it is still English. The same standard should also apply to Spanglish.

Spanglish, as a growing force, is what some have referred to as a type of negative assimilation, that is to say a readiness by Hispanics "to retain their ancestral heritage against all odds and costs" (Stavans 2000a, 7).[9] The goal of this negative assimilation, according to Stavans, is that "we are all to become Latinos *agringados* and/or *gringos hispanizados*; we will never be the owners of a pure, crystalline collective individuality because we are the product of a five-hundred-year-old fiesta of miscegenation that began with our first encounter with the gringo in 1492" (Stavans 2000a, 9). Despite Stavans' suggestion, though, I'm not sure that gringos are more hispanizados now than they were in 2000 when Stavans wrote this. But, the publication of *Yo-Yo Boing!* and *Killer Crónicas*, both written by bilingual authors, is a statement that affirms his notion of the authors' resistance to assimilation. In other words, Braschi and Chávez-Silverman can conform to English or Spanish publication norms. They choose not to.

Since the emergence of prose written in Spanglish, the language has also blossomed in audiovisual media. This ranges from professional YouTube content which began to emerge around 2005 to an increasing presence of Spanglish in TV and film (Attig and Derrick 2021). While some of this is restricted to dialogue, there are also instances in which Spanglish is the dominant language

---

[9] Further reading on the tenuous relationship between US citizenship and a sense of belonging to the US cultural sphere among Latinx millennials can be found in Flores-González (2017).

of these works. Time will tell as to whether Spanglish has reached its zenith on the silver screen or is only in its infancy.[10]

Doulas and Radical Spanglish Writing

Now that we've explored the path of Spanglish from its infancy to its current status as a language with a body of literature from a range of genres, let's turn our attention to the *literary doulas* who moved this work forward. While there are myriad possible doulas that I could highlight, each of whom has made important contributions to the evolution of Spanglish, I've chosen to focus on two whose work has most influenced my own: Gloria Anzaldúa and Susana Chávez-Silverman.

Gloria Anzaldúa, whose work has already appeared several times in this book, was born in 1942 in the Rio Grande Valley of southern Texas. A seventh-generation Chicana/Tejana, Anzaldúa was one of the great theorists of early intersectional feminism, publishing her seminal work *Borderlands/La Frontera: The New Mestiza* in 1987. Prior to this she had written numerous other essays and poetry. Throughout her work she uses Spanglish—often with Spanish elements set off by italics—to discuss her life story, the history of the US-Mexico border regions, spirituality, intersectionality, and queer Chicanx identity.[11]

The theme that most directly connects with this book, however, is her work on the intersections between language and identity. Anzaldúa rejects the idea that her identity, nay her reality, can be captured in standardized English or in standardized Spanish. These languages are, she suggests, antagonistic to her own life story. She is at once ethnically Mexican, but US educated. In Spanish, Mexican linguistic conventions—informed themselves by the Real Academia Española, the Madrid-based institution charged with defending the purity and setting the standard for how Spanish should be used globally—are imposed. In English, any Spanish presence is impure. To live up to the standards of either

---

[10] While a robust discussion of the presence of Spanglish in audiovisual media is important, this development is not paralleled to the same degree in Portuñol and in Judeo-Spanish, and thus is ultimately beyond the scope of this project. For more on this, see Taylor and McQuillen (2018), Attig (2019a), Beseghi (2019), Corrius and Zabalbeascoa (2019), Attig and Derrick (2021), and Derrick and Attig (ND).

[11] Anzaldúa usually uses the terms "Chicana" and "lesbian" to refer to herself, but given the intersectional and poststructural epistemological orientations of her research, I am confident that, if she were writing today, the terms "Chicanx" and "Queer" would pepper her descriptions of self.

official language variety, then, she's left with no choice but to minimize her own authentic voice. In short, for her words to be read, her voice must be silenced.

Anzaldúa does not accept this paradigm, however, and discusses the complex realities of navigating multiple sociolects as loci of belonging. She brings this into her own poetry and prose writing and thus becomes one of the early writers in Spanglish. While her writing was linguistically radical in the 1980s, her passing in 2004 meant that she is not around to see how the next generation of *literary doulas* build on her work and take Spanglish creativity to even more radical levels.

Our second *literary doula*, Susana Chávez-Silverman, was born in Los Angeles to a Chicana mother and Jewish father who, incidentally, was a renowned researcher of Judeo-Spanish oral literature, thus connecting her through circumstance to later chapters of this book (Chávez-Silverman 2004, xviii). She spent her childhood between California, Madrid, and Guadalajara, but would later live in numerous other cities, including Boston, Buenos Aires, and Pretoria (Montalvo Arts Center n.d.). Chávez-Silverman studied Spanish in which she earned her PhD in 1991 from the University of California, Davis. In 1989 she joined the faculty of Pomona College where she is a professor of Latin American and US Latinx literature and queer sexualities in Latin America (Pomona College). Queer herself, she is the author of three Spanglish books and numerous individually published crónicas that tell the story of her life through short vignettes. Chávez-Silverman's writing style is considered by Roshawnda Derrick, drawing inspiration from Torres, to be "radically bilingual" in a way that is not typical of other bilingual writers. Derrick analyzes the language use in one of Chávez-Silverman's books, *Killer Crónicas*, and concludes that only about 18 percent of the sentences are in English with no presence of Spanish, a number she contrasts with Junot Díaz's work where she found approximately 90 percent of the text to be in English (Derrick 2015, 100–3). She goes on to break down the writing into a number of subcategories, including monolingual English, monolingual Spanish, English-based bilingual, Spanish-based bilingual, and hybrid sentences. The largest single category consists of what Derrick terms "hybrid sentences" at 45 percent (102–3). This category is essentially composed of sentences that have "no base language" from which certain elements can be said to depart. Derrick suggests that this level of code-switching is used as a resistance to dominant culture (129). While Derrick explains her findings in terminology quite different to the terms that I use to discuss *linguistic labor* and *literary doulas*, this evaluation of Chávez-Silverman's writing provides clear and quantifiable data that helps illustrate what I mean when I speak about Spanglish in prose.

Spanglish writing exists on a spectrum, in some cases the presence of translinguistic elements is rather light, as Derrick found to be true of Díaz's work, and at times it is far more radical, such as in the case of Chávez-Silverman's writing. There are few examples of studies that provide quantifiable linguistic statistics to help illustrate this difference, but Derrick's research does just that. Through her analysis she helps us see that while some writing is more radical than others, it's all Spanglish. And Spanglish, written in any form, transgresses the monolingual norms imposed by mainstream publishers. Given this context, publishing in Spanglish is radical and emancipatory for its speakers.

3

Portuñol

Portuguese and Spanish have shared borders since they began their evolution from Latin during the Roman control of Hispania beginning in the second century BCE (Fear 2000, 21). Moorish presence in the region from the eighth to fifteenth centuries resulted in similar types of Arabic influence on both languages. Furthermore, they have historically formed part of a dialect continuum that includes Galician, Asturian, and Leonese, as well as many other Romance languages, some of which are now extinct or endangered. Because of this, the two languages share a very high degree of mutual intelligibility, particularly in the written form (Fernández 2011, 77).

Nevertheless, despite Spain and Portugal sharing a monarch for sixty years beginning in 1580—or perhaps because of such a history—Spanish and Portuguese readers have traditionally maintained a strong separation between their two literary corpora, reading each other's works only when presented in translation (Fernández 2011, 77).[1] In the Americas, however, this dialect continuum didn't exist like it did in Iberia, so when the two languages came into prolonged contact in the border regions between Brazil and Spanish-speaking countries—particularly with countries on Brazil's southern borders—a new language variety emerged.[2]

Portuñol, alternatively spelled Portunhol in keeping with Portuguese orthographic conventions, also goes by many other names, including Fronterizo and "Uruguayan dialects of Portuguese" (Elizaincin, Behares, and Barrios 1987,

---

[1] This isn't universal, particularly in Renaissance theater. For a discussion about how language is used in the works of Gil Vicente, see Chapter 7, "O Sistema bilingue de Gil Vicente" in Teyssier (2005).
[2] There is evidence of a type of Portuñol on the border of Spain and Portugal but given the situation of the millennia-old dialect continuum there, the situation is too far removed from the one that is at the core of this chapter for its extended consideration to be relevant. For more information, see chapter 4 of Elizaincin (1992).

Carvalho 2003, 126, Bertolotti et al. 2005, 58, Fernández 2011, 85).[3] In this book we'll follow the lead of recent authors who have carved out a niche for what they've termed Portuñol literature, particularly in Uruguay, but it's worth recognizing that this term may not be used by all speakers.

Before discussing the emergence of a literature in Uruguayan Portuñol, I'd like to take a moment to discuss what Portuñol is, in broad strokes. I'll then consider three different varieties of Portuñol spoken outside the Uruguay-Brazilian border region: tourism contact varieties, contact varieties of commercial Portuñol, and so-called Portuñol salvaje spoken on the Paraguay-Brazil-Argentina border. The goal in exploring all three of these varieties is to note that the idea of Portuñol exists in a wide range of sociolinguistic contexts, but we will see that the case of Uruguayan Portuñol stands out against the others as something truly unique.

What Is Portuñol?

What exactly Portuñol is depends on who you ask. Given the significant grammatical overlap between the languages, a description of Portuñol that follows the type of description provided for Spanglish or Judeo-Spanish is not helpful, as most of what distinguishes Portuñol from either Spanish or Portuguese is at the lexical level. John Lipski suggests that "closely related varieties such as the Spanish-Portuguese dyad do not fit easily into structural and sociolinguistic models designed for bilingual speech communities in which the languages are more distinct from one another" (Lipski 2006, 1). Nevertheless, a sociolinguistic description that reflects on how, where, and why Portuñol has emerged is useful in considering the language and emergence of literature in this language.

Spanish and Portuguese translanguaging exists in many contexts in which Spanish and Portuguese coexist for one reason or another. Sometimes it responds to a speaker of one language's need to communicate with a speaker of the other where neither is proficient in the other's language. In cases like these, since the two languages are sufficiently similar, the speakers capitalize on mutual intelligibility to communicate while sprinkling in occasional vocabulary of the other language to mitigate potential miscommunication. Sometimes,

---

[3] In this book, I've chosen to spell the name of the language as Portuñol to be consistent with how the term is used in Uruguay; however, both spellings are equally valid, and the reader should not consider my choice of one over the other to be a judgment on the matter.

though, this strategy exacerbates the language distance, for example, when false cognates appear. In the following pages I identify and discuss three such lingua franca contexts in which Portuñol emerges, I've categorized them as Tourism Portuñol, Border Commerce Portuñol, and Paraguayan Portuñol Salvaje. Though these groupings are my own, extant research—to the degree to which such exists— suggests that all three are unstable varieties of Portuñol that are highly individual to each speaker. Following these discussions, I turn my attention to the only stable community-wide variety of Portuñol in Latin America, Uruguayan Portuñol.

Tourism Portuñol

Tourism Portuñol, a term I'm using for the purpose of this study though it has not been widely applied elsewhere, is a manifestation of Portuñol that results from a limited acquisition of either Spanish or Portuguese by a proficient speaker of the other. This form is different to other forms of Portuñol, not necessarily in its linguistic features, but in its removal from geographic borders and its role at promoting tourism rather than facilitating border region commerce or as a language of a strong regional identity.

Tourism Portuñol can be heard, for example, when Cuban airport employees in Miami inject some elements of the Portuguese that they've learned into their Spanish when speaking with Brazilian travelers. Similarly, Brazilian tourism workers in Florianópolis who are not fluent in Spanish may, nevertheless, adopt some Spanish vocabulary to improve communication with Argentine tourists or vice versa.[4]

Tourism uses of Portuñol are the ones identified in the display about Portuñol in the Museu da Língua Portuguesa in São Paulo. It reads:

---

[4] Some Brazilians believe that Tourism Portuñol is ubiquitous in hotspots like Florianópolis which receive large amounts of Argentine and Uruguayan tourists; in the research for this book, many people who helped in the planning of my field research nonchalantly mentioned it as characteristic of the region by those living there. Despite the belief that it is commonplace, however, I found that there were many Brazilians who were fluent in Spanish working in the tourism industry, albeit with the accent one would expect given the circumstances. Any overt use of Portuñol, however, was almost universally avoided unless Brazilians were given no other option but to attempt some Spanish. This suggests that Tourism Portuñol may not be as common as it is anecdotally believed to be, though further studies on Tourism Portuñol are needed. While interpersonal interactions are impossible to measure with the methods used in this study, linguistic landscape research showed no presence of written Portuñol, though normative Spanish did appear alongside Portuguese on a limited number of signs, menus, or in relation to other services marketed to tourists.

Como o português e o español têm muito em comum, os falantes de uma das línguas acreditam que é possível falar a outra com pequenas modificações na própria. "Falar espanhol é muito fácil," pensam os brasileiros. Água é agua; sol é sol; açúcar, azúcar. É verdade. Mas lenço é pañuelo. E a palabra correta para sorvete é helado.

O argentino ou uruguaio que pasa férias numa praia brasileira vai usar logo o "você" e colocar, no meio do seu espanhol, alguma outra palabra que tenha ouvido nesses días, pensando que dessa maneira facilita a compreensão—é a armadilha do parecido.

Esse fenómeno criou até uma "língua" nova: o portunhol ou portuñol.

Mesmo caótica, cheia de palabras erradas, essa "língua" misturada e informal é útil na comunicação entre os brasileiros e seus vizinhos hispanofalantes.

(Museu da Língua Portuguesa 2023)

[Since Portuguese and Spanish have a lot in common, speakers of one of the languages believe that it is possible to speak the other with small modifications to their own. "Speaking Spanish is very easy," Brazilians think. Água is agua; sol is sol; açúcar, azúcar. It's true. But lenço is pañuelo. And the correct word for sorvete is helado.

An Argentine or Uruguayan who spends vacation on a Brazilian beach might use the term "você" and place, in the middle of their Spanish, some other word that they may have heard in recent days, believing that in this way they're facilitating comprehension—the similarity is a double-edged sword.

This phenomenon has even created a new "language": Portunhol or Portuñol.

Despite being chaotic and full of mistaken words, this mixed "language" is informal and useful for communication between Brazilians and their Hispanophone neighbors.][5]

Here the term Portuñol is applied to a translanguaging practice that prioritizes function. It would appear that Argentines, Brazilians, and others in these contact situations do not use Portuñol with their compatriots; rather, they reserve it as an attempt to bridge a language divide when traveling. Lipski suggests that such language use may be seen as "ignorant" or "lazy" by others (Lipski 2006, 3). Such a judgment is, indeed, present in the Museu da Língua Portuguesa's description. However, terms like "ignorant" or "lazy" should be deployed with care as this

---

[5] Translation is the author's.

is a natural human practice, and it's not reasonable to expect tourists to gain fluency in a language simply because they spend a week there every year or two. I would argue that any effort at all is well beyond the realm of ignorance; instead, it demonstrates a desire of hosts and guests to connect on some level.

In the case of Tourism Portuñol, what's important to note is that this type of Spanish-Portuguese mixing is a translanguaging practice that is not reflective of a natural linguistic identity, but instead a manifestation of communicative accommodation theory (CAT). CAT posits that speakers often consciously or unconsciously bring their language use closer to that used by their interlocutor (a phenomenon known as convergence), or distance themselves from it (divergence). This may be motivated by any number of reasons, including to establish connections, to improve comprehension, or, in the case of divergence, to establish stronger boundaries or distance (Giles and Ogay 2007, 326–7).

María Jesús Fernández suggests that this type of Tourism Portuñol can serve an ideological purpose as well. In online communities a convergence-based, rather than border or identity-based, Portuñol mixes Hispanic and Lusophone cultural reference points and art forms as a symbol of South American fusion or integration (Fernández 2011, 86). This is an interesting suggestion and one that is reminiscent in some respects to Spanglish authors who attempt to reflect in writing an identity that joins the Latinx and the Anglo worlds. However, Fernández is clear that this is an "artificial" Portuñol. This manifestation of Portuñol doesn't attempt to replicate the comfortable and authentic language use of any community's vernacular. Instead, it uses Portuguese and Spanish translanguaging practices to communicate across South America in an attempt to promote a desired shared identity, but one that is not—at least not yet—based on a shared linguistic identity.

Border Commerce Portuñol

Another convergence form of Portuñol that exists at the geographic borders of the Brazilian subcontinent is what I'll term Border Commerce Portuñol. This speech variety is also a convergence practice that brings together Spanish and Portuguese elements into a type of lingua franca to facilitate communication and commerce in remote border communities. Generally, except for the Argentina-Brazil-Paraguay triple border region, the communities where Border Commerce Portuñol is spoken are quite small and distant from the larger population centers of their respective countries. Take, for example, the case of

Santa Elena de Uairén, Venezuela, which has been documented as demonstrating Spanish-Portuguese mixing (Chinellato Díaz 2016). Located near Pacaraima, Brazil, Santa Elena de Uairén is roughly 500 km from Ciudad Guyana, the nearest major city in Venezuela, and nearly 250 km from Boa Vista, Brazil. Commerce between Santa Elena de Uairén and Pacaraima is essential given their remote location, and a Portuñol lingua franca facilitates such exchanges. Even more remote are the triplet cities of Leticia (Colombia), Tabatinga (Brazil), and Santa Rosa de Yavarí (Peru), which are connected to the nearest major cities of Iquitos (Peru) and Manaus (Brazil) only by very long boat rides: Bogotá is accessible only by air. In these and other similar frontier communities, isolation from major national centers is the norm and regular cross-border exchanges are essential. Consequently, each region has developed its own way of mixing Spanish and Portuguese.

Unfortunately, none of the Border Commerce Portuñol varieties have been extensively studied and documented. This lacuna has left linguists in the dark as to whether these communities have developed their own stable varieties of Portuñol, or if their practices are individual speaker-based adaptations tailored to their own language mastery and their immediate needs as dictated by the situation. Since the main purpose of the present study is to consider the emergence of literature in these varieties, it is noteworthy to clarify that there appears to be no literature written by Leticianos, Pacaraimenses, or others in their respective varieties of Border Commerce Portuñol.

The Portuñol presence in Foz do Iguaçu, BR, Puerto Iguazú, AR, and Ciudad del Este, PY is used as a lingua franca for commercial purposes more so than for speaking with compatriots; thus, it has been grouped here with Border Commerce Portuñol. Nevertheless, it is in rather close proximity to other Portuñol-speaking communities (Lipski). Portuñol spoken in these small communities may be more appropriately grouped with Uruguayan Portuñol, but there is, to date, little research on these communities and they seem to be largely ignored in the literary and broader cultural sphere, with the notable exception of Papo Curotto's 2016 film *Esteros* which is set in Corrientes, AR (Curotto 2016).

Paraguayan Portuñol "Salvaje"

Brazilian authors Wilson Bueno and Douglas Diegues have both written in a variety of Portuñol that incorporates not only Spanish and Portuguese elements, but also Guaraní, the indigenous language spoken throughout Paraguay, Northeastern Argentina, and Southeastern Brazil. Diegues refers to this as "Portuñol Salvaje."

Despite the existence of this literature, there has been far less research into the historical and current sociolinguistics of these communities. Of this so-called Portuñol Salvaje, Diegues says that it not only includes elements from Spanish, Portuguese, and Guaraní, but may also include fake English or fake French to capture the feel that the author or speaker is trying to achieve (Museu da Língua Portuguesa 2023). In the absence of an extensive body of research into this manifestation of Portuñol, we can only imagine that the use of invented terms meant to invoke English or French is merely performative and would likely require explanation in a way that the Spanish, Portuguese, and Guaraní elements would not for speakers where those three languages coexist.

However, it is in this manifestation that the first novel in which Portuñol was the dominant language variety of both the dialogue and the narration emerged. This is Wilson Bueno's *Mar paraguayo*. First published in 1992, *Mar paraguayo* is a short novel/novella that mixes Spanish, Portuguese, and Guaraní to tell the torrid tale of La Marafona, a character of ambiguous cultural and gender identity who contemplates their life at a pivotal moment in the resort town of Florianópolis (Larkosh 2016, 553). That Bueno, a queer author from the southern Brazilian city of Curitiba, would embed queer themes that mimic the inherent queerness of border spaces in this novel is remarkable. Still, he was not from the border region himself and the degree to which he would have been exposed to, adopted, and later written the natural varieties of Portuñol that form the backbone of this chapter is unclear. What we do know from Néstor Perlongher's introduction to the novel is that Bueno's prose employs an invented Portuñol that doesn't necessarily reflect the linguistic practices of border communities themselves (Bueno 1992, 7). This is certainly true of communities on the border between Uruguay and Brazil, as Guaraní is not strong on that border; conversely, Guaraní is an important part of life at on the Paraguayan side of the triple border it shares with Brazil and Argentina. Regardless of its authenticity, queerness requires play, coloring outside the lines of the colonial, class, and patriarchal structures that have been imposed on us, as will be explored more in Chapter 5. Bueno does this and his exploration has led, perhaps unwittingly, to the emergence of a new wave of Portuñol prose.

Uruguayan Portuñol

The most well-documented variety of Portuñol is thriving at the southern frontier of Brazil, particularly in the northern Uruguayan departments of Artigas, Rivera, and Cerro Largo and in Argentine communities along the Uruguay River (Behares, Díaz, and Holzmann 2004, 5). Uruguayan Portuñol, also known as Portuñol Riverense, Fronterizo, or "Dialectos Portugueses de Uruguay," is the only stable form of Portuñol in South America, which is to say that its use follows predictable patterns rather than being unique to each speaker, though idiolects exist as they do in all languages (Lipski 2009, 10). This Portuñol has evolved due to centuries of Portuguese and Spanish coexistence along the border between southern Brazil and the Spanish-speaking countries of the Southern Cone. The most studied varieties of Uruguayan Portuñol extend along a strip beginning at the Uruguayan border with Brazil and extending south roughly 50 km, though some have suggested the strip is wider still (Elizaincin 1992, 96–7).

Uruguay, Paraguay, the Argentine provinces of Misiones and Corrientes, and southern Brazil have had an established European presence from the early seventeenth century and, due presumably to their more accessible locations, had thriving settler populations quite early as well. Let's contrast this history with the linguistic landscape of the Amazonian communities mentioned only moments ago. Small Jesuit missions aside, the sparsely populated border cities in the Amazon basin were founded very recently: Leticia was founded in 1867, Santa Elena de Uairén in 1923, and Pacaraima only officially in 1993. On the other hand, on both sides of the southeastern borders of Brazil, Spanish- and Portuguese-speaking settlers arrived hundreds of years ago, long before the establishment of any national borders in the region. Consequently, the two languages thrived in contact with one another irrespective of social class (Moyna and Coll 2008, 105).[6]

Unlike the relatively small literary and cultural production in Portuñol from Brazil, Paraguay, or Argentina, in Uruguay literature written in Portuñol has gained national and international attention. This is, I suggest, owing to the nation's history which has a unique relationship with Brazil that isn't shared with other South American countries. Whereas the Portuguese influence in Paraguay and Argentina and the Spanish influence in Brazil are restricted to small

---

[6] For more historic background on this region and a much more in-depth explanation of the linguistic features of Portuñol than will be covered here, see Elizaincin (1992).

segments of the population and thus not an essential element of the national myth, the presence of both Spanish and Portuguese in Uruguayan territory is fundamental to the national identity, which has resulted in Uruguay being the leader in the publication of Portuñol literature.

The History of Uruguayan Portuñol

From first settlements in Uruguay, Spanish and Portuguese have coexisted in the territory. Colonia del Sacramento was founded by the Portuguese in the 1680s under the name Nova Colônia do Santíssimo Sacramento (Vianna 1972, 63). The Spanish settled the area around what is now Montevideo in the early decades of the 1700s (Elizaincin 1992, 97). Though officially part of the Spanish Empire for most of its colonial history, control of modern-day Uruguay, the neighboring Brazilian state of Rio Grande do Sul, and some bordering areas of what is now Argentina and Paraguay, passed between Spain and Portugal until the Treaty of San Ildefonso set the border in 1777 (Vianna 1972, 147, Owens 1993, 22–3, Bertolotti et al. 2005, 11). That border, however, would be called into question only decades later after the Provincias Unidas del Río de la Plata—the successor territory to the colonial Viceroyalty of Rio de la Plata, including parts of modern-day Argentina, Uruguay, Paraguay, Bolivia, and to a lesser extent Chile and Brazil—acquired their independence from Spain in 1810.

During the colonial period, Uruguay, known at the time as the Banda Oriental, was colonized by Spanish and Portuguese speakers in overlapping geographies. Portuguese speakers were present both in the north, near the modern border with Brazil, but also in Colonia del Sacramento, Montevideo, and other areas (Bertolotti and Coll 2014, 62–3). Likewise, Spanish speakers were scattered throughout the country. Documents from this period demonstrate that the Uruguayan society was bilingual more than it was diglossic, which is to say that throughout society both languages were used irrespective of their contexts rather than one language being privileged in government or formal situations and the other in informal speech. Sources suggest that even if such diglossic categorizations did exist in theory, they weren't rigidly respected (Mena Segarra 2004, 7).

Following the independence of the Provincias Unidas del Río de la Plata from Spain, the Banda Oriental would go on to form the easternmost province of that country. Uruguay's bilingual character was a particular liability during this period, as the Orientales struggled to define a regional identity as distinct not only from the former colonizers, but also from the larger powers of Argentina and Brazil on either side (Barrios 2013, 197). Portugal occupied the Banda Oriental in 1816 and fully annexed it in 1821 (Vianna 1972, 248–50). Brazil gained its independence from Portugal the following year and the Banda Oriental became known as the Cisplatina Province of the newly formed Empire of Brazil (Caetano 2020, 50). Uruguay would not gain its independence until 1828, and then not from European colonial powers, but from Brazil as a result of the Cisplatine War (Vianna 1972, 349–50, Caetano and Rilla 2016, 39, Caetano 2020, 40, 52). In this way the national history of Uruguay is far more intimately intertwined with Portuguese and Brazilian influences than is any other country in Latin America besides Brazil itself.

Despite this political history, Virginia Bertolotti and Magdalena Coll suggest that it had a relatively small influence on the linguistic situation in Uruguay. A much larger influence came from the constant influx of Portuguese—and later Brazilian—farmers and ranchers who settled in northern Uruguay (Bertolotti and Coll 2014, 63). These settlers, Bertolotti and Coll suggest, were not initially motivated by the State, as was the case in other Latin American land grabs, but by their own interests and the available land in the region (Bertolotti and Coll 2014, 63).

The linguistic divisions between Uruguay and Brazil have always been porous and somewhat artificial. In the colonial years and well into independence, Portuguese and Spanish could be found alongside each other in government documents, with bureaucrats often alternating between the two in the same document. For example, in the corpus of historic documents studied by Bertolotti, Caviglia, Coll, and Fernández, between 1833 and 1856, 41.1 percent of official documents from Tacuarembó mixed Spanish and Portuguese. This contrasts with 57.4 percent that are in Spanish and 1.4 percent in Portuguese (Bertolotti et al. 2005, 20). In other words, while it was clear that government documents kept only in Portuguese were rare, bilingual documents were quite common. These bilingual texts are some of the first written examples of Portuñol, which incidentally appear at about the same time as early examples of Spanglish.

Throughout the nineteenth century, the presence of Portuguese in Uruguay held strong, which drew the attention of many in the corridors of power. In the 1850s and early 1860s Montevideo encouraged the foundation of Spanish-speaking communities in the north—curiously one of these, Artigas, is the birthplace of one of the Portuñol authors we'll consider later (Bertolotti and Coll 2014, 65). Spanish was seen as an "instrument for the affirmation of nationality, which basically meant establishing differences with Brazil and eliminating Portuguese" (Barrios 2013, 201). Later, in the 1870s, Spanish was declared the language of education, thus seeking to kill two birds with one stone by combatting the presence of Portuguese in the north and the presence of an increasing number of European immigrant languages in the south (Barrios 2013, 203, Bertolotti and Coll 2014, 67). Finally, in 1878, it was decreed that official documents should be kept in Spanish (Bertolotti and Coll 2014, 64). These efforts did see the growth of Spanish in the Republic, but not necessarily a decline in Portuguese. Instead, large bilingual communities emerged such as in the Department of Tacuarembó where 43 percent of the population was bilingual (74).[7]

In the presence of this bilingualism, language evolved: by 1922 the resulting "lowly dialect" of Spanish and Portuguese mixing had drawn the attention of Uruguayan politician Justino Zavala Muniz (Behares, Díaz, and Holzmann 2004, 237). During the Uruguayan dictatorship, which spanned from 1973 to 1984, the official policy of the government was to eliminate Portuguese—by which it also meant Portuñol, a term not yet in common use for the tongue—in Uruguay (Barrios and Pugliese 2004). As with many such linguistic purity policies enacted from on high by repressive governments, this policy was destined to fail, though it did contribute to the internalized stigma that speakers had for their own native language.

Over time, and despite the best designs of central Uruguayan governments to limit the use of Portuñol, it persisted. In this geography, influence from both Spanish and Portuguese allowed for Portuñol to redefine words—sometimes playing off false cognates between the languages—and to create new ones (Bertolotti and Coll 2014, 78). Eventually Uruguayan Portuñol would be deemed a stable language in its own right (Lipski 2009, 7, 10). While prestige varieties of Spanish and Portuguese are taught and used in official settings on both sides of the border, it would appear that an organic evolution of the language has led to the emergence of myriad nonstandardized regional varieties and idiolects of Portuñol that vary from one speaker to another, and from one community to the next, despite the stability that Lipski has identified.[8]

---

[7] What exactly bilingualism means in these studies is not made explicit. We can assume that the literacy rates in the region would have been low in the late nineteenth century. Consequently, we don't know if these numbers reflect language skill level, and if so how, or if these are self-reported and thus may reflect identity values.
[8] For an in-depth discussion of variation in Uruguayan uses of Portuñol, see Elizaincin (1992, 100–56).

As mentioned before, some linguists refer to the results of this linguistic evolution as "Uruguayan Dialects of Portuguese" much in the same way that we saw that Spanglish described as a North American variety of Spanish with heavy English influence. However, there are a few reasons that we'll stick with the term Portuñol in this study. First, while Portuñol is an important part of the culture of Northern Uruguay, it's not unique to there. As mentioned, Portuñol exists in southern Brazil, Paraguay, and to a lesser extent in the northeastern Argentine provinces of Corrientes and Misiones. Though Uruguayan varieties of Portuñol are by far the most studied and Uruguayan authors are the most prolific, literature and cultural products are emerging in this language from across the region, so referring to Portuñol as an "Uruguayan" phenomenon seems reductionist if we limit our understanding of the word to be in reference to the nation state itself. However, the fluvial border between Argentina and Brazil that extends from just south of Iguazú to the northern border of Uruguay is marked by the Uruguay River; thus, the name "Uruguayan Portuñol" retains this double meaning. Nevertheless, given the prolific writing of authors from Uruguay and the academic interest in the varieties of Portuñol located in that country, this study will focus most heavily on the situation there. Second, as we've seen, language is not merely a series of linguistic features or influences; it is an essential element of its speakers' identity, and giving the language its own name is an act of pride for some communities, even when they disagree on what that language should be called. Writing, singing, or performing in that language is a way of expressing their pride and identity. Still, it seems that in recent years the term Portuñol has become the most used among its speakers and is the name reflected in their 2015 application to UNESCO for the language to be recognized as an Intangible Cultural Heritage of Uruguay (Da Rosa 2015).

Experimenting with a Literary Language

Though Portuñol existed in Uruguayan government documents, mostly in the form of bilingual side-by-side texts, and in personal correspondence from across the region, it didn't make the leap into literature until sometime later (Varsi de López 1967, Bertolotti et al. 2005, 16). When it did, as we've seen to be the case in other forms of *linguistic labor*, it emerged first in poetry or as dialogue within texts that were otherwise narrated in a more normative Spanish or Portuguese, such as those by Brazilian author João Simões Lopes Neto (Simões Lopes Neto and Kades 2015). Only much later did they appear as the dominant variety of the text. That the appearance of dialogue in Portuñol in an otherwise dominant-language text (i.e., with a normative Spanish-speaking narrator) often was for comedic or *costumbrismo* purposes also is a trend that appears in Spanglish literature.

Early examples of Portuñol in poetry can be seen in the works of Agustín Ramón Bisio, from the first half of the twentieth century (Gutiérrez Bottaro 2014). Foundational texts that demonstrate Portuñol dialogue in prose and theater can be seen in the work of his contemporaries, Eliseo Salvador Porta and José Monegal (Monegal 1958, López 1993). All were born in Northern Uruguay at the twilight of the nineteenth century and wrote until their deaths in the middle of the twentieth century. Of Bisio's poetry, Brenda López asserts that it is authentic in content and language, mixing "Gaucho" and Portuguese to tell culturally relevant stories about the border (López 1993, 68–9). However, regarding Porta and Monegal, who wrote prose, López says that they incorporate authentic myths, culture, and vocabulary from the border region, but their use of Portuñol is fragmented (López 1993, 30, 122).

Portuñol poetry and theater are strong currents that remain in the literature today with notable authors such as Michel Croz, Marianella Moreno, and Raphael Ficher publishing in the genres. Similarly, musicians Ernesto Díaz and Andrés Rivero have taken the language to the stage in other formats.

Prose

The primary interest of this book is to explore the emergence of prose literature in Portuñol, a shift Saul Ibargoyen Islas is often credited for beginning. However, at a closer look, we see that Ibargoyen Islas' use of Portuñol was also often limited to dialogue, while the narrator still speaks in an unaccented standardized Castilian.

In 2010, however, Fabián Severo, published, in a prose poetry form, his *Noite nu Norte: Poemas en Portuñol* (Severo 2010).[9] Following his success of this first work and several subsequent poetry collections, he broke the hold that normative Spanish has had on the narrator's tongue in his 2015 novel *Viralata* (Severo 2015).

---

[9] Severo has republished several of his works under edited titles and with adjustments made to the way he represents Portuñol.

Born in the far northern frontier town of Artigas, Severo now resides in the Montevideo metro area where he's a literature professor and creative writing workshop coordinator. In total he's published six books which consistently demonstrate engagement and a heightened linguistic awareness (*surconscience linguistique*) of his relationship to Portuñol. One such example is in poem "Trinticuatro" of *Noite nu Norte*; here he describes his role as a child language broker. He says:

> Mi madre falava muy bien, yo intendía ….
> Mas mi maestra no intendía.
> Mandava cartas en mi cuaderno
> todo con rojo (igualsito su cara) y firmava imbayo.
>
> Mas mi madre no intendia
> *Le iso pra mim ijo* y yo leía.
>
> (Severo 2022, 70)

> [My mother spoke very well, I understood …
> But my teacher didn't understand.
> She would send letters in my notebook
> full of red (just like her face) and would sign below.
>
> But my mother didn't understand
> Read this to me, son and I would read it.][10]

Similar topics about his community's language use reverberate throughout his work, though as with all of the *literary doulas* studied in this volume, it is far from the only theme he addresses. Other topics include the center-periphery divide between Artigas, the most remote of Uruguay's cities, and Montevideo which manifests on the one hand in structures imposed from afar to keep Artigas from tumbling over the cultural precipice into Brazil, while on the other hand stigmatizing Artiguenses and allowing infrastructure to lie in waste. Of his writing, he mentioned in a tweet that some Artiguense politicians are embarrassed at how he portrays the town and region as stagnant or backwards.

---

[10] Translation is the author's.

Reception of Portuñol Literature

In the Uruguayan context, there are strong stigmas of poverty and backwardness generally associated with the interior, which is to say any area outside of the larger Montevideo metropolitan area where two-thirds of Uruguayans live. Portuñol is a manifestation of this. It persists despite the aforementioned history of education efforts and reforms meant to eradicate it.

In the forward to the 2022 edition of Noite nu Norte, Uruguayan poet Javier Etchemendi reflected these preconceptions when he penned the following:

> Este libro es un atrevimiento y por eso no lo perdono. NO está escrito ni en español de España, al que tanto imitamos, ni en portugués de Brasil, al que ya quisiéramos poder imitar. Es un libro concebido en portuñol. Me rechina, me molesta y, aun así, es un texto que me fascina.
>
> Me encuentro sentado cómodamente en Montevideo y alguien me dice que existe literatura y, peor aún, poesía en portuñol. Displicentemente leí este texto. Extrañamente amé este texto.
>
> El idioma (dialecto, podrán decir algunos más patrióticos que yo) transforma este libro en una rara avis dentro de nuestro panorama literario, más acostumbrado a las experiencias circenses que a los destellos de buena poesía. Ni de Uruguay ni de Brasil, ni en español ni en portugués.
>
> (Etchemendi 2022, 13–14)

-

[This book is daring in a way I do not forgive. It is written neither in Spanish from Spain, which we try so hard to imitate, nor in Brazilian Portuguese, which we wish we could imitate. It is a book conceived in Portuñol. It bothers me, it annoys me and, even so, it is a text that fascinates me.

I am sitting comfortably in Montevideo, and someone tells me that there is literature and, even worse, poetry in Portuñol. Dismissively, I read this text. Strangely, I loved this text.

…

The language (dialect, some more patriotic than me may say) transforms this book into a oddity within our literary landscape, more accustomed to circus experiences than to flashes of good poetry. Neither from Uruguay nor from Brazil, neither in Spanish nor in Portuguese.][11]

---

[11] Translation is the author's.

However, in the face of this, as Etchemendi points out, Severo's work has garnered overwhelming attention. His works have been published in translation—a challenge to which I'll return later—and in 2017 his book *Viralata* won him the Premio Nacional de Literatura, Uruguay's highest literary commendation. He's regularly a presenter at national and international book fairs and has appeared in countless readings and interviews.

Conclusion

In the previous pages I've told a story of the cohabitation of Portuguese and Spanish in a variety of geographies across South America, from isolated jungle towns to resort cities and airports. I've also shown that the centuries-old manifestation that appears in Uruguay is unique among them all. It's not merely a lingua franca to facilitate communication between those who do not speak the same language. Instead, it's a mother tongue that has been highly stigmatized and education efforts have fought to teach it out of existence. In the face of this, we've seen that *literary doulas* are putting in the work to bring forth a literature that celebrates this tongue. In recent years it has been published over and over again, performed on stage, and has garnered national and international attention. In a small country flanked by giants we find another example of linguistic leadership.

4

Judeo-Spanish

Today the Judeo-Spanish-speaking population is largely concentrated in Israel, but this has only been true for the last few decades. This community's journey from the ancient shores of the eastern Mediterranean to the Iberian Peninsula and back spans thousands of years and tells the tale of high-ranking court officials, conquests, philosophers, expulsions, colonization, extermination, secularization, Zionism, and the struggle between language revitalization and language death. We'll focus most of our attention on the historical elements that lead to the evolution of Judeo-Spanish into a distinct language variety from Modern Spanish after the Jews' expulsion from Spain (and later Portugal) at the end of the fifteenth century and the ensuing struggle of the community to write and preserve their own language variety. Let's start at the beginning, over two millennia ago.

Ancient sources are uncertain as to when the Jewish diaspora first arrived to the region that is now Spain; some folk traditions suggest that Jerusalem's aristocracy settled in the Iberian Peninsula following the Babylonian exile sometime around 586 BCE (Gerber 1994, 2). Other sources propose that the Jews arrived during Roman times (King 1972, 131, Flavius Josephus 2017, 7:2). What we can know for certain is that by the time the Visigoths conquered Hispania (the Roman province corresponding to modern-day Spain and Portugal) in the fifth century, the Jewish diaspora of the area was significant.

The Visigoths ruled Iberia from the fifth to eighth centuries. As Christians, the Visigoths forced the Sephardim (the Iberian Jews—from the Hebrew word for Hispania, Sepharad) to renounce their faith, advocated for the extermination of the Jews, and passed multiple anti-Jewish decrees including declaring all Jews to be slaves and forcing their children to be raised by Christians (King 1972, 131-6).

Given such a treatment by the Visigoths, and by extension by Christian society at large, it's no surprise that the Jews saw the Muslim armies led by Tariq as liberators when they arrived in Spain in 711 CE (Gerber 1994, 18). Arab chronicles paint a vivid picture of Christians fleeing their cities as the Muslim forces swept through the peninsula, leaving Jewish patrols as allies to support the Arab advance. Despite this alliance, Jews were not considered equals with Muslims in the parts of the Iberian Peninsula that came under Muslim rule, then known as Al-Andalus. However, they were able to practice their religion in peace, provided of course that they pay the tax required of them as non-Muslim monotheists, or *dhimmis* (Menocal 2002, 72–3).

Muslim rule in Al-Andalus lasted, in one form or another, until 1492 CE. During this period Jewish civilization thrived and was highly integrated into the multicultural society composed of Muslims, Christians, and Jews. Some of the greatest Jewish minds of the age resided in Córdoba, the capital of Al-Andalus, and contributed to its emergence as the intellectual center of the medieval world. Some renowned Andalusi Jews include Maimonides, who wrote Jewish philosophy that is still cited today; Yehuda Halevi, whose poetry changed Jewish liturgy; and Hasdai ibn Shaprut, whose medical discoveries saw him promoted to a royal administrator for Calif 'Abd ar-Rahman III (Glick 1979, 172, 256, Menocal 2002, 79–80).

Jews were influential in court life in Christian-ruled areas of the Peninsula as well. In the twelfth and thirteenth centuries, the Toledo School of Translators relied heavily on educated Sephardim to translate philosophical and scientific texts from classical Arabic into Latin and later into Castilian (Foz 1998, 5). After all, many of the Jews of the time spoke the local language, be it Castilian, Portuguese, Catalan, Galician, Valencian, Arabic, or others, though sometimes with Hebrew loanwords (Bunis 1992, Rodrigue 2002). Jewish texts in these languages during this period have been lost to time, if ever they existed. Rather than writing in their vernaculars, many Jews of the time wrote instead in Hebrew, Latin, or Arabic. Linguist David Bunis suggests that the elements preserved in Judeo-Spanish now would lead us to believe that medieval Sephardim likely spoke in a way very similar to their non-Jewish neighbors (Bunis 1992, 403). And, like other Iberians, the Sephardim were not part of any linguistically homogeneous population.

Over the course of the Muslim rule of Al-Andalus, the Christians never gave up trying to assert their authority over the entirety of the Peninsula. As they slowly pushed the Muslims out, the Christians again became hostile to the Jews. In 1391 a massive pogrom began in Seville. By the time it had swept north through Castile a year later, 300,000 Jews had been affected. Christian extremists had had murdered 100,000 Jews; a similar amount converted to Christianity to save their lives. A third of those affected fled or went into hiding. This violence set the stage for the complete expulsion of the Jews from Spain a century later (Gerber 1994, 113,14).

Many associate 1492 with Columbus' first voyage to the Americas; others remember it as the year that Ferdinand and Isabella conquered Granada, the last Muslim stronghold in Spain. But it is also the year that an estimated 150,000 Sephardim were presented with a choice, to convert or leave Spain within four months (Pérez 2007, 14). Many fled to Portugal, only to be expelled again five years later (Soyer 2008, 33). When they left, the Sephardim could take very little with them. What they didn't leave as they fled into exile were all of the languages and dialects they had spoken in the diverse regions in which they had lived across the Iberian Peninsula.

Diaspora, Again

Many of the Sephardim settled in the Ottoman Empire; others moved to Morocco.[1] In exile the various Iberian languages evolved separately from those in Spain and Portugal. In some respects, they evolved more quickly, in others more slowly (Bunis 2005, 58). In addition, Hebrew, Greek, Turkish, Arabic, Bulgarian, Bosnian, and Serbo-Croatian influenced the nascent Judeo-Spanish (Moreno Fernández 2009, 439). These eastern Mediterranean and North African languages did not exert the same influence on the languages back in Spain and Portugal. But what is most interesting is that in the post-expulsion diaspora (those living in a "diaspora of a diaspora") the Iberian languages also evolved in close contact with one another (Wacks 2015, 1–3). Whereas in the Iberian Peninsula Portuguese, Aragonese, Catalan, and Castilian would have been separated at times by great distances or by important geographic divisions, in Morocco and the Ottoman Empire, Jews from across the Iberian Peninsula found themselves intermixing in great numbers for the first time. While these communities initially maintained their linguistic distinctions by establishing synagogues and socializing with those from the same areas of the Peninsula,

---

[1] The history of Moroccan Jewry and the evolution of Haketía there are not dealt with extensively in this volume. For more information, see Schroeter (2002), Elmaleh and Ricketts (2012), and Hart (2016).

eventually these different Iberian languages blended together and formed what we now know as Judeo-Spanish (Penny 2002, 26–9). Judeo-Spanish is not, however, a monolith; it is divided into at least two main Ottoman dialects, each differing in how they use elements of Castilian, Catalan, and Portuguese (Wexler 1977, Saul 1983, 327). Moroccan Judeo-Spanish has its own name known as Haketía (also spelled as Jaquetía or Yaquetía). Initially, though, Judeo-Spanish was the spoken language, but Hebrew remained the language of Sephardic Jewish literature.

While many Jews left Spain and Portugal following the edict of expulsion, not all did. Those who remained were surrounded by a new notion of racial purity that was not common during the centuries of Muslim rule. To prevent Jews from amassing political power, aspirants to positions of influence in many Iberian jurisdictions were required to prove they did not have Jewish blood. Furthermore, many Jews publicly converted to Christianity (known as conversos), but practiced their own religion secretly, hoping to evade the judgment of the Inquisition. This pressure to remain hidden, systemic oppression, and precarity was too much for most to bear and the Spanish and Portuguese conversos slowly trickled out and joined their coreligionists in Morocco and the Ottoman Empire (Gerber 1994, 163).

Written Ladino

As one might imagine, those Jews who left Spain and Portugal after 1600 had spent a century without institutionalized Jewish practice or formal education and had quite a low level of Jewish textual literacy. Nevertheless, they did have a strong Jewish identity and strong cultural reference points. To bolster their Jewish education, rabbis translated Hebrew-language didactic literature, known as *musar*, into Judeo-Spanish ... sort of. What they created was calque or word-for-word translations that respected Hebrew syntax and grammar but replaced Hebrew words with Judeo-Spanish ones. This was called Ladino. It wasn't Judeo-Spanish the way the people spoke it; instead, it facilitated the study of Hebrew-language literature by making it more accessible to a segment of the population who was not able to access the literature in the source. Jacob Huli's *Meam Loez* (first instalment in 1730) and Abraham Asa's translation of the Bible (1739) were the first two such works (Lehmann 2005, 34). Written Ladino was not meant to be read by individuals; rather, it was to be read in a group setting known as a *meldado*. For anyone who has read calque translations, it should come as no surprise that, while they are didactic tools, they are not always the most easily accessible types of literature to those who are not at least moderately familiar with the source language. Still, this was the first attempt at writing Judeo-Spanish—in the Hebrew alphabet of course—and this sort of hybrid form of Ladino remained the dominant written variety of Judeo-Spanish until the middle of the nineteenth century.

Western European Colonization

Having contributed to, and benefited substantially from, the secularization that came from the Enlightenment in Western Europe, Jews from Paris (and to a lesser extent Vienna) set up schools in many Jewish communities across the Ottoman Empire. The Alliance Israélite Universelle (AIU), the largest umbrella organization for these schools, had 115 schools in 47 cities by the early twentieth century. As a result, 80,000–100,000 Ottoman Sephardim spoke French (Saul 1983, 333–6). At first glance this might seem like an act of charity from the wealthier and ever more upwardly mobile enlightened Western European Jews toward their less fortunate coreligionists in the Ottoman Empire. However, this benevolence shrouded the fact that the AIU was also a tool of cultural colonization that emerged from contemporary Western European imperialist designs that were playing out in Africa and Asia. After all, colonization was frequently conducted under the auspices of charity, but with a goal for the colonizer to benefit disproportionately by spreading their culture and language at the expense of the other, all the while gaining economic advantage. This is precisely what happened with the Ottoman Sephardim.

Under the influence of the French Jews, the Ottoman Sephardim slowly abandoned the Hebrew alphabet. The first major step toward the adoption of the Latin alphabet was in 1886 when a Judeo-Spanish newspaper was first published in the Latin alphabet rather than using the Hebrew alphabet (Saul 1983, 338). Whereas Judeo-Spanish had developed spelling conventions in the Hebrew alphabet, those disappeared in favor of fluctuating phonetic transcriptions of the sounds based on the Latin-alphabet orthographies of French, Italian, and eventually Turkish (Bunis 1975, 2). French literature was imported into Judeo-Spanish, but was again translated not as the people spoke, but with an eye for moving the community closer toward French norms (Sephiha 1986). This desire to evolve Judeo-Spanish toward French was replicated as the Sephardim began to create their own secular literature.

From the Fall of the Ottoman Empire to the Second World War

In 1923 many Sephardim celebrated the declaration of the Turkish Republic, a secular state modeled on Enlightenment ideals that had been imported from the West. Five years later, the Turkish language reforms replaced the Arabic-based script that had been traditionally used to write Turkish with a newly adapted version of the Latin alphabet. The Sephardim followed suit and abandoned what little use of the Hebrew alphabet they had retained for Judeo-Spanish prior to this shift.

At the same time, increased transportation options and stronger ties to Western Europe put Judeo-Spanish speakers in regular contact with Castilians for the first time in centuries. Until then, the Judeo-Spanish-speaking community was unaware that their vernacular was so far removed from the literary standard of Spain. When confronted with this, and already believing their language an inferior jargon devoid of cultural production—a sentiment that stemmed from the belief that Hebrew, Turkish, Greek, French, and other languages had a literature, while Judeo-Spanish did not—some of the bourgeois Judeo-Spanish population attempted to adopt Castilian norms (Díaz-Mas 2009, 93). This added yet another competing spelling system to the already cluttered landscape of Judeo-Spanish orthography.

In the period between the fall of the Ottoman Empire and the Second World War Turkey transferred the major Judeo-Spanish center of Salonica, modern-day Thessaloniki, to Greece as part of a land and population exchange between the two countries. The Judeo-Spanish speakers chose overwhelmingly to remain in their home city, but in so doing again found themselves, 450 years later, surrounded by an ethnic nationalism that had not existed under the previous rulers (Ginio 2002, 238). Greece thus became home to two distinct Jewish communities, a Greek-speaking community centered in Athens, and a Judeo-Spanish population based in the north. Whereas their Turkish coreligionists were an active part of the establishment of a new political project, the Turkish Republic, and engaged in secular community life in Turkey, the Jews of Salonica struggled to adapt to the new cultural and linguistic context. While in the multi-ethnic Ottoman Empire the Jews were one of many cultural communities and could move freely between languages depending on the situation. Greece, on the other hand, was a nation built around an ethnic identity. Consequently, learning Greek was essential for employment and full participation in civic life. In this context an accent marked most of the Judeo-Spanish speakers as Others. The Jews, try as they might, were unable to integrate quickly enough.

In April 1941, Greece was occupied by the Axis forces and nearly the entire Jewish population of Salonica was exterminated. Broadly speaking 86 percent of Greek Jews were killed, mostly in the gas chambers of Auschwitz (The National WWII Museum 2017). Those who survived were overwhelmingly Greek-speaking and could more successfully hide among the majority (Ginio 2002, 255). The Judeo-Spanish-speaking communities of Yugoslavia and Romania were also decimated. Only the Sephardic communities of Turkey and Bulgaria emerged largely unscathed from the war.

Despite the survival of these two communities, Judeo-Spanish in the eastern Mediterranean had been dealt a fatal blow. The horrors of the Holocaust pushed many Sephardim to leave their homes and relocate, most to the newly created State of Israel. Two ideologies, neither new, but both gaining traction, contributed to the further decline in the population of native Judeo-Spanish speakers: the identity of a Turkish secular republic and Zionism.

Death by Ideology

The secular Turkish Republic was supported by most of Turkey's Jews. Over time the Turkish community abandoned Judeo-Spanish as the language of the community and adopted Turkish, first in the public and later in the private sphere. The younger generation ceased to transmit Judeo-Spanish to their children. As of the late 1990s the language was in dramatic decline in Turkey (Altabev 1998a). There is no data to suggest that it is returning as the dominant language of any community.

Similarly, Judeo-Spanish speakers who left Europe and Turkey for Israel did so because of the draw of Zionism. Zionism is the political belief that the Jewish people should form a national homeland rather than continuing to live in disparate diaspora communities around the world. The movement gained traction in the late 1800s and resulted in the formation of the State of Israel in 1948.

One can imagine the optimism and motivation to help build a new nation for your people in the aftermath of near total annihilation of your minority community at the hands of others. However, the Jews arriving in Israel did not constitute a cultural or linguistic monolith, despite sharing a religious heritage. Instead, they were highly diverse. In addition to Judeo-Spanish, among the new immigrants Yiddish, Persian, Arabic, English, French, Russian, Polish, German, and many other languages could be heard. The early Zionists, recognizing the struggle to unify such a linguistically diverse people, revived Hebrew which had remained the traditional and liturgical language of the Jews despite having fallen into disuse as a spoken language centuries earlier. Upon independence in 1948, Hebrew was declared the official language of the new country. This again situated Judeo-Spanish as the language of a minority and speaking it instead of Hebrew was at odds with the nation-building project that Zionism was promoting. So, the younger generations instead adopted Hebrew and English (Schwarzwald 2004, 575, Harris 2011, 51). Ironically Israel, a nation created to ensure the survival of the Jewish people, was a major force in the decline of Judeo-Spanish.

At last count (in 2011) an estimated 11,000 native speakers remained; many were well over seventy and had varying degrees of fluency (Harris 2011, 58). Over the last few decades, the current population and other interest groups have been attempting to revitalize the language. Consequently, literature in Judeo-Spanish has been emerging like never before. In 1996 the Knesset (Israeli parliament) established the Autoridad Nasionala del Ladino (ANL) to promote and protect the language. The ANL went on to suggest a standard spelling system for the language using the Latin alphabet to resolve the confusion of the various existing orthographies in circulation (Navon 2011, 4–8).

In 2018 a new Academia Nacional del Judeoespañol en Israel was founded with a mandate to accomplish a similar mission to that of the ANL, but in partnership with Spain's national language governing body, the Real Academia Española. This academy was founded with the intention of it integrating as a full member of the Asociación de Academias de la Lengua Española, the unifying body of all of the Spanish language academies. Of course, with so few remaining speakers—and as an initiative largely driven by non-native (or non-heritage) speakers of Judeo-Spanish, most notably Ashkenazi and European philologists—this begs the question for whom exactly the Academia Nacional del Judeoespañol en Israel is attempting to standardize the language and why a new organization was needed given that the Autoridad Nasionala del Ladino had been in operation for over twenty years.

In 2019, reports emerged of founding members asking these same questions. Aldina Quintana, one such founding member, suggests that this academy has been founded from a top-down approach. Despite her initial participation in the founding of the academy, she has withdrawn her support stating that she would prefer to dedicate herself to research rather than to an organization that will have little impact on the language use itself (Morales 2019).

As we've seen, Judeo-Spanish, as a unique language variety, has a history of just over 500 years. During that time, it has been dispersed among various empires and countries, but has nearly always occupied a minoritized position relative to Hebrew, as the liturgical and literary language of the Jewish intelligentsia, and the imperial or national languages used by the dominant groups of those among whom the Sephardim were living. Given this political reality, it is little wonder that the Judeo-Spanish community was slow to write literature in a way that truly represented their own speech patterns instead of seeking to conform to the styles and literary conventions of these high-prestige varieties. It took a metaphoric "terminal diagnosis" to move the oral language into the literary sphere.

Writing Judeo-Spanish Folktales as Linguistic Palliative Care

Since the 1980s one woman, Matilda Koén-Sarano, known by the Judeo-Spanish-speaking community simply as Matilda, has published the vast majority of the literature emerging in Judeo-Spanish. Koén-Sarano's work deviates from much of that published before her in that her work is copied from the oral tradition in a way that transcribes the informal language as it is spoken in its community, rather than recreating calque or highly Gallicized works as we've seen were typical of the literary translations that tended to precede her. In the coming pages we will look at Koén-Sarano's life, her motivations, the life-cycle of her community, and other emerging Judeo-Spanish language initiatives that are serving as a type of linguistic palliative care which seeks to preserve the language variety as it first transitions away from being the native language of large communities, then moves through a period in which it's the heritage language of a smaller community, before eventually becoming a post-vernacular language used in certain restricted settings.

Matilda's Life and Passion

In order to understand Matilda's passion and motivation, let's begin by considering how her own life shaped her experience. Alfredo Sarano, Matilda's father, was born in Aydın, Turkey in 1906. In 1912 he moved with his family to the island of Rhodes, which had been taken from the Turks by Italy in the Italo-Turkish war. Though the Dodecanese islands (of which Rhodes is one) were meant to be under Italian occupation only temporarily, in 1924 the Fascist Italian government made this control permanent (Bosworth 2006, 49, 296). In 1926 Alfredo left Rhodes, a decision that proved lifesaving. Since the Rhodian Jewish community had no escape route to flee the invading German army in 1944, almost all were deported to concentration camps. Following his departure, Alfredo settled in Milan where he met Matilda's mother, Diana Hadjés. Diana was also a native of Aydın but had moved to Izmir as a child and remained there until 1937 when she relocated to Milan, no doubt at least in part motivated by the Thrace Pogroms of 1934 (Bayraktar 2006). Diana and Alfredo married in 1938 and stayed in Italy until their immigration to Israel in 1969. The native language of both Alfredo and Diana was Judeo-Spanish.

On November 17, 1938, Fascist Italy enacted a set of laws known as the Manifesto of the Race (*Manifesto della razza*). This was a series of racial purity laws that showed heavy Nazi influence. Under the Manifesto, ethnic Italians were affirmed as belonging to the Aryan race and restrictions were placed on non-Aryans (including Jews). These restrictions limited their professions, abolished the right for Aryans and non-Aryans to intermarry, and allowed for the confiscation of property belonging to non-Aryans. Jews, in particular, were required to register their status with the municipality. Prior to the establishment of these laws, anti-Semitism in Italy was uncommon and the enactment of these laws provoked a backlash from the Italian population toward this overt discrimination. Even the Catholic Church ostensibly endeavored to protect the Italian Jews (Bosworth 2006, 414–21). The Italian laws defined who was Jewish less strictly than did the race laws of the Third Reich. Whereas in Germany one was identified as Jewish if one grandparent was Jewish, regardless of one's own religious or cultural practice, in Italy even conversion to Christianity was enough to escape the law. Still, Italian Jews undoubtedly feared that laws would later be amended to parallel more closely those of Germany. It was into this environment that Matilda Koén-Sarano was born in 1939 in Milan.

In 1943 Italy signed an armistice with the Allied forces and was occupied by the Third Reich. It was only then that deportation of Jews to concentration camps began, and only in German-occupied areas of Italy. Being immigrants to Italy and involved in the Jewish community there—Alfredo worked for the Jewish Community of Milan—it would have been almost impossible for the Sarano family to hide their Jewishness from the larger society. So, endangered by the constant bombing of Milan and the implementation of the Nazi's Final Solution in Italy, the Sarano family fled to Mombaroccio in the Province of Pesaro e Urbino. In this small village in the mountains of Italy the Sarano family hid for a year (Koén-Sarano 2006, 66–72). In order to make ends meet Alfredo sold the family's gold jewelry and occasionally taught math lessons that the local priest secured for him. Matilda describes this year as one of austerity and fear. After a year, allied soldiers took the Sarano family first to Pesaro, then to Rome. Following the liberation of Milan, the Sarano family finally returned home (Koén-Sarano 2012). Three years had passed since their flight.

After the war, when the family had returned to Milan, Alfredo became the secretary of the local Jewish community. There Matilda grew up speaking Spanish at home (or so she thought) and Italian in public.

In 1956 Matilda began her university studies in Foreign Languages and Literatures at the Università Bocconi. It was there that she became aware that the Spanish that she knew was different from the Spanish that she was being taught in the classroom. After telling her father, he secured a Mexican tutor for her. Through exposure to the Spanish Renaissance novella *Lazarillo de Tormes* (1554) Matilda realized that the language that she had grown up with was not standard Modern Spanish; instead, she referred to it as "Old Spanish" (espanyol antiko), since it more resembled the Spanish of that text than it did the modern language that she was being taught in university (Koén-Sarano 2006, 116). This distinction became particularly evident when the professor had a hard time translating certain parts of *Lazarillo de Tormes* to the class in Italian; these same passages seemed to Matilda to be very close to her everyday speech.

Shortly thereafter, in 1960, Matilda married Aharon Cohen (later spelled Koén). In 1962 they joined the growing number of Zionists immigrating to Israel. They settled in Jerusalem. Matilda had three children before starting a career at the Ministry of the Exterior from which she retired in 1997 after twenty-three years of service. In 1987 Matilda graduated with a BA degree from the Hebrew University, having specialized in Italian Literature, Folklore, and Judeo-Spanish, thus completing the university studies that she had begun in Milan many years before. Aharon worked as a school principal.

Despite having full-time careers in unrelated areas, Aharon and Matilda labored pro-actively to ensure the survival of the Judeo-Spanish language. Aharon became the director general of the Autoridad Nasionala del Ladino, an organization dedicated to the preservation of the Judeo-Spanish language and culture; in the late 1970s Matilda began collecting folktales that would later be published in her first book *Kuentos del folklor de la famiya djudeo-espanyola* (1986). While compiling these stories Koén-Sarano was on occasion invited to broadcast about Sephardic and Italian folktales and music on Kol Israel (Israel's public radio service); in 1995 she became host of their Judeo-Spanish news broadcast. Koén-Sarano continues educating others and researching about Judeo-Spanish folktales and music through a storytelling group and a traditional music group that she coordinates. Due to recent efforts to preserve the performative element of Judeo-Spanish storytelling and music, Matilda can now be seen lecturing, telling tales, and singing on the YouTube channel *autoridadladino*.

In the introduction to *Kuentos del Folklor de la Famiya Djudeo-Espanyola* Matilda credits her parents with instilling in her a pride for her native language but says that it was not until she moved to Israel in 1962 that she truly learned the value of her language and culture. Upon arriving in Israel, Matilda spoke no Hebrew and many of her first steps to integrate into Israeli society took place with the help of other Judeo-Spanish speakers who aided her in getting adjusted to her new surroundings. Despite developing a life and career in Hebrew, a necessity in Israel and an ideal of the Zionist ideology, Koén-Sarano believes that her native language and traditions should be preserved for posterity. By engaging in this work, she has also enriched her own connection with her parents and heritage. Matilda states that she believes that it is her mission in life to preserve her native language and culture since many Judeo-Spanish speakers were not spared from the Holocaust, as she was.

Matilda Koén-Sarano has taught courses on Judeo-Spanish at the Autoridad Nasionala del Ladino i su Kultura, Ben Gurion University of the Negev, Midreshet Amalia seminary, the Sentro de Musika i Bayle Klasiko Oriental (Jerusalem), and in several short-term courses abroad. She was on the editorial committee for *Aki Yerushalayim*, a magazine published in Judeo-Spanish, and *Los Muestros*, a multilingual magazine that highlights themes of Sephardic interest around the world. Koén-Sarano has published or collaborated on eighteen collections of Sephardic folktales (predominately in Judeo-Spanish with Hebrew translations but also in English, French, and Italian), one cookbook, a complete Judeo-Spanish-Hebrew dictionary, nine musical collections, two textbooks, two didactic books, and a made-for-radio musical (Koén-Sarano 1986, 2006, XVI–XXI).

Other Contemporary Efforts

While Koén-Sarano is certainly the most prolific of authors who have published in Judeo-Spanish since the 1980s; she isn't the only one. Moshe Shaul, former vice-president and founding member of the Autoridad Nasionala del Ladino, was for many years an active supporter of Proyecto Folklor that copied down, recorded, and catalogued thousands of Judeo-Spanish folktales and songs. He was also a regular reporter on Israel's national radio station, Kol Israel, where he broadcast in Judeo-Spanish. Shaul was the editor in chief of *Aki Yerushalayim*, a Judeo-Spanish language periodical that was published from 1979 until 2016, but which eventually shut down due to reader attrition and waning interest (Santacruz 2017). Shaul has also developed several Judeo-Spanish learning materials, both traditional textbook formats and online methods.

Cantor Solly Levy is notable for his work recording Haketía (Moroccan Judeo-Spanish) music (Levy 2012). Others have published old romance novels in Judeo-Spanish; some have embarked on new translation projects into Judeo-Spanish and interested readers can now find Judeo-Spanish versions of *Le Petit Prince*, *Alice in Wonderland*, and *Martín Fierro*, among others. In some cases the titles of these texts imply that they are palliative in nature, referencing the language's impending death; in other cases they seem to be novelties or post-vernacular in nature. For example, given the wealth of translations of *Le Petit Prince* into languages for whom one would struggle to imagine a market, we can only conclude that its Judeo-Spanish translation may be more of a collector's item than anything else. Perhaps some of these authors do hope that their contributions will reignite an interest in the language among young people. More likely, though, is that this writing is ideologically motivated by those who, through writing, are serving as death doulas, helping their community mourn, or mourning themselves, as they slowly watch their traditional language fall into disuse.

Judeo-Spanish, Linguistic Labor, and Literary Doulas

Until now, we've explored a brief history of Judeo-Spanish and a sociolinguistic outline of the state of Judeo-Spanish today. We've also looked at the story of one woman, Matilda Koén-Sarano, whose efforts are unmatched in the realm of Judeo-Spanish linguistic palliative care. Before concluding, however, it's important to link these ideas explicitly back to the theories presented in the introduction, the notion of *linguistic labor* and of the *literary doula*.

As we've seen, despite the best efforts of some native and heritage speakers on the one hand and concerned academics on the other hand, evidence suggests that Judeo-Spanish will soon die as a language of natural communication. However, due to the efforts of authors like Matilda, it leaves a literary legacy of stories, idiomatic expressions, songs, personal memoires, and other genres that will allow interested parties in the future to learn about Judeo-Spanish and to even perhaps use it as a post-vernacular language—which is to say a language that does not serve a primarily communicative function, but rather a nostalgic one (Shandler 2004).

It's essential that we do not view Matilda's efforts through rose-colored glasses, however. This work may be driven by passion, but it is nevertheless *linguistic labor*. When she embarked on this project in the 1980s, she was writing for two audiences, the audience who could read the works and would eventually die, and those who likely could not read it at all, and for whom she ensured the stories were published with accompanying Hebrew translations. She was not writing for the generations of children who would come after her. She was not writing at the request of global publishing houses who would pay her handsomely, promote her work, and nominate her for prestigious awards. She was recording speakers telling hundreds of stories, writing them down, and publishing them—an enormous task—with no expectation of financial compensation or professional return on the investment.

Matilda sat with her community, holding its hand, and listening to its stories as its vitality waned. She watched it move from the living language of her childhood community to the terminal language of the elderly. Matilda, and others like her, did not abandon their language through this decline; instead, they prepared the community so that when Judeo-Spanish eventually passes, those who remain will be able to mourn and remember.

Part II

Queerness, Translation, and Translanguage

5

The Queerness of Linguistic Labor

Linguistic labor is inherently a queer act. In some cases, as we can see in the writing of *literary doula*, Gloria Anzaldúa, it's explicitly related to queer sexual identity, but the notion of queerness is not limited to sexual orientation. While the term queer has increasingly been conflated with sexual identity politics in recent years, Tim Dean suggests a wider application of the term which can enlighten this conversation. He says that queerness "extends the politics of sexuality beyond sex and sexual minorities' civil rights by insisting that 'queer' is opposed not simply to 'straight,' but more broadly to 'normal.' Hence the centrality accorded ostensibly nonsexual categories—such as race, ethnicity, and nationality—in queer theory" (Dean 2000, 227). Given this, the *linguistic labor* discussed in this work is queer as it directly opposes the linguistically homogenizing doxa of nationalist rhetoric that we've discussed throughout the first half of the book. In its attempt to dismantle the relationship with a national identity and a singular unifying language—a theme present in the United States, Uruguay, and Israel—*linguistic labor* encourages the emergence of a chorus of dissent from communities whose linguistic identities have been minoritized for generations, thus representing an artistic form of queer anti-normative activism.

In this chapter I explore the evolution of *linguistic labor* from the beginning of its boom in Spanglish, Portuñol, and Judeo-Spanish around the 1980s. In this period, before the internet facilitated instantaneous communication between people from distant corners of the world, people from remote corners of the Hispanic world embarked on similar projects, to write their vernaculars for the first time.[1] Chapters 2, 3, and 4 outline the ways in which these communities,

---

[1] Throughout the book I've struggled with the notion of referring to these languages as part of a Hispanic collective identity while simultaneously advocating for their legitimacy outside this paradigm. Nevertheless, that they are peripherally related to Spanish is what unites them into this book. Ultimately, we must question these colonial labels, but until we have new vocabularies to conceptualize shared histories without colonial labels, we're stuck with what we have. After all, if we throw out all existing vocabulary that stems from problematic histories, we're left with far fewer tools with which to have a conversation. In this book, I've suggested several terms and problematized others. I hope that others will continue to help us remedy our lexical shortcomings in the future.

each in turn, have a history of being linguistically oppressed or minoritized by the dominant societies in which the speakers live. In the three cases studied in this book, this oppression continues to manifest today. Given this context, the choice to write and to come out of the linguistic closet, demanding visibility in the public sphere for that which had been shameful or hidden for so long, is reminiscent of the coming out of the closet that many queer people either celebrate or endure, depending on their own support networks and social spheres. But, without any evidence to suggest that Spanglish, Portuñol, and Judeo-Spanish speakers were in contact with each other, we must wonder why they began this coming out en masse after hundreds of years of closeted language practices. The answer to this can be found in the ways in which several new theories, which emerged around the same time, were fundamentally reshaping our understandings of the human experience—forcing us to grapple with notions of identity which complicated the rigid categories that imperialism and structuralism had promoted up until then.

In the latter decades of the twentieth century there were a few major streams of thought that built on each other and which inspired intellectuals from around the world, namely poststructuralism and its latter intellectual offspring of postcolonial thought and queer theories. Poststructuralists, as well as postcolonial and queer theorists, created an environment in which very early *literary doulas* began the shift away from normative language uses and worked toward an ever-more radical writing. At first, these were small steps, but later waves of *literary doulas*, such as those studied in this book, pushed language in ever more radical ways in order to create a body of literature that reflected the voice they and their ancestors had been ashamed of for so long.

As I tell the tale of the relationship of *linguistic labor* to queerness, I'll begin well before queer theory was a theoretical framework, with a brief discussion of how poststructuralism and postcolonial thought influenced notions of nation and identity in the lead-up to a first boom of *linguistic labor* from the 1980s to around 2000. I'll then shift my gaze to discuss the second wave of *linguistic labor* that emerged after 2000. This second wave did not seem to take shape in Judeo-Spanish but did in Spanglish and Portuñol and drew inspirations from ideas that emerged from queer theory such as a rejection of capitalist, patriarchal, and racist notions of hierarchies, and a resistance to essentialist or fixed identity categories, preferring individual expressions of self. This chapter will close by linking the theory of *linguistic labor* with Halberstam's concept of the *Queer Art of Failure* and Preciado's *Countersexual Manifesto*, both central ideas to queer theory and essential to the notion of *linguistic labor* as a queer act of liberation.

What Happened in the 1980s?: The First Wave of *Linguistic Labor*

Spanglish, Portuñol, and Judeo-Spanish are nearly as remote from one another as is possible within the larger Spanish-speaking world; yet, all three communities began embarking on this *linguistic labor* at roughly the same time and with no obvious influence from each other, which can only lead us to wonder why. Of course, it's difficult to prove why any new art form emerges, but we can look to the philosophical theories, social movements, and political currents that were in vogue before and during this period to ascertain some influences that might have created the necessary conditions to foster this type of work.

Lead by such theorists as Derrida, Barthes, Foucault, and Deleuze, poststructuralism emerged in the 1960s. Poststructuralism was a critique of the rigid categories that its theoretical predecessor, structuralism, had proposed as a lens through which we could analyze the humanities and social sciences. A main critique that poststructuralists levied against previous theoretical frameworks was that these categories, often binary in nature: (a) were not ontologically real categories but rather were conceived by humans often without questioning the premise behind them and (b) ignored the relationship of power differentials which are ever-present in human interaction. Consequently, poststructuralists believed that structuralism was insufficient to capture the nuances of the human experience. Instead, poststructuralism sought to focus on the power inequities inherent in humanity in order to add nuance to our understandings of the humanities and social sciences.

Poststructuralism gave birth to several other movements that likely more directly impacted or inspired the work of these *literary doulas*, but without poststructuralism, which rejected binary definitions that were previously de rigueur in Western circles, one wonders to what degree a rejection of the marginalization of borderland and so-called hybrid identities would have been possible.

At roughly the same time, early postcolonial theorists such as Fanon and, later, Saïd began studying the structure of colonization and its legacy on the postcolonial societies which were emerging following the withdrawal of primarily English and French colonial governments in South Asia, Africa, and the Middle East. Postcolonial theorists rejected the hierarchy that was applied through colonization whereby European colonial centers were understood as the apex of culture to which the colonies were expected to aspire and conform. Instead, adapting the tools provided by poststructuralism, they focused on the power dynamics that were imposed through colonialism and which often remained in place even after independence. Postcolonial theories extended to language; colonial doxa had perpetuated a view that European languages, spoken and written as in Europe, were supreme to other languages. Scholars as early as Fanon, who wrote in the 1950s, demonstrated that to become legitimate in the eyes of the dominant class it was essential for colonial subjects to speak like a European (Fanon 2008, 2). Incidentally, France, of which Fanon wrote most of his critiques, had yet to decolonize much of its holdings, so it is premature to speak of postcolonial subjects in this context. He goes on to show that whereas languages like Wolof and Fulani may be seen by colonial centers to be of sufficient complexity so as to possess their own literature, languages that are the product of colonization—he cites creoles, but a similar extrapolation can be applied to the cases addressed in this book—are viewed as bastardized forms of a pure language and thus are viewed by colonial structures as "languages of the illiterate" (Fanon 2008, 11). Fanon decries these views, but demonstrates that, prior to the understandings that would result from poststructural and postcolonial theories, Europeans widely promoted those false ideologies. Indeed, these views are still held by many today, particularly where there is an emphasis on the teaching of another language.

By discrediting these absurd views, which are rooted in the raciolinguistic ideologies that I've discussed earlier in this book, theorists empowered early *literary doulas* to reflect on the ways that translating their community's experience into national languages propped up the hegemony of these national or colonial languages. Consequently, it perpetuated the belief that Spanglish, Portuñol, and Judeo-Spanish were bastardized forms of language used only by the illiterate. By the mid-1980s, some members of these communities had begun to see that this tendency robbed them of the ability to create prestige for themselves, which could be achieved by writing in their own language varieties. Instead, it motivated them to seek affirmation for their communities by rejecting the obligation to translate and to choose instead to birth new forms of literature in the languages in which they lived.

The earliest of these *literary doulas* sought to break from these imposed paradigms but had no clear path as to how to achieve this. In cases like these we see a strong desire to focus on stories which promote a postcolonial image of a country or people by showing us how things are different to those of the colonial and national centers. Such stories are present in the works of Anzaldúa, Ibargoyen Islas, Koén-Sarano, and many more. This approach is essentially a unique form of costumbrismo.

Costumbrismo was a literary device typically associated with nineteenth-century Spain, Italy, and post-independence Latin America. This device portrayed ordinary daily ways of life and folklore in writing as a way of strengthening regional identity, be it national or otherwise, by highlighting shared traditional customs that were different to other traditions outside the region in question. This was in large part a response to the urbanization trends sweeping Europe in the mid-nineteenth century, but in the Americas costumbrismo and its successor criollismo focused on strengthening regional identities both against other outside forces—this came on the heels of the subdivision of a newly independent Latin America into smaller countries—and against imposed European cultural forces.

The costumbrismo present in *linguistic labor* centered not on unifying national identity through a focus on local cultural practices, but rather it focused on the local to destabilize the notion of a hegemonic national identity that was based in colonial paradigms. In this first wave of *linguistic labor*, authors use Spanglish, Portuñol, or Judeo-Spanish in dialogue or in highly conversational forms, but the narrator often, though not always, still prefers a national language. For example, in the Portuñol prose of Saúl Ibargoyen Islas, we still find a Spanish-speaking narrator who introduces readers to Portuñol-speaking characters. In the theater of Luis Valdez or the prose of José Antonio Villareal we see English- and Spanish-speaking characters contrasted with Spanglish-speaking characters. For her part, Matilda Koén-Sarano copies down audio recordings of previously oral folktales into whichever orthographic conventions she deems most closely represent the speech of the informants, but always with a Hebrew (or occasionally other language) translation in parallel.

This costumbrismo-inspired approach to minoritized language use emerged as an early wave of *linguistic labor* and grew out of postcolonialism. It harnessed the mundane lives of certain people—this was particularly the case with Uruguay and Israeli literary productions, Spanglish had quite a different history in this regard—to set the countries in question apart from the postcolonial frameworks that they had overwhelmingly been attached to. In the Uruguayan context, this responded to the linguistic purity movements that we saw were imposed by the education system and the dictatorship up until the 1980s; in Israel this was the product of a growing national comfort level in which Hebrew was clearly established as the national language. There minority languages were no longer viewed as a force undermining national unity in a country of brand-new immigrants from a variety of linguistic backgrounds. Instead, regional

Jewish languages began to be celebrated at the national level and across the Jewish diaspora.

For its part, Spanglish remained a threat. On the one hand, it was a symbol of growing Latinx population in the United States, which raised fears among Anglos who were losing political power through the Civil Rights Movement and through demographic changes due to immigration. Latinx people also saw Spanglish as a threat because it fueled the fears that they were losing Spanish as an essential element of their culture. Spanglish, then, was not a manifestation of costumbrismo in the same sense as we see in Portuñol or in Judeo-Spanish, but rather a rejection of US expectations to conform that were imposed on Latinx people, as discussed in Chapter 2.

The presence of a dominant language narrator or a translation, however, doesn't fully liberate the language use from external power structures. In some instances, in fact, this presentation of Spanglish, Portuñol, or Judeo-Spanish alongside a more normative language use on the part of the narrator results in further othering of the already-minoritized characters. When this happens, the speakers of these minoritized languages are portrayed the odd ones, the uneducated, the bumpkin, the quirky. This seems a far cry from the activist reclamation of minoritized identities that I've described throughout this book, but let's hold our judgment for a moment. In the context of literary currents emerging prior to the 1990s—we'll look at 2000s queer currents in a moment—we must remember that any depictions of these communities were novel. Creating a space for this publication, then, required that an established author—in many but not all cases—incorporate it into their work. Someone needed to open the door. Saúl Ibargoyen Islas, Wilson Bueno, Gustavo Pérez Firmat, and many others were already successful literati in the dominant languages of the countries in which they lived before their works emerged in these minoritized languages. Rather than reflect on humble and perhaps imperfect beginnings with an unforgiving eye, let's recognize that in their context at the time, these baby steps were revolutionary.

The Queer Second Wave

Beginning around the 1990s another set of theoretical frameworks which also grew out of poststructuralism began to gain traction: queer theory. Rooted in the works of Foucault, Anzaldúa, and others, queer movements gave us a new lens through which to seek justice: the notion of performativity and the rejection of a fixed category of "normal." Originally attributed to Judith Butler, performativity was understood as the way by which we learn and attempt to mimic society's expectations of us based on our sex (Butler 1988). Butler suggests that there is nothing innate about those expectations, but that we perform them to fit in—to at least be perceived as normal.

Performativity, however, is not restricted to a performance of gender expectations. Instead, it can be applied to a wide range of social categories. We may perform a socioeconomic class to access or retain our social standing. Or, more importantly for the purpose of this book, we may perform language in a way that meets certain social expectations of class, gender, nationality, education level, etc. Traditionally, and even today, society has expected us to perform language in a way that meets colonial norms and conforms to a European or US-based expectations of linguistic standards in order for us to gain social mobility, be perceived as educated, or simply to avoid violence at the hands of others. For centuries, we played along in the hopes that if we played by the rules, we might win the game. For many, they never did.

Some scholars of queer theory have suggested that liberation lies not in conforming, but in breaking the expectation that we conform all together (Warner 2000, Conrad 2014). Jack Halberstam expands on these ideas in his book *The Queer Art of Failure* (2011). Failure is, to Halberstam's mind, a failure not on the part of queer people at what we aspire to accomplish, but rather a choice not to seek to accomplish what is expected of us by society. In other words, the failure is in the eyes of the dominant capitalist society. In the market economy in which we all live, there must be winners and losers. Failure, then, is "refusing to acquiesce to dominant logics of power and discipline" (88). Failure is nonconformity, anticapitalism, and nonreproductive states of being (89). These do not prop up the mechanisms of power which depend on human and financial resources for a state to succeed. How, then, is this failure queer? Queers do not aspire to these goals. The queerness, then, lies not in the notion that we are losing at capitalism, but rather "the queer artist works with, rather than against, the failure and inhabits the darkness" (96). Our *literary doulas* reject aspirations to be best-selling authors and instead produce works that bring them joy at the expense of capitalist success.

The notion of performativity and failure can be applied to nationalist subjects as well. If we concede that national subjects are units of work which, in a capitalist society, are intended to yield productive (or reproductive) benefit in ways that uphold this capitalist and nationalist narrative, which as we've seen often espouses values of linguistic uniformity, the choice to be unproductive in this vein is an embrace of failure as established by these criteria but rejected by queerness. To then create art to celebrate this failure is a radically queer act.

The later *literary doulas*, those who write this second wave of queer theory-inspired work, are seeking out the type of liberation that theorists such as Halberstam have proposed. They are rejecting the obligation to perform their subjecthood. Instead, they seek to liberate themselves and their communities from those expectations. This is the linguistic manifestation of Preciado's invention of new bodies. Of binary understandings of identity, he says: "The invention of new bodies will be possible only through the assemblage and hybridization of experiences from the border of what are traditionally understood as proper identities ... These [proper] identities (which never existed and were only ever fixed points in the power-knowledge regimen of the patriarchal-colonial) are now obsolete" (Preciado 2018, 15). In other words, queer theory is freeing us from the obligation to conform to (post)colonial, national, and capitalist expectations as those were never attainable expectations to begin with. Instead, we are creating, through our experiences of failing at meeting those expectations, new identities. And our doulas write them.

The *literary doulas* considered in this second wave are not as fettered, as were earlier doulas, by a need to mark their own otherness through italics, as we saw was commonplace in the work of Gloria Anzaldúa or Sandra Cisneros, for example. Neither did they predigest their ideas for a wide global readership as was the case for Koén-Sarano who presents most of her work with a parallel translation. Instead, they are comfortable advocating for their position as members of the multiethnic and multilingual fabric that makes up the diverse societies in which they live rather than being cookie-cutter citizens who perpetuate the cultural hegemony, through their intellectual productivity, that the nationalist marketplace seeks to impose.

Furthermore, second wave *literary doulas* such as Fabián Severo, Susana Chávez-Silverman, and others reject the notion that there is any objective singular manifestation of language that must be replicated in order to be valuable or authentic. Instead, they see language as an individual manifestation that is creative and can be—perhaps should be—liberated from the social constraints previously discussed, an issue to which I return in Chapter 7.

On the So-Called Artificiality of *Linguistic Labor*

One critique levied against Portuñol authors Wilson Bueno and Saúl Ibargoyen Islas as well as Spanglish author Ilán Stavans is that some of their works come across as artificial or contrived to native or proficient speakers of the languages in which they write. This is a quandary worth exploring further. After all, a critique on the grounds of authenticity can be fundamentally at odds with the notion of queer liberation. If we're blowing up established categories and embracing failure, what categories remain against which we can measure authenticity? Let's consider this from two angles: on the one hand the relationship between authenticity and the voice of the self, and on the other hand the importance of authenticity in the portrayal of someone else.

In the first case, no one can tell an author that their writings don't reflect their own language use in an authentic way. Sure, there may be inconsistencies in a doula's spelling or grammar choices, but such inconsistencies are often present in their daily language choices as well. In Koén-Sarano's writing, for example, we see a visual representation of the various accents of the informants who told her the folktales she recorded and later transcribed and published. After all, a doula's writing is a manifestation of their own understanding of themselves and their community and what better informant than these can we have? To suggest that their language use is contrived is to question their own relationship to their communities or to themselves, which seems at best an unfruitful observation. Furthermore, distracting from their work toward liberation with a claim of inauthenticity minimizes the work of liberation and instead imposes another norm against which this radical work can be judged and found to be lacking—most likely imposed by the same outsiders against which they are rebelling to begin with. As an art form, this work should be judged by what it achieves, not by what someone else wishes it did.

On the other hand, when authors such as Bueno, Ibargoyen Islas, and Stavans who are not from these communities, though they may indeed have certain ties to them, use these languages in their own writing, the issue is different. In-group members may legitimately critique this work as an inaccurate representation of their communities. This is a fair claim. After all, minoritized communities are often portrayed by people in positions of power in ways which further rob them of their agency and relegate them to a second-class position, well-meaning though these people may be. This is worse still when authors from outside these communities double down on their own misunderstandings of these languages and promote their own ideas as if they were authentic representations, as Lourdes Torres critiques Stavans of doing (Torres 2005). Allyship in this work requires humility; meaning well but causing harm is still harmful.

Despite this potential for harm, even artificial manifestations of these languages from outsiders can further the cause that *literary doulas* promote. Polysystem theory tells us that speakers of languages draw inspiration from the types of works that already exist in their language (Even-Zohar 1990). Both new compositions and translations of genres that had not previously existed inject new life into the language and inspire authors to continue building on the work of those who came before them. We must not forget that novel ideas are rarely perfect when they first come out, if outsider allies are using Spanglish, Portuñol, or Judeo-Spanish and creating a safe space for speakers to take over, that should be celebrated. However, taking someone's language for our own benefit and speaking over those with whom we pretend to stand in solidarity are not acceptable.[2]

Queerness and Linguistic Play

An important aspect of queerness that I have yet to address is its relationship to play. After all, queerness isn't limited to somber activism. Instead, Adrienne Maree Brown speaks to the queerness and activism of play in her book *Pleasure Activism: The Politics of Feeling Good* (Brown 2019). The overarching thesis in this collection of essays is that leaning into pleasure goes against the patriarchal and capitalist expectations imposed upon us. Pleasure, after all, is not productive. It does not build wealth for those in positions of power nor contribute to society in economically measurable ways, thus tying the idea back to Halberstam. Despite this failure to contribute to global capitalism, pleasure radically changes the quality of life for individuals and for the communities in which they live. She says:

---

[2] For more on equity and solidarity in a language context, see Attig (2023b).

So we could say on the spectrum of pleasure, yes, I like to get touched, I like to get fucked, but also, what about for my community, for my people? What is pleasurable in finding a place of grace and well-being and transcending oppression? If we're not imagining where we're going, then it will constantly just be pushing back outside from inside cages.

(Brown 2019, 39)

This type of pleasure is evident in the work of our *literary doulas*. While much of this book has spoken of labor in terms that focus on the work required to bring literatures into being, this work is also playful and fun. We should not underestimate the pleasure that our *literary doulas* bring to the work that they do, challenging though it may be.

By tossing off societal expectations of appropriateness and instead leaning into infinite playful and creative possibilities inspired by their own languages rather than the so-called literary standards, *literary doulas* bring about a radical shift in mindset of what literature can be. Rather than aspiring to externally imposed standards, they are liberated. This oddness, this queerness, centers a resistance to the "normal" and instead privileges the limitless possibilities that emerge when queerness and play come together to promote linguistic equity.

Conclusion

While some might conclude, based on the portrait that I have painted, that this *linguistic labor* constitutes the voice of the subaltern, I would argue that these *literary doulas* are exactly the opposite. When asked to clarify the use of the term "subaltern," Spivak states that the subaltern should not be equated with those who experience oppression. The oppressed who can express their views using the hegemonic discourse are by definition not subaltern. The subaltern who, in her words "cannot speak," is the subject who is unable to access or participate in the hegemonic discourse at all (Spivak 2001). The *literary doulas* that I have explored are educated in Western traditions, they conduct their public lives in the national languages where they live, and they use Western methodologies and literary models to inform their *linguistic labor*. We must not equate their literary production in minoritized languages with limitation, as Fanon criticized in the 1950s. Instead, we must see that, as multilingual people themselves, the choice to reject translation into national languages is a powerful act that seeks to right past wrongs and give literary prestige to languages that are in positions of precarity due to the stigma imposed on them by those in power. These doulas are not ignorant of, nor do they avoid or reject the hegemonic traditions that inform Western discourse; quite the contrary, they employ those theoretical frameworks to seek liberation by speaking the metaphoric language of the discourse in a written language in which the discourse had never been seen. They embrace poststructuralism, postcolonial, and queer conceptualizations, consciously or not, and use those theories to advocate for their own liberation all the while having a gay old time.

6

Translating Linguistic Labor

If we close our eyes and imagine a translator hard at work, many of us will imagine someone working between two national languages in commercial or governmental contexts. Open on their laptop is Trados or another CAT (computer-assisted translation) software, dictionary resources, parallel text software, and perhaps a model of an extant text in the target language to ensure accurate formatting. Alternatively, we might imagine a researcher holding a manuscript of an influential book open with their wrists as they type their translation directly into Word. Still others might think of those who work to subtitle film and TV into any myriad of languages for transnational streaming platforms. Regardless of the mental image that comes to mind, what's common across all images is that we know that a translator must understand the source text and be able to render it with some degree of faithfulness, regardless of how that might be defined, into a translated target text.[1]

Ultimately, what faithfulness in translation means is highly theorized in translation studies and a discussion on this topic is well beyond the scope of this project.[2] However, in order to have a conversation, it's important to share a common definition. For this reason, I'm proposing a definition based on what I believe most people understand as equivalence: rendering a source text into a target text with a prioritization for conveying the *meaning* of the source and, if possible, the form. My use of this idea, however, should not detract from the many ways of understanding equivalence, both within a textual interlingual understanding of translation and beyond (Jakobson 2000, Nida [1964] 2000).

---

[1] This chapter draws from these articles Attig (2019d and 2023b).
[2] The topic of what translation is, and where the idea of "faithfulness" fits in is complicated; some texts that have inspired my own reflection on this include the following: Lefevere (1990), Gentzler (1993), Spivak (1993), Benjamin ([1923] 1997), Berman (2000), Jakobson (2000), Nida ([1964] 2000), Vermeer (2000), Bassnett (2002), Tymoczko (2003), Chamberlain (2004), Holmes (2004), Schleiermacher (2004), Folkart (2007), Apter (2008), Venuti (2008), Cronin (2010), Pym (2011b), and Eco (2012).

The goal of this chapter, however, is not to redefine or engage extensively with theories of equivalence, but to raise some discussion points about how the conventional notion of equivalence may not be the most useful, at least not when used in isolation, as we reflect on translating, or attempting to translate, *linguistic labor* and hence make it accessible to new audiences.

At times the translation of the textual message conveyed by the words of one language into another language is more than adequate, even if it comes at the expense of a deep engagement with sociolinguistic, cultural, paratextual, postcolonial, or other contextual cues contained in the text. Such a translation may be, in fact, the only acceptable strategy for some projects. Examples of texts like these may be translations of classic or religious works for a specialized reader. However, when the source text is a product of *linguistic labor*, the same strategy may undermine the larger more holistic message. The purpose of this chapter is to articulate the challenges that face the translator of this type of labor and thus inform translators', editors', and publishers' decision-making processes when they are working with these texts.

Returning to the image conjured up in the first paragraph of this chapter, the reality of *linguistic labor* is quite distinct. For example, none of the languages studied in this book are likely to have bilingual translation memory databases that could support the use of CAT tools. Only Judeo-Spanish, of the three, has comprehensive bilingual dictionaries. Even with these dictionaries, there are no standardized orthographic conventions shared between them and frequently the spelling in a text may not reflect the spelling in any of the various dictionaries available. Parallel texts don't exist, and there are likely few professional gigs that seek out Spanglish, Portuñol, or Judeo-Spanish speakers. This is in part due to their historic relegation to the domestic sphere, as we've seen in previous chapters. However, *literary doulas'* motivations to conduct *linguistic labor* stem primarily from a desire to liberate their minoritized language varieties from the cultural confinement of the domestic sphere that has historically been imposed upon them. Publishing, then, is a key action that *literary doulas* employ to get their language and literature into the public sphere.

Given these motivating factors, *linguistic labor* is, as I've discussed throughout this book, an act of rebellion against systemic power struggles between those in positions of linguistic power and those whose full linguistic identities are marginalized by nationalist rhetoric and linguistic ideologies. Consequently, the theoretical lens of *linguistic labor* shows us that the textual message of the literature, while still important, is secondary to the form. The primary function of *linguistic labor* lies not in the message that is communicated, but the way in which it is articulated. After all, it is the act of writing in one of these minoritized languages that constitutes the labor, regardless of what the textual message may convey. Therefore, it is of utmost importance for a translator of this literature to address the form and sociolinguistic context whence it emerges—and by extension the relationship between the form and context—for target readers of the translation.

Whereas in a translation exchange between global languages which all share a certain minimum degree of prestige or global recognition, as might be the case between English and Spanish or between Portuguese and Japanese, for example, a focus on conveying a message is central to the translation project.[3] The same cannot be assumed about a translation from Spanglish, Portuñol, or Judeo-Spanish, much less if the translation is into a dominant national language. In these cases, the translator must not only convey the content, but also the rebellion against established linguistic power structures inherent to the linguistic choices made by the authors. How this can be accomplished, though, is not immediately evident. In this chapter, I consider the unique challenges that arise when translating this type of literature and the extant research on minoritized or minority translation. I then raise some questions that translators and publishers of such literature might use to amplify these authors' voices and resist assimilating their work into the linguistic structures of power against which these authors rebel.

Translation and Minority: Background

In her 1987 book *Borderlands/La Frontera: The New Mestiza*, Gloria Anzaldúa says the following of translation:

> Until I can take pride in my language I cannot take pride in myself … Until I am free to write bilingually and to switch codes without having always to translate, while I still have to speak English or Spanish when I would rather speak Spanglish, and as long as I have to accommodate the English speakers rather than having them accommodate me, my tongue will be illegitimate.
>
> (Anzaldúa 1999, 81)

---

[3] For more on comparable degrees of linguistic prestige, see Pomerleau (2017).

Some *literary doulas*, including previously discussed author Susana Chávez-Silverman, have understood this declaration of linguistic independence to be a mandate against textual translation. However, this literal interpretation of Anzaldúa's words is not the only reading available to us. Anzaldúa is not problematizing only a textual or vocal exchange of information as the verb "translate" in this quote might imply. Instead, she is describing a resistance to the requirement that a minoritized subject—in her own case a queer Chicana woman—perform their identity in a way that minimizes an authentic representation of the self. She resents this obligation to conform to the expectations of dominant society in order to gain access to the public sphere. In this sense, translating oneself is a matter of wearing a metaphorical costume that hides one's true nuance from those who cannot be bothered to respect it. This broader-reaching interpretation of Anzaldúa's missive, when combined with the notion of *linguistic labor* as articulated in previous chapters, adds a multifaceted dynamic to the relationship between translation—both textual and metaphorical—and minoritized communities.

Textual translation, on the other hand, if done in a way that magnifies the voices of *literary doulas* rather than assimilating them or domesticating their words, as Venuti cautions against, can provide other communities with tools and models that can inspire the emergence of their own *literary doulas* (Venuti 2008, 1–30). This type of south-to-south communication, albeit through a center, is described by Johan Heilbron:

> The international translation system is, first and foremost, a hierarchical structure, with central, semi-peripheral and peripheral languages. Using a simple definition of centrality, one can say that a language is more central in the world-system of translation when it has a large share in the total number of translated books worldwide ... Distinguishing languages by their degree of centrality not only implies that translations flow more from the core to the periphery than the other way around, but also that the communication between peripheral groups often passes through a center. What is translated from one peripheral language into the other depends on what is translated from these peripheral languages into the central languages. In other words, the more central a language is in the translation system, the more it has the capacity to function as an intermediary or vehicular language, that is as a means of communication between language groups which are themselves peripheral or semi-peripheral.
>
> (Heilbron 2010, 309–11)

Heilbron's suggestion, given our current societal shift to considering issues of representation through the lens of equity and solidarity, may seem shocking.

It seems, at first glance, that he is suggesting that we assimilate literature into the linguistic power structure against which it may be rebelling in order for its message to reach broader audiences than might be possible were it not translated. This hope for a positive impact from the same hierarchical linguistic ideologies that have caused systemic minoritization of the languages in which our *literary doulas* write sounds similar to the notion of a benevolent dictator to whom we must relinquish our own freedom so that he might take care of us. Pragmatically, however, if we are to translate literature to magnify a minoritized voice so that it may support others, this may be the best option. After all, it is hard to imagine how many speakers of Hinglish, the Hindi-English language used in India, might be comfortable enough in Spanglish to translate Chávez-Silverman's Spanglish crónicas directly. Despite this linguistic barrier, speakers of some minoritized languages may desire to understand the realities, challenges, power dynamics, and celebrations of others. From a practical perspective, in the words of Gayatri Spivak, these authors must be "made to speak English" or some other central language (Spivak 2005, 182).

This does not mean, however, that the translation process must invisibilize the *linguistic labor*. On the contrary, several studies have explored ways in which peripheral voices, broadly defined, have been translated in the past (von Flotow 1997, Grutman 2006, Meylaerts 2006, Cronin 2010, Spivak 2010, Tymoczko 2010, Attig 2019d). Sometimes these highlight inequities or challenges, but the most optimistic of these provide us with inspiration for how we might do better in the future (Appiah 1993, Spivak 2005, Epstein and Gillett 2017, Attig 2019c, 2022, 2023b).

If we are to embark upon a translation project, be it as translators ourselves or as editors/publishers of this work, there are several questions that we must consider to ensure that our engagement with this literature preserves not only the textual meaning of the source, but also the cultural meaning that the text and the language of the text both convey. The two main concerns that I will touch on in the following pages are: (1) identifying the target audience and the purpose of the translation (the so-called why of the translation), and (2) the choice of translator and the translation process (the "how"). The purpose here is not to provide answers or dictate acceptable practices to the exclusion of others; after all, a great many approaches to translation can be valid for any one situation. Instead, the goal is to raise questions that translators and publishers may consider as they embark on these projects to help them make decisions that are sensitive to the cultural realities of *linguistic labor*.

The "Why": Target Audience and Purpose

Translation can take a myriad of different forms; as we've seen, it is not always an exchange between equals. Sometimes translation occurs between two global languages in which the target audience of the translation is similar in education and socioeconomic class to the target audience of the source. In this case, the purpose of the translation could be more or less the same as the source text. This is, as mentioned in the introduction to this chapter, the situation that most people imagine when they think about translation. Consequently, this dynamic influences a common understanding of fidelity in translation. However, textual translation can also exist in many other contexts. For example, the translation of an old text for modern readers, the adaptation of literary classics for children, or a translation geared at promoting community services to a clientele with low literacy skills (Reiss 2000). Furthermore, intersemiotic translation can move a text from one semiotic system (such as literary/textual) to another (such as film) (Jakobson 2000). In these situations, fidelity can exist though it may take on a very different shape. To decide what an appropriate degree of fidelity looks like in any given situation, translators must identify who their target audience is and define the desired purpose of the translation.

Let's begin this conversation about target audience by considering some widespread beliefs about translation and then reflect on how those might be different for translators working with source texts that are the product of *linguistic labor*.

There is a lay belief that translation is merely an exchange (often a neutral exchange) of information between two languages, as can be seen in the definition of translation as provided by dictionary.com: "the rendering of something into another language or into one's own from another language." However, if we look more closely, we can see that far too often such an exchange is not neutral at all but is informed by systemic power differentials. The power imbalance inherent in any translation exchange has been discussed at least since Benjamin's 1923 seminal essay "The Task of the Translator" (Benjamin [1923] 1997). Many more seminal debates consider the language exchange through a postcolonial or center-periphery lens (Spivak 1985, Rafael 1988, Appiah 1993, Susam-Sarajeva 2002, Bandia 2010). Additional studies have focused on the translation of multilingualism or the ways in which heteroglossia, idiolects, queer language, or nonstandardized forms are translated for audiences who may not understand the cultural context from which such texts emerge (Grutman 2006, Meylaerts 2006, Démont 2018). Still further conversations have highlighted the overwhelming emphasis on the translation of source texts produced in prestige varieties of national or so-called named languages into prestige varieties of other languages, which comes with its own nationalist bias (Cussel 2021). Such an orientation, Cussel notes, stresses translation that takes place between languages like French, Spanish, and English, but minimizes the importance of translation from, into, or between minoritized languages that do not enjoy the same level of institutional or national recognition. While most theorists take the stance that all texts can be translated in one way or another, we cannot minimize the importance of the context in which writers in minoritized languages reside and the *linguistic labor* that informs their oeuvre.

Without a deep understanding of this context, translators risk mischaracterizing a *literary doula's* work in any number of ways. Speaking about source texts from queer communities, Démont found that such source texts are not always fully understood by translators (Démont 2018). Though Démont was speaking of sexual and gender minorities in his chapter, the queerness of linguistic labor as discussed in Chapter 5 clearly makes these theories applicable here as well. He identifies three modes into which queer texts are often translated: a misrecognizing translation, a minoritizing translation, and a queering translation (157). In this paradigm, a misrecognized translation is one in which the queer elements of the source are not perceived or are minimized by the translator. A minoritized translation, on the other hand, "congeals queerness's drifting nature by flattening its connotative power to a unidimensional and superficial game of denotative equivalences." Finally, a queering translation takes a stance by "developing techniques to preserve, using Kwame Anthony Appiah's expression, the thickness of queer literary texts."

Building on Démont, I argue that perhaps such a misunderstanding of minoritized communities may be more widespread than merely in LGBTQ+ contexts (Attig 2023a). This is especially likely when translators are not deeply engaged with the communities they translate (Attig 2023c). Consequently, their misunderstanding of the source texts, and perhaps source culture, be it through either a misrecognition or a minoritizing fallacy, may result in translations which fail to convey the message—both textual and contextual—that was central to the source. This results in a domino effect of misunderstanding or minimization that can impact available interpretations to readers of the translation. However, if we prioritize why translation of *linguistic labor* is happening and for whom, we can start to ponder a list of considerations that will support more equitable practices going forward.

Most commercial translations are paid for by publishing houses whose primary goal is to sell works to as broad an audience as possible. Within the constraints of global capitalism, this makes logical sense. Consequently, though, this means that translations are expected to conform to the norms of the target language markets. Into English, this means a domesticating norm—in other words, a translation that is not identifiable as a translation to the readers. Other cultures permit translators to use more robust footnotes or other intervention strategies to explain the source text and its cultural context. Regardless of the culture, though, the constraints placed on the translator are not governed by the necessities of the text being translated, but rather by the market expectations. In this sense the target audience and the purpose of the translation can be synthesized into an idea that a translation is produced to sell a work to whomever might consider buying it.

This is a terrible approach to take for *linguistic labor* and does not respect Halberstam's idea of queer liberation through capitalist failure. *Linguistic labor* is, by definition, not written for the broadest audience possible. Instead, it's written to speak to those who either see themselves represented in the work or are willing to put in the necessary effort on their own part to access it. Conversely, *linguistic labor* is not intentionally obtuse or closed-off to outsiders, but *literary doulas* do refuse to frame their narratives in terms that are easily accessible to those from outside the linguistic community. Translating for the broadest audience possible undermines this effort.

Translating, however, for a similarly minoritized audience who might find solidarity in this work—described by Christopher Larkosh as south-to-south translation—yields a different set of considerations (Larkosh 2011). For example, Portuñol works might resonate with Franglais/Frenglish-speaking communities in Quebec; Spanglish works might inspire Singlish speakers in Singapore. While it's true that the most accessible manifestation of this solidarity might look aesthetically similar to a domesticated translation into whatever the language in question is, it might take other forms as well. Translations presented in parallel with the source text, as can be seen with many of Matilda Koén-Sarano's folktales, annotated translations, or translations with extensive translator's notes, are some possible options. In some cases the form may be dictated by the available translators of the work, especially given the aforementioned challenges of finding translators who work directly between minoritized languages. Regardless of the form, the purpose of these translations is fundamentally different. Here the translation serves to inspire groups who have similar linguistic struggles in different geographies; it is not to further line the pockets of those in positions of power who have often been, at best, complicit in the perpetuation of harmful linguistic ideologies.

The line between what is a market-driven translation and what is a solidarity-driven project may seem invisible to the naked eye. Like two oceans bleeding together, the distinction is subtle at first. But it becomes noticeable in minute differences in temperature, salinity, or the color of the water when seen from afar. When considered collectively, though, the differences can be felt.

Given this context, it is essential that any conversation about the translation of minoritized voices fully engage the matter of who is translating their literature and how. It is only by considering the issue through this lens that we can attempt to understand how *linguistic labor* can be approached to minimize the risk of misrecognition or minoritization of the source through the translation exchange.

The "How": Translator Choice and Translation Process

Given the challenges described above, a concerned translator or editor might wonder if all translators are equally able to translate all texts, and what processes might ensure a more nuanced representation of the source text and context in a translation. To consider these questions, we must turn our attention away from the theoretical challenges that arise when we think about translating *linguistic labor* and instead consider two perhaps more practical aspects, the choice of the translator themselves and some thought-provoking questions that may guide the decisions that translators and editors make as they approach this work.

Over the past few years there have been growing conversations about the ways in which privilege and translation intersect. Some of these conversations have suggested that the identities of translators and the authors they translate must overlap. One example of this is the matter of the translator chosen to render Amanda Gorman's 2020 inaugural poem into Dutch, which I addressed in more depth elsewhere (Attig 2023b). Despite this suggestion, which is clearly important in the context of current equity-oriented discourse, we cannot assume that such an ideal is even accessible, particularly when discussing the nuances of *linguistic labor*. After all, many translators are shaped by the languages and cultures that they navigate and the transnational lives that they lead. By contrast, many *literary doulas* are informed by a different set of linguistic and cultural references. The ability to navigate different cultures and languages is a key tool that the translator brings to their métier, but it is also a key difference that makes a full overlap of identities between author and translator impossible.

In the remaining pages of this chapter, I reflect on some ways in which translation of *linguistic labor* can be possible even in the face of these challenges. I do not, however, aspire to provide a set of prescriptive practices that will ensure a keen translator will adequately render *linguistic labor* and all its nuance into a new language. Such methodological suggestions simply don't work with translation; as I tell my students, in translation there is no right answer, though there are many wrong ones. Instead, I hope to provide aspiring translators of *linguistic labor* some questions that they may consider to help them choose projects at which they can excel and deploy the translation strategies that are fitting to the task at hand.

Purpose of the Source and Purpose of the Translation

As we consider for whom we might be translating, let us return momentarily to some widespread ideas about translation and publication. From a profit-driven publishing model in the context of global capitalism, it's easy to imagine that texts should be written and/or translated to reach the broadest audience possible. This should not be understood as a necessary starting point. As Vermeer and Reiss's skopos theory teaches us, every text has a purpose and was created with that purpose in mind (Vermeer 2000). They go on to say that in a similar way each translation has a purpose which may deviate from the purpose of the source text. The purpose of each text will determine how it is rendered for the desired audience.

In the context of *linguistic labor*, where minoritized communities are telling their own stories, the reality is that sometimes the intended audience is far narrower than we might expect given the aforementioned profit-driven assumptions many of us hold. In these cases, creators (authors, filmmakers, etc.) have chosen not to present their work in a way that is equally accessible to all. One example of this, albeit from outside the realm of the languages and communities studied in this volume, is Brandon Taylor whose 2020 debut novel *Real Life* tells the story of Wallace, a gay Black grad student at a midwestern university (Taylor 2020). Wallace describes feeling out of place, being gaslit by white colleagues, and being exoticized by the predominantly white gay community. Taylor, in an interview, clearly stated that the target reader of this novel is not a cis-white-het-male. Instead, he wanted other queer Black young adults to see their experiences reflected in his work (Wheeler 2020). Such a goal of writing for a specific audience is not new. In the 1980s, Gloria Anzaldúa said: "Until I am free to write bilingually and to switch codes without having always to translate, while I still have to speak English or Spanish when I would rather speak Spanglish, and as long as I have to accommodate the English speakers rather than having them accommodate me, my tongue will be illegitimate" (Anzaldúa 1999, 59). And indeed, Anzaldúa published a wide range of poetry in which she used Spanglish to articulate her message to those with whom she thought it would most resonate. For source texts with purposes (skopoi) that seek to prioritize one readership, potentially to the exclusion of others, it's essential to take a good long look at for whom we might be translating the texts and how that will impact the approach we take to the task.

Given that *linguistic labor* fulfills not only a communicative purpose, but also a goal of raising linguistic prestige, we might wonder if such literature should be translated at all. Theorizing non-translation is fascinating and there is space for these conversations, but I think that a rigid posture against translation in contexts such as these limits itself to theory. After all, these texts are being translated, regardless of our opinions as to whether or not they should be. Consequently, my goal isn't to argue that they ought not to be rendered into a new language and opened to a new audience. Instead, I'd like to focus on how the translation of *linguistic labor* may advance the ideas of this type of sociolinguistic work rather than be assimilationist to larger prestige varieties of central languages, and thus potentially undermine the structural change for which *literary doulas* are advocating.

One potential impetus for translation of *linguistic labor* emerges if we consider that there are a great many opportunities for south-to-south translation (translation that builds international solidarity by avoiding passing through central or dominant language varieties) or translations aimed at building solidarity with other minoritized communities who struggle in similar ways against linguistic ideologies of prestige. For the translator, considering how this translation may support the rebellion of other communities against similar ideological structures of oppression can inform how they approach their task more strategically.

Does the Translator Understand the Struggles of the Source Community?

In the case of *linguistic labor*, which is born out of struggle, it's important to consider whether the translator understands the struggle of the source community and why the text they are approaching is rebellious in form, even if it may not always seem to be so in content. Similarly, is the translator able to render the duality of form and content for potential readers? This seems obvious, but too often literary and audiovisual media are not considered to be specialized texts—a term that has often been used to refer to medical, legal, or other such jargon-heavy texts.[4] In specialized translation, we expect a translator to understand nuance in genre, form, vocabulary, and context of a source text and be able to render them into a context-appropriate target text in their specialized areas. In fact, we often require proof or credentials to ensure they can do so. However, when it comes to *linguistic labor*, and literary translation in general, the same rigor is not applied. It should be. Translating *linguistic labor* is a form of social justice translation and by extension specialized translation. As such, translators should be held accountable to no less a degree than they are in medical, legal, or other so-called specialized fields (Attig 2023c, 18).

An example of a translation that achieves very different goals than the source text is evident in the French and Brazilian Portuguese translations of Disney/Pixar's film *Coco* (2018). The source version of *Coco* includes nearly 300 utterances in Spanish in an otherwise English-dominant film (Attig 2019a, 154). This reinforces the border-crossing narrative, which is metaphorized by the need for Miguel, the protagonist, to move undocumented between the land of the living and the land of the dead. This metaphor maps directly on the reality some children experience at the US-Mexico border. Further strengthening the links to modern transnational US-Mexican realities are the linguistic codes used to tell the story; linguistically, Miguel inhabits a borderland in which he can be seen as either Mexican or Mexican American. Spanglish in the film supports this ambiguity. The translations into French and Brazilian Portuguese both conserve the Spanish elements of the source text. However, the resulting linguistic cues paint a very different picture than in the source. Since France and Brazil share land borders with Spanish-speaking regions, translingual forms of speech (employing Spanish and either French or Portuguese elements)

---

[4] For a definition of specialized translation, see Franco Aixelá (2004, 32) and Rogers (2015, 21).

are possible at those borders, as indeed we have seen in the case of Portuñol. However, the border-crossing narratives of undocumented workers, the fear of virulent anti-immigrant action that was pervasive when *Coco* was released, and other such critiques that are illustrated in Disney/Pixar's film are not at all the same concerns as in France or Brazil. Consequently, the resulting translations illustrate Démont's observation that some elements in texts are often miscategorized into a superficial translation of denotative equivalences (Démont 2018, 157). Though Démont was referencing queer-specific contexts when he presented this theory, this example broadens his theories to include a wider range of applications than was originally discussed.

One way that a translator can minimize the risk of misunderstandings when translating *linguistic labor* is to focus on translating works from communities whose struggles they have taken the time to understand. This does not mean that all translators must inherently share a significant overlap of their identity with the authors they translate. After all, there is no guarantee that a Chicanx translator, for example, will necessarily value the *linguistic labor* of publishing in Spanglish rather than in English or Spanish. To suggest that an identity overlap in one area is a quality control mechanism to ensure a translator's understanding of the nuances present in *linguistic labor* is naïve. After all, we all bring our own conscious and unconscious bias to bear on our work, and sometimes we are hardest on those with whom we share close ties. On this the American Literary Translators Association has stated: "We should not use personal identification as the primary criteria that determine a potential translator's ability to work on any given text" (American Literary Translators Association, 2021). But there must be some honest and deep engagement with the communities they are seeking to represent in their work. This is a humbling and ongoing task; there is no end goal at which to arrive. Instead, the goal is a continual integration of this humility and engagement into the practice of translation.

If We Are Going to Translate, How Do We Do It?

For a qualified and sensitive translator, the task of translation, given all the challenges presented above, may seem daunting if not impossible. Given the scarcity of studies on existing translations of *linguistic labor*, we also don't have a lot of strategies to consider in any depth. In this final section of the chapter, my goal is to consider how we *might* translate it given the few existing studies on this topic.

There is no single approach to translating this literature, which I hope to have driven home already, and each individual scenario will require its own set of questions, and by extension its own translation strategy. However, given my subjectivity as a translator and scholar for whom global Englishes and Spanishes are the dominant languages of writing and research, I cannot divorce my reflections on this topic from that context.

Since at least the end of the Second World War, translation in the English-speaking world has been praised, by readers and publishers alike, when "it reads fluently ... in other words, [it looks like it] is not in fact a translation, but the 'original'" (Venuti 2008, 1). Any evidence that the work is a translation is viewed as shoddy or unskilled on the part of the translator. Lawrence Venuti coins this tendency "the translator's invisibility." The burden of digesting a text, removing from it all traces of foreignness, and situating the work within the culture and value system of the translating language (a process he calls domestication) lies with the translator, though editors and publishers certainly have a say.

When the translator is truly invisible, however, there is no expectation that readers will leave their comfort zone and consider the text as the product of any culture besides their own. Instead, the translator's responsibility hinges on "the reconstitution of the foreign text in accordance with values, beliefs, and representations that preexist it in the translating language and culture, always configured in hierarchies of dominance and marginality, always determining the production, circulation and reception of texts" (14). This model, known as a domesticating translation, is exactly the type of translation that I've suggested we avoid. Instead of domesticating a text, however, there are any number of experimental or creative approaches that translators may employ, and which have a long history in the translation tradition (Tymoczko 1999a, 33).

One of these creative strategies, which may seem like a possible solution at first glance, is to seek out literary "dialect" in the target language in order to set the translation apart from normative language uses and thus replicate the ways in which the source deviates from existing linguistic paradigms and conventions. This must be deployed very carefully. After all, as Grutman has observed, sociolects, ethnolects, or other so-called dialects that hint at a speaker's social location are highly indexed to nuanced and culturally bound realities. He points out that Lunfardo is an Argentine sociolect that is indexed to reference the overlap of a specific ethnic group, social class, and age/time period in Buenos Aires. On the other hand, Abruzzese is an Italian language variety that references a different reality. To translate Lunfardo into Abruzzese, or the other way around, is to create the minoritizing translation that Démont criticizes. Consequently, Grutman suggests that translating "dialect into dialect"—imprecise terms which need not be contested in depth here—rarely achieves the desired result (Grutman 2006). Nevertheless, translating from one minoritized language into another may be an exception. For example, in 2019 I translated a short story about the border between Uruguay and Brazil from Portuñol into Spanglish specifically to put these two communities who are both conducting *linguistic labor* at the same time in conversation with each other (Attig 2019b). My goal was not to conflate one community with the other, or to draw parallels where they don't exist, both points which were made clear in my translator's note. Such projects must be intentional and we must not confuse *linguistic labor* with literary "dialect."

Another creative approach is what Kwame Anthony Appiah terms *thick translation* (Appiah 1993). This is the abundant use of the translator's interjections through footnotes or other tools to provide insight to the readers of the translation regarding significant cultural differences which may not be readily apparent. After all, as Susam-Sarajeva observes:

> Researchers of periphery-origin cannot afford to leave certain historical, literary, social or political information implicit in their work, as they cannot assume such a vast erudition on the part of their audience—even though a similarly vast erudition on central practices and traditions of translation is often expected on their part. Therefore, research on peripheral systems is often full of background information, which would not be necessary to anything like the same extent for research on central systems.
>
> (Susam-Sarajeva 200)

Such a thick translation may help to open *linguistic labor* to new audiences while also respecting the social commentary present in the choice of language in which the *literary doulas* write. Many English-language publishers, however, are resistant to including explanatory footnotes in works translated for a broad, rather than academic, readership. We must challenge this in the case of *linguistic labor*.

Other approaches to translating *linguistic labor* will emerge as studies in this field continue to give us new insights into which approaches have been successful at conveying the nuance of this work and which have domesticated or erased essential aspects of the struggle.

Conclusion

In conclusion, if we consider that translating *linguistic labor* is a form of social justice translation, and by extension is specialized translation, it should be treated as such. Only then can we develop practices that will prioritize accurate and nuanced translations of these messages over rushed or assimilationist translations that may mean well but may instead undermine the purpose of the source text, particularly when the language the author has chosen to deliver their ideas is a key element of the message. Some ideas have emerged, but certainly more work is needed in order to understand and establish best practices around this work.

We've seen that not all texts are written to prioritize equal access by all audiences. Neither is it a given that all potential translators should translate all texts, even when there is no doubt about their linguistic competence. Finally, unfettered access to *linguistic labor* by those from classes who have traditionally marginalized these language practices is likely undesirable, but that does not mean that translation is impossible; it simply means that translators of this work must bring to their métier a unique brand of humility and creativity.

7

Spanglish, Portuñol, Judeo-Spanish, and the Translingual

Throughout this book I have referred to Spanglish, Portuñol, and Judeo-Spanish as languages. Specifically, they are languages which are developing or expanding their literature to respond to either an urge to birth a body of works in the language (in the cases of Spanglish and Portuñol) or to prepare a written record of a language in decline before it moves into the realm of the post-vernacular (the case with Judeo-Spanish). However, my assertion that these are languages rather than varieties or dialects and why I haven't started this conversation with a discussion on translanguaging deserves further nuance. In this chapter I will examine these languages and their literatures through three frameworks which have informed my own reflections. First, I will discuss Deleuze and Guattari's notion of minor literature. I will first explore the origin of that term and its relationship to Kafka's writing. I will then move on to discussing the limitations of the term when we're reflecting on linguistic labor. In short, I suggest that linguistic labor is the antithesis of minor literature for reasons which will be spelled out below. Second, I will return to Lise Gauvin's idea of a *surconscience linguistique*, a linguistic hyper-awareness, which we see is present in minoritized (but not "minor") literatures. While Gauvin's ideas stem from the context of French literature written in Québec where French is minoritized against a larger English-Canadian context, I will relate her ideas to *linguistic labor* more broadly and suggest that the term can be useful in a wider range of contexts than the one in which she coined it. Finally, I will explore the relationship of these languages to the emerging theories of translinguistics and trans-theory, particularly focusing on how translinguistics can draw from Paul Preciado's *Countersexual Manifesto*. I then discuss how the identities reflected in the *linguistic labor* studied in this volume complicate the notion of translinguistics. Rather than accept translinguistics writ large, I present an argument that suggests that linguists must redefine our discipline with translinguistics, as a value system, at the center. This will, I suggest, remove the need for a trans- prefix to discuss natural language uses in ways consistent with descriptivist linguistics.

Minor Literature

In 1975, French philosophers Gilles Deleuze and Félix Guattari published *Kafka: Towards a Minor Literature*, in which they reflected on the relationship between the ethnic and linguistic identity of Bohemian author Franz Kafka and German, the language in which he wrote. They were concerned by what we might now consider the intersectional identity and imperial subjectivity of Kafka. After all, he was an Ashkenazi Jew, whose historic ethnic language would have been Yiddish: he was also born in Czech-speaking Prague but spoke and wrote in German because it was the language of social mobility in the Austro-Hungarian Empire of which Bohemia was a part (Deleuze and Guattari 1986, 17). Deleuze and Guattari coined the term *minor literature* to refer to works that reflect the intertwined relationship between the dominant imperial language and the subjectivity of minoritized communities present within those empires, as was the case with Kafka's work (16). They were interested in Kafka's choice, or obligation, to speak and write in German for social mobility rather than either Yiddish or Czech, which would have been a culturally or geographically more logical choice if it were not for the contextual obligations the empire imposed on him. Kafka was, we believe, raised speaking German—though some suggest he might have spoken with a Czech accent—so the "choice" to speak and write in German was not necessarily a conscious one he made for himself (Koelb 2010, 12). In other words, even before birth the structure of empire was impacting him. Nevertheless, as Deleuze and Guattari clarify, there was no other language available to this Bohemian Jewish author but to write in the language of the empire in which he lived, as it was the only language that he considered himself to speak fluently (Deleuze and Guattari 1986, 16). That Kafka only spoke German fluently was part of the imperial baggage that Deleuze and Guattari found so fascinating. In short, at some point in Kafka's family history, the languages of Yiddish and Czech fell out of favor due to German being the language of the Austro-Hungarian Empire. Therefore, Kafka, while left with no choice in the matter himself, wrote in a language to which he had no ethnic or geographic connection.

It bears clarifying that for some authors of minor literature, the language in which their works are written—which must be language of the halls of power for their works to be considered minor literature—is also their dominant or perhaps only language as we see with Kafka. Not all authors of minor literature are multilingual. That Kafka's Ashkenazi Jewish ethnicity ostensibly linked him to Yiddish—a claim based on what I view as an outdated linguistic essentialism—albeit perhaps with one or two generations of distance, it was not his native language, and he only took interest in Yiddish later in life (Koelb 2010, 12). A similar situation likely arises for many postcolonial authors whose ancestral language may occupy the place of a post-vernacular or heritage language. A post-vernacular language is one which is present in a ritual rather than communicative capacity. For example, Shandler points out how some Jewish communities use Yiddish expressions and songs because of tradition, even when the community members are not fluent in Yiddish themselves. In these cases, as Shandler points out, communities who use post-vernacular languages may not be certain of the meaning of what they say or sing, but reference it simply because of nostalgia (Shandler 2004).

Heritage languages, though, are a bit more complex to pin down and there are several different definitions of the term. Consequently, I'll take a moment to consider how I use the term here and how that applies to the *literary doulas* considered in this book. Polinksy and Kagan provide a useful definition that builds off Valdés' previous work. They state:

> She [Valdés] refers to heritage speakers as individuals raised in homes where a language other than English is spoken and who are to some degree bilingual in English and the heritage language.[1] Although the original definition is English centered, any other dominant language can be substituted for English. The crucial criterion is that the heritage language was first in the order of acquisition but was not completely acquired because of the individual's switch to another dominant language.
>
> (Polinsky and Kagan 2007, 369–70)

They go on to clarify that often this shift to another dominant language is in part due to the arrival of the child to school where national or regional languages dominate. Consequently, heritage speakers' acquisition of the language exists on a spectrum. High-proficiency speakers on one side of the continuum often have a high degree of contact with a vibrant heritage community. On the other end of the spectrum are low-proficiency speakers who may only hear the language from their own immediate family and may be unable to

---

[1] Source cites Valdés (2000).

read and write (371).² Across this range, however, a common throughline is that heritage speakers have incomplete input in their language development; after all, it would be truly unusual for a child to acquire all their academic knowledge in both the language they speak at home and the language they speak at school to the same degree of comfort. Similarly, some social situations, such as government interactions, may not be available in all languages. Even among the most fluent speakers of a heritage language, often a full range of linguistic registers to fit all situations is not part of their repertoire.

When considered in the light of this definition, most of the authors studied in this book should be considered heritage speakers of the languages in which they write. Gloria Anzaldúa writes extensively about the linguistic violence she suffered when forced to speak only English at school and the struggle against Spanish-language essentialism that she found in Mexico (Anzaldúa 1999, 76–7). Susana Chávez-Silverman was educated in the United States and Spain, in both English and Spanish (Chávez-Silverman 2004, XIX–XXI). Still, Spanglish was not part of her formal education. Fabián Severo discusses his role as a language broker—a child who facilitates language interpreting or translation for their parents—in communicating between his teacher, who only spoke Spanish, and his mother (Severo 2017, 58). Portuñol was stigmatized and thus he was not educated in this language. Matilda Koén-Sarano was educated in Italian and didn't even realize that her home language was not normative Spanish until she reached university and enrolled in a Spanish class for the first time (Koén-Sarano 2006, 115–16).

We'll return to the relationship of writers to their own linguistic identity when we discuss their *surconscience linguistique* momentarily, but for now I simply want to illustrate their position as heritage speakers rather than what we often understand as native speakers. This does not lessen or demean their linguistic identity; rather, it describes the reality that all the authors here do speak the languages in which they are writing but were educated in the national languages of the countries in which they lived, adding one more level of complexity to their linguistic identities. Writing literature in a heritage language in which the author did not receive a formal education isn't unique to the authors enumerated here; rather, it's the case at the birth or death of any language. All languages have a literary generation zero. This is a generation who was educated

---

[2] Terms like high-proficiency and low-proficiency risk stigmatizing heritage speakers and should not be accepted without problematizing them in the ways I attempt to throughout this book.

in another language and yet becomes the generation to provide texts that later generations will use to study and understand the newer language. Even Spanish, a language we've seen in previous chapters to be held on a pedestal as a global language, saw a generation zero boom in literary production under the reign of Alfonso X (1252–84). During this period, books were translated en masse into Castilian rather than Latin for the first time (Foz 1998, 65). Those texts provided a foundation upon which other texts would be written and studied—a literary genealogy that we can trace even today. Our *literary doulas* provide the generation zero texts that are being studied in this book and by speakers of their languages in their own geographies.

With this new context, let's return to the matter of whether this is or is not minor literature, which can be understood to be literature written by minority or minoritized subjects in the language of the dominant society in which they live (Deleuze and Guattari 1986, 16). While for some the national or imperial language may be the language in which the authors are most comfortable, that is itself the case because the State has exerted linguistic power over them to ensure either that any minoritized languages would be suppressed or that authors would view these minoritized languages as a less desirable option in which to write and publish their works. This can come through mechanisms of direct linguistic violence, as we've seen explicitly in the writings of several of our *literary doulas*, or due to economic realities. Whatever the cause, the outcome is the same; authors write in the language of the State because that is what is required of them in order to advance. Consequently, *linguistic labor* is the antithesis of minor literature.

Linguistic labor is the choice of an author to write in a language that has been minoritized specifically because of the lack of prestige that the language possesses in an effort to break the cycle of low prestige. Without *linguistic labor* minoritized language forms are not written, thus do not gain linguistic or literary prestige, and consequently remain minoritized. *Literary doulas*, as we've seen, aspire to break that cycle. They are activists and are aware of the role they play in the creation of prestige for their languages, a topic we'll return to later in this chapter. Nevertheless, *literary doulas* do have some experiences in common with authors of minor literature, namely that both sets of authors are educated in the languages of the State. Unlike authors of minor literature who harness this education to produce literature in the dominant language, *literary doulas* rarely have a codified language in which they can articulate their thoughts. Instead, in addition to conjuring up compelling stories for their readers, they must take on the additional challenge of devising their own writing system. This can take a few forms; in some of her collections, Matilda Koén Sarano has written Judeo-Spanish phonetically according to the pronunciations of her informants. On the other hand, she has also collaborated with the Autoridad Nasionala del Ladino to establish a literary standard orthography. Fabián Severo writes Portuñol phonetically based on Spanish orthography (rather than Portuguese conventions or a system of his own device) but has edited his Portuñol in subsequent editions of his work to tweak it so that it more closely resembles natural speech patterns. Others, such as Susana Chávez-Silverman, rely mostly on the orthographies of the dominant global languages which influence her writing but depart occasionally to reflect their own uses (such as her spelling of the word "anyway" as "anygüey"). Still others use the orthography and lexicon of one influencing language to write words of another, as Jonathan Rosa terms "inverted Spanglish" (Rosa 2019, 144–76).

Creating a writing system is no small task, particularly in an age in which we all depend so heavily on technology to ensure uniformity across our texts based on standardized orthographies. The presence of constant spellchecks and autocorrect options frequently rewrites texts into normative varieties against which some may be rebelling.[3] This is one more form of labor that *literary doulas* must conduct, rewarding though it may be, before their words can make it to an even narrower readership than they would have had if they had instead chosen to write a minor literature in the dominant language of the society in which they live.

Surconscience Linguistique

A second theoretical framework we'll return to in this chapter is that of a *surconscience linguistique* as theorized by Lise Gauvin. Writing about the use of French by Québécois authors in a Canadian context dominated by an Anglophone literary scene, Gauvin explains that they consistently reference

---

[3] As an anecdote to these challenges, let's consider my doctoral quandary. Since my Ph.D. dissertation employed significant excerpts in Judeo-Spanish and Spanglish, spellcheck did not work. It identified so many so-called mistakes in the text, once all the chapters were compiled into one document, that it crashed Word over and over. Eventually I disabled spellcheck completely for the entirety of the document, which left the door open for more errors than I would have liked. Many thanks to my thesis committee and external examiner for their grace and understanding as to the challenges that writing in and about minoritized languages presents.

or reflect on their language in a way that is atypical of writers in dominant languages (Gauvin 2000, 8–9). This *surconscience linguistique*, which might be translated as a sort of heightened linguistic awareness, is evidenced in the frequency with which Québécois works directly address the positionality of French in a Canadian context, which Gauvin outlines in detail in the remaining chapters of her book. In contrast, Gauvin asserts that Anglo-Canadian authors rarely speak about their linguistic identity in such direct terms.

This *surconscience linguistique* is not, however, unique to the Québécois context. Rather, it's present in all the languages studied in this volume. Limiting myself to the *literary doulas* that I've already discussed, we find extended discussions about language and linguistic identity in Susana Chávez-Silverman's Spanglish writing, in Fabián Severo's Portuñol works, and in Matilda Koén-Sarano's short stories, collection of sayings, and her Hebrew-Judeo-Spanish dictionary (Koen-Sarano 1994, Chavez-Silverman 2004, XIX–XXI, Koén-Sarano 2006, 2010, Severo 2017, 58). These are just a few examples, though, and scholars of works in these languages and others will find that this *surconscience linguistique* is widespread.

This *surconscience linguistique* is yet one more form of *linguistic labor*. Whereas in dominant language contexts authors can write about whatever strikes their fancy with little concern for addressing their choice to write it in one language rather than another, the politicized nature of writing in a minoritized language compels many authors to explicitly address their linguistic choices. This perceived obligation—though perhaps self-imposed—means that authors in minoritized languages are not expending their effort writing with the same unfettered creativity as are their dominant-language counterparts, but instead spend a disproportionate amount of energy on advocating for their linguistic choices. Consequently, authors in the minoritized languages studied here inevitably become linguistic advocates or a sort of language caretaker, which was hinted at in the introduction, whether they want to be or not.

Whereas authors in dominant languages can write about topics that interest them with little to no need to defend their choices to write in one language instead of another, our *literary doulas* must also serve as spokespeople and activists, both through their work and often to the media and other interested parties. The reasons behind this go back to the earlier notions discussed, that these languages have historically been seen as corruptions or uneducated varieties of dominant language forms (i.e., the erroneous belief that Spanglish is the Spanish or English spoken by uneducated people who are not sufficiently bilingual so as to speak proper Spanish or proper English).

The history of linguistics has perpetuated this belief that some languages are legitimate and worthy of study, while others are not (Reagan 2019, 1–28). While many linguists have embraced broader understandings of the discipline that are non-hierarchical and descriptive in nature, many in adjacent fields such as area studies, literature, and language pedagogy are still clinging to antiquated understandings of language prestige that are impeding our ability to give well-deserved attention to important literary movements outside of the colonial European or dominant global language context.

This approach to education, namely one in which languages are mandated to be used only as discrete from each other and which inculcate in the minds of students the belief that a mastery of one language requires that it have no influence from outside sources, has been found to be detrimental to students who navigate more than one language (Flores and Rosa 2015). Furthermore, it supports narratives that enable us to discriminate along linguistic lines, equating "language mixing" or translanguaging with a lack of education—most often a complaint levied against black and brown people—even though we know this is often not the case.

The *surconscience linguistique*, as Gauvin describes it, is thus a sort of linguistic anxiety. It's a constant justification for using a language about which the authors are self-conscious but in which they want to be proud and encourage others to be proud about as well. This anxiety may be assuaged if we decolonize linguistics by leaning into the push for a more nuanced understanding of the field that translinguistics provides.

Translinguistics and the Problem with Trans

Theories of translinguistics gained traction with the education-based research of Ofelia García. García, numerous coauthors, and many who have built on their work later argue that language in the mind does not exist in discrete categories between which speakers move based on the named language they're trying to speak (García 2009). In other words, a Spanish and English speaker does not choose subconsciously to open the Spanish box to speak with other Spanish speakers and then close the Spanish box, open the English box, and begin speaking English. Instead, García says, language exists as a singular system from which we choose features to use with different audiences. Working from an education perspective, Flores and Rosa clarify that students need to be able to grapple with ideas using the full breadth of their linguistic toolkit rather than be forced to learn in a subtractive bilingualism environment in which each language[4] must appear "pure" and without influence from others (Flores and Rosa 2015).

Translinguistics has evolved beyond the educational setting, however, and now we also understand the trans- prefix to be reflective of a shared human experience of moving between many different registers to navigate various situations. This is true for multilingual but also monolingual speakers. For example, the fundamental notion of choosing the best linguistic features to communicate our intentions to our interlocutors can apply whether we're speaking Spanish rather than Portuguese, presenting an academic paper, having drinks with friends, or discussing queer topics with queer friends rather than broader topics with non-queer interlocutors. This is not a new aspect of linguistics as we might assume when we consider the somewhat new term "translinguistics." Rather, it's a core element of linguistics that linguists have studied for decades. Despite this decades-old history, it's often been considered in one imperial or colonial language at a time rather than across a spectrum of humanity in which all language varieties and registers are variables. Translinguistics, then, isn't particularly novel despite the name; rather it's a broadening of traditional understandings of linguistics beyond imagined linguistic borders.

However, there is a problem with the trans- prefix which is misleading. It implies the existence of a cis- prefix for linguistics.[5] After all, translinguistics does not stand out as different against a normative unmarked "linguistics." No, we all translanguage all the time. In fact, it would seem that no one cislanguages ever, since we all—monolinguals included—must navigate a wide range of linguistic features in a way that allows us to communicate not only our ideas, but also aspects such as the seriousness or formality of the situation, the intimacy of friendships and romantic relationships, the reduced vocabulary necessary to speak with children, the religious or cultural spheres to which we belong. The list is endless.

---

[4] Here the term "language" refers to named languages which often have some sort of clear, though artificial, boundaries that correspond to nation-states. A significant amount of this educational translinguistics research focuses on students who learn in English and speak a language other than English at home (Spanish, French, Mandarin) and consequently reflects that context.

[5] Trans- is a prefix meaning "on the other side" or "beyond"; cis- is a prefix meaning "on this side."

Since, I argue, that no one cislanguages—by which I mean no one only uses the same set of linguistic features all the time—how can we say that translanguaging exists at all? After all, how absurd would it sound if we navigated all social situations as if we were in a bar with friends? What about if all social situations sounded like a job interview? This simply isn't how language works. Translanguaging is languaging. Translinguistics is linguistics. Cislanguaging doesn't exist. Cislinguistics is pretend. To translanguage is, as I view it, simply *to language*. We must stop marking the most common manifestation of linguistics as other to a static form of linguistics that is not reflective of human patterns.

Paul Preciado sheds some light on language through his discussion of sexuality. His book, *Countersexual Manifesto*, encourages us not to focus on traditional sex organs to distinguish humans from each other. As long as humanity is divided based on whether someone has a penis or a vagina, Preciado says, we are missing the point of sexuality. Instead, we should focus on that which is universal to human sexuality, a flexible approach to pleasure, derived from any number of sources—Preciado specifically speaks to the universality of the anus as a locus of pleasure. Sexualities, sexual practices, and sexual identities, like languages, are learned. Also, like language, we typically come of age with one option imposed on us; it might be one colonial language or one sexuality. Both cases establish a dichotomy of those like us versus those unlike us. Yet, Preciado suggests, "we could have entered into any other sexuality under a different regime of knowledge, power, and desire" (Preciado 2018, 8). The same is true of language. Had linguistics as a field embarked upon the study of language through a different regime of knowledge and power, we might now understand language to be something very different than the dominant narrative that we hold today. Fortunately, it's never too late to make a change.

Like the universality of the anus as a locus of pleasure, there are universalities to language as well. At a base level, we all aspire to make ourselves understood and understand others. As we move beyond that minimum, we aspire to love, to belong. We want to experience joy, share that joy with others, and feel their joy as well. We also want to cry and be held. All of these universals of humanity can be expressed and experienced in the languages studied in this book.

This brings us full circle to my original point in the introduction: Spanglish, Portuñol, and Judeo-Spanish are languages. They may share a considerable amount of grammar and vocabulary with other languages, but they are a natural manifestation of a particular set of linguistic tools which are deployed by speakers and authors to communicate an idea to a desired audience. To assign terms such as "hybrid language" or "translanguage" to them requires us to presume that there exists a pure form of language somewhere in the world. Some might suggest that the major imperial and national languages of the world are such forms: I do not concede this point.

Linguistics, as a discipline, emerged from philology which placed classical and biblical sources on a pedestal and viewed modern languages as removed from divine or classical ideals. In the context of fixed texts being translated for global audiences, often with an eye for proselytizing, it's clear why a standardized version of a text would be idealized. But modern linguistics has moved beyond this and is a descriptive rather than prescriptive field. As such, while it is important to be able to talk about linguistic systems with regional names to identify them, simply to know what we're discussing, we must be open about the imprecision of these terms. In recent years the term "global Englishes" has emerged to recognize there is no unified English, while still using the term "Englishes" to indicate that we're not discussing varieties of Mandarin or Swahili. In the same way, we can embrace the imprecision of terms like Spanish, Portuguese, Spanglish, Portuñol, Judeo-Spanish, or others to provide some context, all the while recognizing that what we now know as translinguistics is ever-present and is a simple reflection of natural linguistics.

Conclusion

In concluding this chapter, I suggest that we as linguists and those in adjacent fields reconsider our understandings of language and languages to be rhizomatic rather than discrete. All language manifestations are languages with equal value in their ability to express ideas and in the cognitive functions required to produce and comprehend them. Nevertheless, I concede that language names are useful as identity markers and adjectives. By opening the notion of language to a spectrum of human expression, an approach we currently associate with translinguistics, much of the conversations of minor literatures, of a *surconscience linguistique*, of so-called linguistic hybridity, can be reframed as what they are, vestiges of colonial or imperial power imbalances. By redirecting linguistics away from discrete linguistic essentialism, we can make space for conversations which can use linguistics to support the development of more equitable societies rather than as a tool to perpetuate discrimination along linguistic lines.

In short, we can drop the prefix trans-. After all, what translinguistics aspires to study is simply linguistics without all the baggage that colonial notions of prestige have imparted on the discipline.

8

Conclusion

In the preceding chapters I've discussed the history of three languages, Spanglish, Portuñol, and Judeo-Spanish. All three have been minoritized and faced systemic efforts to "educate" them away, assimilate speakers into national dominant cultures, or otherwise exterminate them. Nevertheless, some authors choose to write in these minoritized languages and to publish their work to bring their languages out of the closets of the domestic space and into the public sphere. This, combined with the social standing of these languages, has led me to reflect on what that says about the decision to publish in these languages. Such an act, which I've named *linguistic labor*, is political and activist. It seeks to bring a language from orality into publishing for the first time or, in the case of Judeo-Spanish, it is a form of linguistic palliative care that can prepare a community for the impending death of their traditional language. The authors conducting this work, to follow the metaphor of birth and death, I've introduced as *literary doulas*. The figure of the doula emerged into Western consciousness in the 1970s as a support worker who is present to help another person through a significant health journey. This is most often applied in the context of childbirth; however, doulas can also support through miscarriage, abortion, and even death. In the latter case, they support not only the dying, but also their family.

Part I of the book presents a deep dive into these languages, the lifecycles, literature, and sociolinguistic reality of each language in turn. This serves to connect the languages to each other and to the theories of *linguistic labor* and *literary doulas* that were described in the introduction. Though their individual histories are quite different one from the other, their relationship to minoritization, identity, and a fervor to promote them beginning in the 1980s was shared.

In Part II, I laid out three overarching themes that these theories complicate. Chapter 5 presented the story of the queer nature of *linguistic labor* and drew from theories of performativity of social expectations, much in the way that gender is performed, and these doulas' decision to transgress such expectations. I then spoke of the power that comes from a rejection of a capitalist-informed model of success and described how the doulas considered in this book have instead preferred what Halberstam describes as the queer art of failure.

In Chapter 6 we saw the challenges that emerge as we consider a less theoretical and more practical choice—that of translation. Translation is not, in instances such as these, necessarily a matter of regurgitating textual information into a different language for a different audience, but rather considering how the underlying sociolinguistic context, and by extension the rebellion against established norms, can be communicated to new readers.

Finally, we situated the scholarship in this volume within linguistics as a field. After discussing how these theories engage with Deleuze and Guattari's notion of minor literature, and Gauvin's theory of the *surconscience linguistique*, I turned my attention to the emerging disciplinary orientation of translinguistics. Translinguistics is, in short, a holistic and poststructural understanding of language that challenges the belief that languages are monoliths from which a range of dialects depart, but rather that language exists on a spectrum that we all navigate to communicate with our interlocutors. I closed that chapter by recognizing that translinguistics is simply linguistics and encouraging a reframing of linguistics to include this approach at its core, rather than as a growing wave from the fringes which is marked by a curious prefix.

Throughout this volume there has been an elephant in the room, and the time has come in the conclusion to address it. That problem is one of terminology. Throughout the text, I have chosen certain terms to express complex and nuanced ideas without the space to discuss the challenges that each of those terms present. Sometimes I have given more attention to terms, but at other times I have glossed over some which, at a second glance, may seem misleading. This has, in large part, been because I want to highlight the stories that need to be told, and I feel that too many asides, definitions, and problematizing of terminology can distract from these important stories and the theoretical frameworks that I'm proposing. Nevertheless, I'd like to take the following few pages to address the challenges of writing and researching this subject matter with a decidedly poststructural approach.

Language is ontologically structural: it can be no other way. Words are the tools that we use to communicate our ideas. To differentiate one idea from another, though, languages must impose boundaries—through the definitions of words—so that we are all on the same page when we are communicating. For example, the term "humankind" is a category that is inclusive of all genders but excludes any non-human species. Similarly, "humankind" is subdivided into other structural categories such as "man" and "woman." Despite the very many characteristics men and women have in common with each other, the relatively minor differences between them are structurally codified by language and essentialized in the minds of the speakers of any given language in ways that don't always reflect the nuances of reality. In one language a certain set of differences may be magnified while in another the same differences may be minimized. An example of this is the way that various languages understand color; whereas English has an overarching category of blue, to which we then add adjectives like light or dark, Russian has no corresponding overarching category. Instead, it forces speakers to choose between darker blues (синий) and lighter blues (голубой) which, lexically speaking, are as different to them as blue and purple are to English speakers. Much like vocabulary codifies ideas into lexical categories, grammar helps us establish temporal, numerical, and relational structures which, in turn, let us articulate our thoughts. But, these categories don't always map cleanly onto our ideas. Language is, theoretically, capable of expressing even the most abstract and nuanced concepts, but eloquence is not guaranteed. Sometimes, when the ideas expressed challenge traditional understandings, the expression of nuance can become quite clunky. This has been a perpetual challenge in this book, particularly insofar as the expression of language and community realities is concerned.

Talking about Language

Dictionary.com provides the following definitions for language (truncated for relevance):

1. a body of words and the systems for their use common to a people who are of the same community or nation, the same geographical area, or the same cultural tradition;
2. communication by voice in the distinctively human manner, using arbitrary sounds in conventional ways with conventional meanings—speech;

3. the system of linguistic signs or symbols considered in the abstract (opposed to speech);

4. any set or system of such symbols as used in a more or less uniform fashion by a number of people, who are thus enabled to communicate intelligibly with one another; and

5. any system of formalized symbols, signs, sounds, gestures, or the like used or conceived as a means of communicating thought, emotion, etc.

These definitions reinforce a few key assumptions about language that seem at odds with the way that I've used the term in this book. Namely, the first, second, fourth, and fifth acceptations define the notion of language as ontologically uniform, codified, formalized, and conventional across all speakers of the same language. This is not how the languages studied in this book should be understood. Instead, we've seen that many *literary doulas* reject a need to standardize their language practices, preferring instead to present their own authentic selves (or others) in writing without suggesting that their own language practices form the basis for a new monolithic or centralized language. Instead, our doulas use a wide range of orthographic innovation to represent their own, and others', pronunciation. Each author also has their own way of drawing from two or more lexicalizing languages to communicate their thoughts with no expectations that their choices become normalized.[1] Furthermore, the above definitions also suggest that speakers must find some similar manner of expression for communication to take place. That is not necessarily a given; there are many examples of communities in which the form of expression of interlocutors may differ greatly from each other without impeding communication. Communication accommodation theory (CAT) teaches us that we often adapt our speaking style to more closely approximate that of our interlocutors to establish relationships of closeness with them (Giles 2007). Alternatively, we may choose to speak differently to create emotional distance between us and the people with whom we are speaking. These are natural human phenomena that are part of language, though they don't correspond well to the definition presented.

---

[1] A lexicalizing language in the case of contact or creole languages is the language from which speakers draw their vocabulary. For example, in Spanglish it would be predominantly Spanish and English, whereas in Jamaican Patois it would be English.

Some scholars have attempted to bridge the incongruencies between the definitions above by providing alternative terms or ideas, each of which carries its own semantic weight, and none of which, I feel, can be fully applied to the cases studied in this book. The most notable three that I'd like to address are the notions of hybridity, code-switching, and translanguaging. Throughout the book these three terms appear; however, this is largely because we must use language in order to weave our tale, and sometimes the whole of the story is more important than the words we use to tell it. But, the time has come to interrogate some of these terms.

Hybridity

The theoretical framework of hybridity as we now understand, and as Nikos Papastergiadis describes it, emerged from postcolonial scholarship in the 1990s in rejection to the notion of purity as a central or racialized aspect of identity (Papastergiadis 2015, 257). Prior to this shift, he goes on to argue, hybridity was seen as a marker of contamination. While there is no singular understanding of hybridity, and indeed many scholars disagree as to how cultural hybridity plays out, the term presents many curious problems when applied to a language and a language community. Here, I'll address the problems I see with using the term hybridity in a linguistic context given the findings of the present study.

The term hybrid is used often enough to refer to languages in ways that do not engage with postcolonial discourse, particularly when discussing border or transnational—rather than postcolonial—contexts. Outside of the context of extended postcolonial theorization that problematizes identities through the lens of hybridity, the term retains, I fear, the lay meaning as is articulated by dictionary.com: "a person or group of persons produced by the interaction or crossbreeding of two unlike cultures, traditions, etc." This understanding of the term fixates on the bringing together of two different central or dominant cultures/languages. By extension, the term categorizes languages and those who speak them as somehow in between two monolithic colonial powers; it does not call into question the legitimacy of those monoliths nor their origin. In other words, to suggest that a language is hybrid is to orient it as the sum of its more important parts, rather than to give it credence in its own right.

Such an understanding of the term continues to replicate the anti-miscegenation and ethnic purity rhetoric that the term conveyed well before Bhabha, Spivak, and Hall argued for more nuanced, albeit conflicting, understandings of the term as referencing a third space that is neither one established category nor another.

Code-Switching

Code-switching (also written code switching or codeswitching) is an alternation between two or more languages in a single conversation. This was historically viewed by prescriptivist linguists as a low-prestige linguistic practice and is still viewed by many in society at large as a marker of low education, low literacy levels, or poor command of the national language. Research on code-switching, however, has taught us that people who live in complex linguistic landscapes manage to move between a range of different languages and registers in structured ways. This structure provides an internally consistent grammatical foundation that allows the speaker to move between languages while still respecting the different grammars of each (Budzhak-Jones 1997).

However, despite the ways in which an understanding of code-switching has pushed linguistics forward—and despite that the term may appear some in this book—it is not without problems when applied to the languages discussed here. Most notably, as Nelson Flores points out, "code-switching presupposes the existence of discrete languages which are, in fact, socio-historical constructions that have been used to marginalize bilingual language practices that do not fit neatly into these discrete languages" (Flores 2014). Similar to the term hybridity, code-switching starts from an orientation that central structures, in this case languages rather than cultures, are ontologically real. By extension it is possible to move between these structures and, one must then logically assume, it is possible to exist outside them. I do not concede that such a structural understanding of language is an accurate representation of reality, quite the contrary. This view can be used to perpetuate the ideology of languagelessness, which is the belief that bilingual or multilingual people who may have accents in all their languages are, rather, without a language at all (Rosa 2019, 126–43). Tragedy and disability aside, no one is without language.

Despite the problems with the term code-switching, I recognize that a quantification of language practices can be useful in discussing how one community uses language differently than another. Code-switching is one such lens through which we can quantify that difference. Another lens, one which does not depend on an a priori belief in the discreteness of languages, is translanguaging.

Translanguaging

Translanguaging, as previously described, is an understanding of language use that considers the ways in which bilingual or multilingual speakers navigate their linguistic repertoire. While it describes the same linguistic practices as does code-switching, it takes a fundamentally different posture on the issue. In Nelson Flores' succinct blog post he reminds us that whereas code-switching is built on the premise that languages are discrete from one another and that it is therefore possible to move between then—whence the "switching" part of the term—translanguaging works from a different starting point. Translanguaging, he is quick to point out, argues that languages are not monoliths between which speakers can switch (Flores 2014). Rather, language exists in the minds of all humans on a spectrum. We are subconsciously aware that certain features of language fit certain situations, and other features fit other contexts. How we choose to deploy different features in different interactions is determined in part by the reactions of our interlocutors, as we saw with CAT, and in part by societal expectations.

Translanguaging is, at first glance, a great way of understanding *linguistic labor* as described in this book. However, there is a gap between how the term is used by many who have not explored the literature in depth, often relegating it to a new term to refer to bilingual and multilingual practices. This gap is why I have not committed to using the term translanguaging throughout this monograph. Returning to Flores' critique from 2014, he states the following:

> Translanguaging is presented as the language practices of the Other–as something exotic or more complex than the bland monolingual White middle class norm. Yet, in actuality, translanguaging offers a new framework for understanding the language practices of all people. Everybody, whether they are positioned as monolingual, bilingual, or multilingual has to negotiate the socio-historical construction of languages, dialects, registers, etc. and often do this in ways that deviate from the arbitrary linguistic boundaries produced by these socio-historical constructions.
>
> (Flores 2014)

This understanding of translanguaging as common to all of us, monolingual and non-monolingual alike, is still not clear among academics now, nearly a decade later. Consequently, to speak of the *linguistic labor* here as translanguaging of some ilk would perpetuate the poorly informed view that translanguaging is something that only happens when people navigate more than one language. To suggest that these *literary doulas* are translanguaging would falsely imply that other authors are not.

Translanguaging, as a disciplinary orientation, is absolutely one that I hope to have employed throughout this work, but the terminology at this juncture seems, in some ways, to undermine the intention of the scholarship around translanguaging. Some scholars seem to hide work which ultimately serves to perpetuate the colonial and classist beliefs in the supremacy of standardized named languages over others, behind a screen of progressive words. Translanguaging—and all its related forms—has become such a buzz word which, when used out of its proper theoretical context, can create as many problems as it resolves.

Conclusion

If I can leave readers with a final thought as you close this book and walk away, it's this: Language is complex, it's ever changing, and it holds power. Let's ditch the belief that languages are ontological realities that are fixed and that language dynamics are inconsequential. Instead, let's celebrate the hard work that has gone into creating literacy, building a body of literature, and supporting these languages, through education and language policies, into being the conduits by which we express art and knowledge that they are today. But let's also recognize that our languages had to get here, and to get here they needed people to believe they could. *Literary doulas* of centuries past conducted the *linguistic labor* needed to garner the prestige now enjoyed by the major global languages of today. Let's observe in awe how others are doing that work in their own languages now.

As you do, push the limits of my concepts of *literary doulas* and *linguistic labor*. How common are they? Where else do they appear? They might be more common than we suspect.

Bibliography

Abitbol, Michel. 1993. "Juifs d'Afrique du Nord et expulsés d'Espagne après 1492." *Revue de l'histoire des religions* 210:49–90.

Adams, Rachel. 2004. "Hipsters and Jipitecas: Literary Countercultures on Both Sides of the Border." *American Literary History* 16:58–84.

Agence France-Presse. 2020. "'Hidden Language': Hongkongers Get Creative against Security Law." *The Guardian*, July 4. https://www.theguardian.com/world/2020/jul/04/hidden-language-hong-kong-security-law-residents-wordplay.

Aikhenvald, Alexandra Y. 2003. "Multilingualism and Ethnic Stereotypes: The Tariana of Northwest Amazonia." *Language in Society* 32 (1):1–21. doi: 10.1017/S0047404503321013.

Aiu, Pua'ala'okalani D. 2010. "Ne'e Papa I Ke Ō Mau: Language as an Indicator of Hawaiian Resistance and Power." In *Translation, Resistance, Activism*, edited by Maria Tymoczko, 89–107. Amherst, MA: University of Massachusetts Press.

Albertoni, Pablo. 2016. "Ideologías lingüísticas sobre el contacto español-portugués en el departamento de Rocha: la otra frontera." In *Miradas sobre educación y cambio*, edited by Fernando Acevedo, Karina Nossar, and Patricia Viera, 247–58. Montevideo: Universidad de la República.

Alexander-Frizer, Tamar. 2008. *The Heart Is a Mirror: The Sephardic Folktale*. Detroit: Wayne State University Press.

Alexander, Tamar. 1985. "Folktales in 'Sefer Hasidim.'" *Prooftexts* 5:19–31.

Alexander, Tamar. 1986. "The Judeo-Spanish Community in Israel: Its Folklore and Ethnic Identity." *Cahiers de littérature orale* 20:131–52.

Alexander, Tamar. 1987. "A Legend of the Blood Libel in Jerusalem: A Study of a Process of Folk-Tale Adaptation." *International Folklore Review* 5:60–74.

Alexander, Tamar. 1990. "The Woman Demon in Jewish Customs and Folktales." *Jewish Folklore and Ethnology Review* 12:21.

Alexander, Tamar. 1991. "La figura de Maimónides en la narrativa popular sefardí." Sobre la vida y obra de Maimónides: I Congreso Internacional, Córdoba.

Alexander, Tamar. 1992. "Theme and Gender: Relationships between Man and She-Demon in Jewish Folklore." *Jewish Folklore and Ethnology Review* 14:56–61.

Alexander, Tamar. 1993. "Second Purim: Literary Tradition, Family, Self-Image and Ethnic Identity." *Jewish Folklore and Ethnology Review* 15:39–48.

Alexander, Tamar. 1998. "Elementos hispánicos y jaquéticos en los refranes judeo-españoles de Marruecos." *Jewish Studies at the Turn of the Twentieth Century*, Toledo.

Alexander, Tamar, and Michal Govrin. 1989. "Story-Telling as a Performing Art." *Assaph* 5:1–34.

Altabev, Mary. 1998a. "The Effect of Dominant Discourses on the Vitality of Judeo-Spanish in the Turkish Social Context." *Journal of Multilingual and Multicultural Development* 19:263–81. doi: 10.1080/01434639808666356.

Altabev, Mary. 1998b. "The Role of Judeo-Spanish in the Framework of the Turkish Jewish Collective Identity." *Jewish Studies at the Turn of the Twentieth Century. Volume II: Judaism from the Renaissance to Modern Times*, Toledo.

Alvar, Manuel. 1960. "Cantos de muerte sefardíes." *Revista do livro do Instituto Nacional do Ministério da Educação e Cultura* 5:19–31.

Alvar, Manuel. 1965. "Un 'descubrimiento' del judeo-español." In *Studies in Honor of M. J. Benardete (Essays in Hispanic and Sephardic Culture)*, 363–6.

Alvar, Manuel. 1983. "El ladino." *Yelmo* 56–57:38–9.

Amantea, Carlos. 2010. "Killer Crónicas Book Review." *Ralph Mag*.

Amantea, Carlos. 2010. "Scenes from La Cuenca de Los Angeles y Otros Natural Disasters Book Review." *Ralph Mag*.

American Literary Translators Association. ND. "ALTA Statement on Racial Equity in Translation." https://mailchi.mp/literarytranslators/alta-statement-on-racial-equity-in-translation.

Andermann, Jens. 2011. "Abismos del tercer espacio: Mar Paraguayo, portuñol salvaje y el fin de la utopía letrada." *Revista Hispánica Moderna* 64 (1):11–22. doi: 10.1353/rhm.2011.0013.

Anderson, Benedict. 2006. *Imagined Communities: Reflections on the Origin and Spread of Nationalism*. revised ed. London: Verso.

Anselmo Peres, Alós. 2012. "Wild portuñol: from the 'language of contact' to the poetics of the frontier." *Cadernos de Letras da UFF* 22 (45):283–304. https://doi.org/10.22409/cadletrasuff.2012n45a473.

Antush, John V. 1994. "Editing the Bilingual Text at Cross-Cultural Purposes." *Text* 6:345–57.

Anzaldúa, Gloria. 1999. *Borderlands/la Frontera: The New Mestiza*. San Francisco: Aunt Lute Books.

Anzaldúa, Gloria. 2009. *The Gloria Anzaldúa Reader*. Edited by AnaLouise Keating. Durham: Duke University Press.

Aparicio, Frances. 1988. "La Vida es un Spanglish Disparatero: Bilingualism in Nuyorican Poetry." In *European Perspectives on Hispanic Literature of the United States*, edited by Genvieve Fabre, 147–60. Houston, TX: Arte Público Press.

Aparicio, Frances R., and Susana Chávez-Silverman. 1997. *Tropicalizations: Transcultural Representations of Latinidad*. Hanover: University Press of New England.

Appiah, Kwame Anthony. 1993. "Thick Translation." In *Translation Studies Reader*, edited by Lawrence Venuti, 417–29. London: Routledge.

Apter, Emily. 2008. "Untranslatables: A World System." *New Literary History* 39:581–98.

Ardila, Alfredo. 2005. "Spanglish: An Anglicized Spanish Dialect." *Hispanic Journal of Behavioral Sciences* 27:60–81. doi: 10.1177/0739986304272358.

Arditti, Adolfo. 1986. "More on Sephardic Mexican Spanish." *Jewish Language Review* 6:24–6.

Armistead, Samuel G. 1992. "Judeo-Spanish Traditional Poetry: Some Linguistic Problems." *Zeitschrift für romanische Philologie* 108:62–71.

Armistead, Samuel G., Reginetta Haboucha, and Joseph H. Silverman. 1982. "Words Worse Than Wounds: A Judeo-Spanish Version of a Near Eastern Folktale." *Fabula* 23:95–8.

Armistead, Samuel G., Iacob M. Hassán, and Joseph H. Silverman. 1972. "La literatura oral del ladino de Damián Alonso García: sobre una reciente chapucería romanticística." *Sefarad* 32:451–73.

Armistead, Samuel G., and Joseph H. Silverman. 1970. "Arabic Refrains in a Judeo-Spanish 'Romance.'" *Ibero-romania* 2:91–103.

Asad, Talal. 1995. "A Comment on Translation, Critique, and Subversion." In *Between Languages and Cultures: Translation and Cross-Cultural Texts*, edited by Anuradha Dingwaney and Carol Maier, 325–32. Pittsburgh: University of Pittsburgh Press.

Asad, Talal. 2010. "The Concept of Cultural Translation in British Social Anthropology." In *Critical Readings in Translation Studies*, edited by Mona Baker, 7–27. New York: Routledge.

Ascher, Gloria J. 2001a. "Sephardic Songs, Proverbs and Expressions: A Continuing Tradition." *Shofar: An Interdisciplinary Journal of Jewish Studies* 19:25–39.

Ascher, Gloria J. 2001b. "Teaching 'Ladino Language and Culture' and 'Aspects of the Sephardic Tradition': Hopes, Fruits, Experiences." *Shofar: An Interdisciplinary Journal of Jewish Studies* 19:77–84.

Asencio, Pilar. 2004. "Una frontera sociolingüística en el Uruguay del siglo xix: Lengua española e identidad nacional." *Spanish in Context* 1 (2):215–39.

Ashcroft, Bill, Gareth Griffiths, and Helen Tiffin. 2002. *The Empire Writes Back. Theory and Practice in Post-Colonial Literatures*. 2nd ed. London: Routledge.

Attig, Remy. 2012. "Did the Sephardic Jews Speak Ladino?" *Bulletin of Spanish Studies* 89:831–8. doi: 10.1080/14753820.2012.712320.

Attig, Remy. 2018. "Translation in the Borderlands of Spanish: Balancing Power in English Translations from Judeo-Spanish and Spanglish." PhD, Modern Languages and Literatures, University of Ottawa.

Attig, Remy. 2019a. "Book Review: *Specialized Translation: Shedding the 'Non-Literary' Tag* by Margaret Rogers." *JoSTrans: The Journal of Specialized Translation* (31):294–5.

Attig, Remy. 2019b. "*Coco* and the Case of the Disappearing Spanglish: Negotiating Code-Switching in the English and Spanish Versions of Disney and Pixar's Animated Film." In *Hybrid Englishes and the Challenges of/for Translation: Identity, Mobility and Language Change*, edited by Karen Bennett and Rita Queiroz de Barros, 151–62. New York: Routledge.

Attig, Remy. 2019c. "El clock de la estación." *PORTAL Journal of Multidisciplinary International Studies* 16 (1/2):141–2.

Attig, Remy. 2019d. "Foreignization and Heterogeneity in the English Translation of Two Judeo-Spanish Folktales by Matilda Koén-Sarano." *The AALITRA Review* 14:123–30.

Attig, Remy. 2019e. "Intralingual Translation as an Option for Radical Spanglish." *TranscUlturAl: A Journal of Translation and Cultural Studies* 11 (1):23–35.

Attig, Remy. 2019f. "Transnational Translation: Reflections on Translating from Judeo-Spanish and Spanglish." *TTR: traduction, terminologie, rédaction* 32 (2):61–79.

Attig, Remy. 2019g. "What's in a Name?: An Onomastic Interpretation of a Sephardic Folktale." *Bulletin of Hispanic Studies* 96 (7):683–94. doi: 10.3828/bhs.2019.41.

Attig, Remy. 2022. "Doule literackie przeciw tłumaczeniu iberyjskich języków peryferyjnych" [The Figure of the Literary Doula in the Birth and Death of Three Hispanic Literatures] – Translated into Polish by: Wojciech Tokarz – *Przekłady Literatur Słowiańskich* 12 (1): 1–24. doi: 10.31261/PLS.2022.12.01.10.

Attig, Remy. 2023a. "Translating the Queerness of Spanglish in Audiovisual Contexts." *Mutatis Mutandis: Revista latinoamericana de traducción* 16 (1):36–51.

Attig, Remy. 2023b. "Translation, Equity, Solidarity." *PMLA* 138 (3):741–7.

Attig, Remy. 2023c. "A Call for Community-Informed Translation: Respecting Queer Self-Determination across Linguistic Lines." *Translation and Interpreting Studies* 18 (1):70–90. doi: 10.1075/tis.21001.att.

Attig, Remy, and Roshawnda A Derrick. 2021. "Dubbing Othering and Belonging: The Latinx Voice as the Self in *One Day at a Time*." *Bulletin of Spanish Studies* 98 (4):635–64. doi: 10.1080/14753820.2021.1926722.

Attig, Remy, and Ártemis López. 2020. "Queer Community Input in Gender-Inclusive Translations." *COZIL Pride Month Blog*, June 23. https://www.linguisticsociety.org/post/queer-community-input-gender-inclusive-translations.

August-Zarebska, Agnieszka. 2017. "Contemporary Judeo-Spanish in Its Rediscovery of the Past." In *Sepharad as Imagined Community: Language, History and Religion from the Early Modern Period to the 21st Century*, edited by Mahir Şaul and José Ignacio Hualde, 257–74. New York: Peter Lang.

Autoridad Nasionala del Ladino i su Kultura. 2011. "לש תורפסמה שגפמ - ונידאל ונארס זהכ הדליתמ Ladino - Las kontaderas." youtube. www.youtube.com/watch?v=RRqJ9MzE12M.

Autoridad Nasionala del Ladino i su Kultura. 2018. "YouTube Channel: Autoridad Nasionala del Ladino i su Kultura." Accessed March 10, 2018. https://www.youtube.com/user/AutoridadLadino.

Azevedo, Milton M. 1998. "Orality in Translation: Literary Dialect from English into Spanish and Catalan." *Sintagma: Revista de Lingüística* 10:27–43.

Baer, Yitzhak. 2001a. *A History of the Jews in Christian Spain Vol. I*. Skokie, IL: Varda Books.

Baer, Yitzhak. 2001b. *A History of the Jews in Christian Spain Vol. II*. Skokie: Varda Books.

Baker, Mona, and Gabriela Saldanha. 2009. *Routledge Encyclopedia of Translation Studies*. 2nd ed. New York: Routledge.

Bandia, Paul. 2010. "Post-Colonial Literatures and Translation." In *Handbook of Translation Studies, Volume 1*, edited by Yves Gambier and Luc van Doorslaer, 264–9. Amsterdam: John Benjamins Publishing.

Bandia, Paul. 2015. "Code-Switching and Code-Mixing in African Creative Writing: Some Insights for Translation Studies." *TTR: traduction, terminologie, rédaction* 9:116–39. doi: 10.7202/037242ar.

Barnard, Alan, and Jonathan Spencer. 2010. *The Routledge Encyclopedia of Social and Cultural Anthropology*. 2nd ed. New York: Routledge.

Barrett, Rusty. 2017. *From Drag Queens to Leathermen: Language, Gender, and Gay Male Subcultures*. Oxford: Oxford University Press.

Barrios, Graciela. 2013. "Language Diversity and National Unity in the History of Uruguay." In *A Political History of Spanish: The Making of a Language*, edited by José Del Valle, 197–211. Cambridge: Cambridge University Press.

Barrios, Graciela, and Leticia Pugliese. 2004. "Política lingüística y dictadura militar: Las campañas de defensa de la lengua." In *El presente de la dictadura*, edited by Aldo Et. Al. Marchesi, 156–68. Montevideo: Ediciones Trilce.

Barros-Lémez, Alvaro. 1983. "Uruguay: Una literatura sin fronteras." *Revista de Crítica Literaria Latinoamericana* 9 (17):195–206. doi: 10.2307/4530093.

Barros, Cristiano Silva. 2020. "Tradução de literatura chicana: entre pontes, muros e fronteiras." *Abehache* 17 (1):69–98.

Barthes, Roland. 1967. "The Death of the Author." *Aspen* 5–6.

Basalamah, Salah. 2004. "Du droit à l'éthique du traducteur." *TTR: traduction, terminologie, rédaction* 17:67–88.

Basalamah, Salah. 2007. "Translation Rights and the Philosophy of Translation." In *In Translation. Reflections, Refractions, Transformations*, edited by P. St-Pierre and P. Kar, 117–32. Amsterdam: John Benjamins Publishing.

Bassnett, Susan. 1998. "The Translation Turn in Cultural Studies." In *Constructing Cultures. Essays on Literary Translation*, edited by Susan Bassnett and André Lefevere, 123–40. Clevendon: Multilingual Matters.

Bassnett, Susan. 2002. *Translation Studies*. 3rd ed. London: Routledge.

Bassnett, Susan, and Harish Trivedi. 2002. *Postcolonial Translation: Theory and Practice*. London: Routledge.

Bayraktar, Hatice. 2006. "The Anti-Jewish Pogrom in Eastern Thrace in 1934: New Evidence for the Responsibility of the Turkish Government." *Patterns of Prejudice* 40:95–111. doi: 10.1080/00313220600634238.

Becker, Kristin R. 1997. "Spanish/English Bilingual Codeswitching: A Syncretic Model." *Bilingual Review* 22:3–30.

Behares, Luis Ernesto, and Carlos Ernesto Díaz. 1997. *Os som de nossa terra: Productos artístico-verbales fronterizos*. Montevideo: Universidad de la República.

Behares, Luis, Carlos Ernesto Díaz, and Gerardo Holzmann. 2004. *Na frontera nós fizemo assim: Lengua y cocina en el Uruguay fronterizo*. Montevideo: Librería de Facultad de Humanidades y Ciencias de la Educación.

Ben-Ari, Nitsa. 2010. "Reclaiming the Erotic: Hebrew Translations from 1930 to 1980." In *Translation, Resistance, Activism*, edited by Maria Tymoczko, 129-48. Amherst: University of Massachusetts Press.

Benjamin, Walter. [1923] 1997. "Task of the Translator." In *Selected Writings Volume 1: 1913-1926*, 253-63.

Benor, Sarah. 2009. "Do American Jews Speak a 'Jewish Language': A Model of Jewish Linguistic Distinctiveness." *Jewish Quarterly Review* 99:230-69.

Benor, Sarah Bunin. 2003. "Jewish Malayalam." Jewish Language Research Website. http://www.jewish-languages.org/jewish-malayalam.html.

Benor, Sarah Bunin. 2012. Jewish-English Lexicon.

Benor, Sarah Bunin, and Tsvi Sadan. 2018. Jewish Language Research Website.

Berman, Antoine. 1992. *The Experience of the Foreign. Culture and Translation in Romantic Germany*. Albany, NY: State University of New York Press.

Berman, Antoine. 1999. *La traduction et la lettre, ou, L'auberge du lointain*. Paris: Seuil.

Berman, Antoine. 2000. "Translation and the Trials of the Foreign." In *The Translation Studies Reader*, edited by Lawrence Venuti, 284-97. New York and London: Routledge.

Berman, Antoine. 2012. "El albergue de lo lejano." *Doletiana* 4:1-10.

Bermann, Sandra, and Michael Wood. 2005. "The Ethics of Translation." In *Nation, Language and the Ethics of Translation*, 93-174. Princeton: Princeton University Press.

Bernstein, Cynthia. 2017. "New Perspectives on Language Variety in the South Lexical Features of Jewish English in the Southern United States." In *New Perspectives on Language Variety in the South: Historic and Contemporary Approaches*, edited by Michael D. Picone, Catherine Evans Davies, Bridget L. Anderson, and Guy H. Bailey. Tuscaloosa: University of Alabama Press.

Bertolotti, Virginia, Serrana Caviglia, Magdalena Goll, and Marianela Fernández. 2005. *Documentos para la historia del portugués en el Uruguay*: Facultad de humanidades y ciencias de la educación Universidad de la República.

Bertolotti, Virginia, and Magdalena Coll. 2014. *Retrato lingüístico del Uruguay: Un enfoque histórico sobre las lenguas en la región*. Montevideo: Ediciones Universitarias - Universidad de la República.

Beseghi, Micòl. 2019. "The Representation and Translation of Identities in Multilingual TV Series: *Jane the Virgin*, a Case in Point." *MonTI* (Multilingüismo y representación de las identidades en textos audiovisuales/Multilingualism and representation of identities in audiovisual texts. Special Issue 4):145-72.

Besso, Henry V. 1951. "Judeo-Spanish in the United States." *Hispania* 34:89-90.

Besso, Henry V. 1961. "Sefardismo: Don Ramón Menéndez Pidal and the 'Romancero Sefardí'." *Sefarad* 21:343-74.

Betti, Silvia. 2011. "El Spanglish En Los Estados Unidos: ¿Estrategia Expresiva Legítima?" *Lenguas Modernas* 37:33-53.

Bhabha, Homi K. 2000. *Nation and Narration, City*. London and New York: Routledge.

Blech, Benjamin, Elaine Blech, D. Iagnosis, and Chun Lu. 1999. *Your Name Is Your Blessing: Hebrew Names and Their Mystical Meanings*. Vol. 89. Northvale, NJ: Jason Aronson Inc.

Blumenthal, Fred. 2009. "Biblical Onomastics: What's in a Name." *Jewish Bible Quarterly* 37:124–8.

Bonnefoy, Yves. 2004. "La traduction de la poésie." In *Entretiens sur la poésie*. Paris: Mercure de France.

Bornes-Varol, Marie-Christine. 1995. "Djoha juif dans l'Empire ottoman." *Revue du monde musulman et de la Méditerranée* 77–78:61–74.

Bornes-Varol, Marie-Christine. 2005. "La langue judéo-espagnole en Turquie aujourd'hui." *Outre-Terre* 10:387–9. doi: 10.3917/oute.010.0387.

Borovaia, Olga. 2002. "The Role of Translation in Shaping the Ladino Novel at the Time of Westernization in the Ottoman Empire (A Case Study: Hasan-pasha and Pavlo y Virzhinia)." *Jewish History*:263–82.

Borovaya, Olga. 2003. "The Serialized Novel as Rewriting: The Case of Ladino Belles Lettres." *Jewish Social Studies* 10:30–68.

Borovaya, Olga. 2008a. "Jews of Three Colors: The Path to Modernity in the Ladino Press at the Turn of the Twentieth Century." *Jewish Social Studies* 15:110–30.

Borovaya, Olga. 2008b. "New Forms of Ladino Cultural Production in the Late Ottoman Period: Sephardi Theater as a Tool of Indoctrination." *European Journal of Jewish Studies* 2:65–87.

Bosworth, R. J. B. 2006. *Mussolini's Italy: Life under the Fascist Dictatorship, 1915–1945*. New York: Penguin Books.

Bourdieu, Pierre, and John B. Thompson. 2001. *Language and Symbolic Power*. Cambridge, MA: Harvard University Press.

Boyden, Michael, and Helder De Schutter. 2006. "Language Ideologies in 'American' Literary History." *Comparative American Studies An International Journal* 4:285–306. doi: 10.1177/1477570006066774.

Braschi, Giannina. 2011. *Yo-Yo Boing! (Spanglish)*. Las Vegas: AmazonCrossing.

Brisset, Annie. 1996. *A Sociocritique of Translation: Theatre and Alterity in Quebec (1968–1988)*. Ottawa: University of Ottawa Press.

Brisset, Annie. 2000. "The Search for a Native Language: Translation and Cultural Identity." In *The Translation Studies Reader*, edited by Lawrence Venuti, 343–75. New York: Routledge.

Brisset, Annie. 2003. "Alterity in Translation. An Overview of Theories and Practices." *Translation, Translation* 21:101–32.

Broussy, Marie-Pierre, and Haïm Vidal Sephiha. 2002. "Le Judéo-espagnol de Mathilda Koen-Sarano tel qu'il apparaît dans son recueil de contes intitulé 'Kuentos del folklor de la familia djudeo-espanyola'." Atelier national de reproduction des thèses.

Brown, Adrienne Maree. 2019. *Pleasure Activism: The Politics of Feeling Good*, Emergent Strategy. Chico, CA: AK Press.

Brown, Francis, Edward Robinson, S. R. Driver, and Charles A. Briggs. 1979. *The New Brown, Driver, Briggs, Gesenius Hebrew and English Lexicon: with an Appendix Containing the Biblical Aramaic*. Peabody: Hendrickson.

Budzhak-Jones, Svitlana, and Shana Poplack. 1997. "Two Generations, Two Strategies: The Fate of Bare English-Origin Nouns in Ukrainian." *Journal of Sociolinguistics* 1 (2):225–58.

Bueno, Wilson. 1992. *Mar paraguayo, IlumiUras*. Curitiba, Brazil: Secretaria do Estado da Cultura de Paraná.

Bugel, Talia. 2009. "Explicit Attitudes in Brazil towards Varieties of Portuguese." *Studies in Hispanic and Lusophone Linguistics* 2 (2):275–304. doi: 10.1515/shll-2009-1053.

Bullock, Barbara E., Gualberto Guzmán, and Almeida Jacqueline Toribio. 2019. "The Limits of Spanglish?" 3rd Joint SIGHUM Workshop on Computational Linguistics for Cultural Heritage, Social Sciences, Humanities and Literature, Minneapolis, MN.

Bullock, Barbara E., and Almeida Jacqueline Toribio. 2009. *The Cambridge Handbook of Linguistic Code-Switching*. Cambridge: Cambridge University Press.

Bunis, David M. 1975. *A Guide to Reading and Writing Judezmo*. Brooklyn: Adelantre!: The Judezmo Society.

Bunis, David M. 1981. *Sephardic Studies: A Research Bibliography*. New York: Garland Publishing.

Bunis, David M. 1992. "The Language of the Sephardim: A Historical Overview." In *Moreshet Sepharad: The Sephardi Legacy II*, edited by Haim Beinart, 399–422. Jerusalem: Magnes Press.

Bunis, David M. 2003. "Modernization of Judezmo and Haketia (Judeo-Spanish)." In *The Jews of the Middle East and North Africa in Modern Times*, edited by Reeva Spector Simon, Michael Menachem Laskier, and Sara Reguer, 116–28. New York: Columbia University Press.

Bunis, David M. 2005. "Judeo-Spanish Culture in Medieval and Modern Times." In *Sephardic and Mizrahi Jewry from the Golden Age of Spain to Modern Times*, edited by Zion Zohar, 55–76. New York: New York University Press.

Bunis, David M. 2016. "Twenty-First-Century Talk about Judezmo on the Ladinokomunita Website." In *Languages of Modern Jewish Cultures: Comparative Perspectives*, edited by Joshua L. Miller and Anita Norich, 321–60. Ann Arbor: University of Michigan Press.

Burgos, Cristina. 2011. "Sunday Evening Cafecito y 'Killer Crónicas.'" *Life in Spanglish*. lifeinspanglish.com/2011/01/09/sunday-evening-cafecito-y-killer-cronicas/.

Bürki, Yvette. 2003. "La alternancia de códigos en la literatura neorriqueña." *Revista Internacional de Lingüística Iberoamericana* 1 (2):79–96.

Bürki, Yvette. 2013. "The status of Judeo-Spanish in the Ottoman Empire." In *A Political History of Spanish: The Making of a Language*, edited by José Del Valle, 335–49. Cambridge: Cambridge University Press.

Busch, Hans-Jörg. 2017. *A Complete Guide to the Spanish Subjunctive*. London: Routledge.
Butler, Judith. 1988. "Performative Acts and Gender Constitution: An Essay in Phenomenology and Feminist Theory." *Theatre Journal* 40 (4):900–11. doi: 10.2307/3207893.
Caetano, Gerardo. 2020. *Historia mínima de Uruguay*. Edited by Pablo Yankelevich. 4ª ed. Ciudad de México: Colegio de México.
Caetano, Gerardo, and José Rilla. 2016. *Historia contemporánea del Uruguay: De la colonia al siglo XXI*. Montevideo: Editorial Fin de Siglo.
Callahan, Laura. 2001. "Metalinguistic References in a Spanish/English Corpus." *Hispania* 84:417–27. doi: 10.2307/3657776.
Callahan, Laura. 2003. "The Role of Register in Spanish-English Codeswitching in Prose." *Bilingual Review* 27:12–25.
Callahan, Laura. 2014. "The Importance of Being Earnest." *Spanish in Context* 11 (2):202–20. doi: 10.1075/sic.11.2.03cal.
Calvo, José Ramón, and Isabel Balteiro. 2011. "Translating Linguistic Creativity: Dubbing and Subtitling of Slang in a Clockwork Orange into Spanish." In *New Approaches to Specialized English Lexicology and Lexicography*, edited by Isabel Balteiro, 189–206. Newcastle upon Tyne: Cambridge Scholars.
Caminero-Santangelo, Marta. 2009. *On Latinidad: U.S. Latino Literature and the Construction of Ethnicity*. Gainesville: University Press of Florida.
Carvalho, Ana. 1998. *The Social Distribution of Uruguayan Portuguese in a Bilingual Border Town*. Edited by Milton M. Azevedo. Ann Arbor, MI: ProQuest Dissertations Publishing.
Carvalho, Ana Maria. 2003. "Rumo a uma definição do português uruguaio." *Revista Internacional de Lingüística Iberoamericana* 1 (2):125–49.
Carvalho, Ana. 2014a. "Introduction: Towards a Sociolinguistics of the Border." *International Journal of Sociolinguistics* (227):1–7.
Carvalho, Ana. 2014b. "Linguistic Continuity along the Uruguayan-Brazilian Border: Monolingual Perceptions of a Bilingual Reality." In *Spanish and Portuguese across Time, Place, and Borders*, edited by Laura Callahan, 183–99. New York: Palgrave Macmillan.
Carvalho, Ana Maria. 2004. "I Speak Like the Guys on TV: Palatalization and the Urbanization of Uruguayan Portuguese." *Language Variation and Change* 16 (2):127–51. doi: 10.1017/S0954394504162030.
Carvalho, Ana Maria. 2006. "Politicas linguisticas de seculos passados nos dias de hoje: O dilema sobre a educacao bilingue no norte do Uruguai." *Language Problems & Language Planning* 30 (2):149–71. doi: 10.1075/lplp.30.2.04car.
Cashman, Holly R. 1999. "Language Choice in U.S. Latina First Person Narrative: The Effects of Language Standardization and Subordination." *Discourse* 21 (3):132–50.
Cashman, Holly R. 2005. "Book Review. Spanglish: The Making of a New American Language by Ilan Stavans." *Chasqui* 34:216–19. doi: 10.2307/29741958.

Cashman, Holly R. 2015. "Queer Latin@ Networks: Languages, Identities, and the Ties That Bind." In *A Sociolinguistics of Diaspora: Latino Practices, Identities and Ideologies*, edited by Rosina Márquez Reiter and Luisa Martín Rojo, 66–80. New York: Routledge.

Casielles-Suárez, Eugenia. 2013. "Radical Code-Switching in the Brief Wondrous Life of Oscar Wao." *Bulletin of Hispanic Studies* 90 (4):475–87. doi: 10.3828/bhs.2013.30.

Castillo, Debra A. 2005. *Redreaming America: Toward a Bilingual American Culture*. Albany: State University of New York Press.

Catullus, Gaius Valerius, Celia Thaew Zukofsky, Louis Zukofsky, and Paul Zukofsky. 1969. *Catullus Fragmenta: Translation by Celia and Louis Zukofsky, Music by Paul Zukofsky*. London: Turret Books.

Cepeda, María Elena. 2010. *Musical ImagiNation: U.S.-Colombian Identity and the Latin Music Boom*. New York: New York University Press.

Cerón, Ella. 2017. "What Disney's *Coco* Means to Me as a Mexican-American." *Teen Vogue*, November 28.

Cervantes Saavedra, Miguel de, Ilan Stavans, and Roberto Weil. 2018. *Don Quixote of La Mancha in Spanglish*. University Park, PA: Pennsylvania State University Press.

Chamberlain, Lori. 2004. "Gender and the Metaphorics of Translation." In *Translation Studies Reader*, edited by Lawrence Venuti, 306–21.

Chapdelaine, Annick. 1992. "Faulkner in French: Humor Obliterated." *The Faulkner Journal* (Fall 1991/Spring 1992):43–60.

Chapdelaine, Annick. 1994. "Transparence et retraduction des sociolectes dans The Hamlet de Faulkner." *TTR: traduction, terminologie, rédaction* 7:11–33. doi: 10.7202/037179ar.

Charron, Marc. 2004. "Don Quijote en espanglais: réflexions autour de la traduction d'Ilan Stavans." *TTR: traduction, terminologie, rédaction* 17:189–94.

Chávez-Silverman, Susana. 2004. *Killer Cronicas: Bilingual Memories*. Madison: University of Wisconsin Press.

Chávez-Silverman, Susana. 2010. *Scenes from la Cuenca de Los Angeles y otros Natural Disasters*. Madison: University of Wisconsin Press.

Chávez-Silverman, Susana. 2014. "All Green Will Endure Chrónicle." *Asymptote*.

Chávez-Silverman, Susana. 2017. "Personal Correspondence March 16, 2017."

Chen Ying-yu, Irene. 2009. "Monkey King's Journey to the West: Transmission of a Chinese Folktale to Anglophone Children." *Bookbird: A Journal of International Children's Literature* 47:26–33.

Chesterman, Andrew. 2009. "The Name and Nature of Translator Studies." *Hermes – Journal of Language and Communication Studies* 42:13–22.

Ch'ien, Evelyn Nien-Ming. 2004. *Weird English*. Cambridge: Harvard University Press.

Childers, William. 2006. *Transnational Cervantes*. Toronto: University of Toronto Press.

Chinellato Díaz, Alessio. 2016. "El portuñol en la frontera Venezuela-Brasil: contacto, actitudes e ideologías lingüísticas." *Estudios de lingüística del español* 37.

Church, Meredith. 2007. *Portuñol and Border Identity in Rivera, Uruguay: Reconciling Identities and Claiming Space in the National Imaginary*, edited by Mehrangiz Najafizadeh: Ann Arbor, MI: ProQuest Dissertations Publishing.

Cintas, Jorge Díaz. 2009. *New Trends in Audiovisual Translation: Topics in Translation*. Edited by Jorge Díaz-Cintas, *New Trends in Audiovisual Translation {Topics in translation}*.

Clyne, Michael, Edina Eisikovits, and Laura Tollfree. 2001. "Ethnic Varieties of Australian English." In *English in Australia*, edited by David Blair and Peter Collins, 223–38. Amsterdam: John Benjamins Publishing.

Clyne, Michael, Edina Eisikovits, and Laura Tollfree. 2002. "Ethnolects as In-Group Varieties." In *Us and Others: Social Identities across Languages, Discourses and Cultures*, edited by Anna Duszak, 133–57. Amsterdam: John Benjamins Publishing.

Cobos, Rubén. 2003. *A Dictionary of New Mexico & Southern Colorado Spanish*. Santa Fe: Museum of New Mexico Press.

Coll, M. 1997. "The Narrative of Saul Ibargoyen Isla as a Literary Representation of a Linguistic Frontier." *Hispania – A Journal Devoted to the Teaching of Spanish and Portuguese* 80 (4):745–52.

Coll, Magdalena. 2008. "La frontera Uruguay-Brasil Analisis linguistico de un corpus del siglo XIX." *Spanish in Context* 5 (1):20–39. doi: 10.1075/sic.5.1.03cav.

Concannon, Kevin, Francisco A. Lomelí, and Marc Priewe. 2009. "Imagined Transnationalism: U.S. Latino/a Literature, Culture, and Identity." doi: 10.1057/9780230103320.

Conrad, Ryan, ed. 2014. *Against Equality: Queer Revolution, Not Mere Inclusion*. Oakland, CA: AK Press.

Contreras, Sheila Marie. 2017. "Chicana, Chicano, Chican@, Chicanx." In *Keywords for Latina/o Studies,* edited by Vargas, Deborah R., Nancy Raquel Mirabal, and Lawrence M La Fountain-Stokes, 32–5. New York: New York University Press.

Corriente, F., and A. Sáenz-Badillos. 1994. "Nueva propuesta de lectura de las 'xarajat' con texto romance de la serie hebrea." *Revista de Filología Española* 74:283–9. doi: 10.3989/rfe.1994.v74.i3/4.456.

Corrius, Montse, and Patrick Zabalbeascoa. 2019. "Translating Code-Switching on the Screen: Spanglish and L3-as-Theme." *Journal of Audiovisual Translation* 2 (2):72–91.

Cotelo, Enrique. 2011. *"Eu estou pronto apagar se os mais bizinhos pagarem": Lenguas en contacto e identidades nacionales en documentos de la frontera de Uruguay con Brasil (1860-1864)*. Edited by John Gutierrez, Diane Marting and Antonio Reyes. Ann Arbor, MI: ProQuest Dissertations Publishing.

Coupland, Nikolas. 2003. "Introduction: Sociolinguistics and Globalisation." *Journal of Sociolinguistics* 7 (4):465–72.

Coutinho, Eduardo de Faria. 1983. *The "Synthesis" Novel in Latin America: A Study on João Guimarães Rosa's Grande Sertão: Veredas*. Chapel Hill, NC: University of North Carolina Press.

Covarrubias Orozco, Sebastián de, Ignacio Arellano, and Rafael Zafra. 2006. *Tesoro de la lengua castellana o española*. [Pamplona]; Madrid; Frankfurt am Main: Universidad de Navarra: Iberoamericana: Vervuert.

Craig, Richard B. 1971. *The Bracero Program: Interest Groups and Foreign Policy*. Austin: University of Texas Press.

Cronin, Michael. 2010. "The Cracked Looking Glass of Servants: Translation and Minority Languages in a Global Age." In *Critical Readings in Translation Studies*, edited by Mona Baker, 247–62. New York: Routledge.

Cruess, Susan Leah. 2011. "A Study of Elena Poniatowska's Amanecer en el Zócalo: The Contemporary Mexican Crónica in Translation." PhD, Modern Languages and Literatures, University of Ottawa.

Cruz, Bill, and Bill Teck. 1998. "The Official Spanglish Dictionary: un user's guía to More than 300 Words and Phrases That Aren't Exactly español or inglés."

Curotto, Papu. 2016. *Esteros*. Argentina, Brazil, France: Outplay Films.

Cussel, Mattea. 2021. "Methodological Nationalism in Translation Studies: A Critique." *Translation and Interpreting Studies* 16 (1):1–18.

Da Rosa, Enrique. 2015. *Jodido Bushinshe: Portuñol como patrimonio cultural inmaterial*. Montevideo: Ministerio de educación y cultura.

Dalleo, Raphael, and Elena Machado Sáez. 2007. "The Latino/A Canon and the Emergence of Post-Sixties Literature." *The Latino/a Canon and the Emergence of Post-Sixties Literature*. doi: 10.1057/9780230605169.

De Fina, Anna. 2015. "Language Ideologies and Practices in a Transnational Community: Spanish-Language Radio and Latino Identities in the US." In *A Sociolinguistics of Diaspora: Latino Practices, Identities and Ideologies*, edited by Rosina Márquez Reiter and Luisa Martín Rojo, 48–65. New York & London: Routledge.

de Jongh, Elena M. 1990. "Interpreting in Miami's Federal Courts: Code-Switching and Spanglish." *Source: Hispania* 73:274–8.

De Kock, Leon. 1992. "Interview with Gayatri Chakravorty Spivak: New Nation Writers Conference in South Africa." *ARIEL: A Review of International English Literature* 23 (3):29–47.

de Mojica, Sarah. 2002. "Sujetos híbridos en la literatura puertorriqueña: ' Daniel Santos y Yo-Yo Boing.'" *Revista de Crítica Literaria Latinoamericana* 28:187–203.

de Onís, Federico. 1968. "Los sefardíes y el idioma castellano." *Revista hispánica moderna* 34:176–94.

de Paula Figueiredo, Nilze, Edgar Aparecido da Costa, and Beatriz Lima de Paula. 2011. "Os elementos do espaco turistico da Fronteira Brasil-Bolivia.(Report)." *Ra'e Ga* (21):105.

de Souza, Livia S. 2019. "Por una traducción latino-americana: un análisis de las traducciones de Achy Obejas." V Coloquio Internacional Latinos en los Estados Unidos.

Dean, Tim. 2000. *Beyond Sexuality*. Chicago, IL: University of Chicago Press.
DeCosta-Willis, Miriam. 2004. "Sandra María Esteves's Nuyorican Poetics: The Signifying Difference." *Afro-Hispanic Review* 23:3–12.
Decter, Jonathan P. 2005. "Literatures of Medieval Sepharad." In *Sephardic and Mizrahi Jewry: From the Golden Age of Spain to Modern Times*, edited by Zion Zohar, 75–100. New York: New York University Press.
Deleuze, Gilles, Félix Guattari, and Robert Brinkley. 1983. "What Is a Minor Literature?" *Mississippi Review* 11 (3):13–33.
Deleuze, Gilles, and Felix Guattari. 1986. *Kafka: Towards a Minor Literature*. Minneapolis, MN: University of Minnesota Press.
Démont, Marc. 2018. "On Three Modes of Translating Queer Literary Texts." In *Queering Translation, Translating the Queer: Theory, Practice, Activism*, edited by Brian J. and Klaus Kaindl Baer, 157–71. New York: Routledge.
Derrick, Roshawnda A. 2015. "Code-Switching, Code-Mixing and Radical Bilingualism in U.S. Latino Texts." PhD, Detroit, MI: Wayne State University.
Derrick, Roshawnda, and Remy Attig. ND. "Translating Boyle Heights: Radical Bilingualism and Spanish Dubbing of Chicanx Voices in *Gentefied* and *Vida*." *Diálogo, an Interdisciplinary Studies Journal*.
Derrida, Jacques, and Alan Bass. 1978. *Writing and Difference*. Chicago: University of Chicago Press.
Díaz-Campos, Manuel. 2011. *Handbook of Hispanic Sociolinguistics*, Blackwell Handbooks in Linguistics. Malden, MA: Wiley.
Díaz-Campos, Manuel, and Gregory Newall. 2014. *Introducción a la sociolingüística hispánica*. Chichester: Wiley Blackwell.
Díaz-Mas, Paloma. 2009. "Folk Literature among Sephardic Bourgeois Women at the Beginning of the Twentieth Century." *European Journal of Jewish Studies* 3:81–101.
Diegues, Douglas. 2023. Interview with Douglas Diegues in "Imigrantes". São Paulo, Brazil: Museu da Língua Portuguesa.
Dietz, Jon Eric. 2011. "Sistahs African American Vernacular English Translation of Les Belles-Soeurs A Foreignization Approach." MA, Department of Translation Studies, Concordia University.
Douglas, Kendra. 2004. *Uruguayan Portuguese in Artigas: Tri-dimensionality of Transitional Local Varieties in Contact with Spanish and Portuguese standards*. Edited by Ray Harris-Northall. Ann Arbor, MI: ProQuest Dissertations Publishing.
Duany, Jorge. 2000. "Nation on the Move: The Construction of Cultural Identities in Puerto Rico and the Diaspora." *American Ethnologist* 27 (1):5–30.
Eagleton, Terry. 2008. *Literary Theory: An Introduction*. Minneapolis: University of Minnesota Press.
Eco, Umberto. 2012. *Experiences in Translation*. Toronto: University of Toronto Press.
Elizaincin, Adolfo. 1976. "The Emergence of Bilingual Dialects on the Brazilian-Uruguayan Border." *Linguistics* 177 (Aug):123–34.

Elizaincin, Adolfo. 1992. *Dialectos en contacto: español y portugués en España y América*. Montevideo, Uruguay: Arca.

Elizaincin, Adolfo. 2008. "Diacronía del contacto español-portugués." In *La Romania americana: Procesos lingüísticos en situaciones de contacto*, edited by Norma Díaz, Ralph Ludwig, and Stefan Pfänder, 255–61. Frankfurt: Iberoamericana Editorial Vervuert.

Elizaincín, Adolfo. 2004. "Las fronteras del español con el portugués en América." *Revista Internacional de Lingüística Iberoamericana* 2 (2):105–18.

Elizaincin, Adolfo, Luis Behares, and Graciela Barrios. 1987. *Nos falemo brasileiro: Dialectos portugueses en Uruguay*. Montevideo: Amesur.

Elliott, J. H. 1984. "Spain and America in the Sixteenth and Seventeenth Centuries." In *The Cambridge History of Latin America*, edited by Leslie Bethell, 287–340. Cambridge: Cambridge University Press.

Elmaleh, Raphaël, and George Ricketts. 2012. *Jews under Moroccan Skies: Two Thousand Years of Jewish Life*. Santa Fe, NM: Gaon Books.

Epstein, B. J., and Robert Gillett, eds. 2017. *Queer in Translation, Routledge Advances in Translation and Interpreting Studies*. Oxon, UK: Routledge.

Esformes, Maria. 2001. "Three Sefardic Folktales from Salonika, Greece." *Shofar: An Interdisciplinary Journal of Jewish Studies* 19:15–24.

Espitia, Marilyn. 2004. "The Other 'Other Hispanics': South American-Origin Latinos in the United States." In *The Columbia History of Latinos in the United States since 1960*, edited by David G. Gutiérrez, 257–80. New York: Columbia University Press.

Etchemendi, Javier. 2022. "Un lugar en donde el agua no toca la tierra." In *Noite nu Norte*, 13–16. Montevideo: Estuario Editora.

Evans, Jonathan, and Helen Ringrow. 2017. "Introduction: Borders in Translation and Intercultural Communication." *TranscUlturAl* 9 (2):1–12.

Even-Zohar, Itamar. 1990. "Polysystem Theory." *Poetics Today* 11 (1):9–26.

Even-Zohar, Itamar. 2004. "The Position of Translated Literature within the Literary Polysystem." In *The Translation Studies Reader*, edited by Lawrence Venuti, 199–218. London: Routledge.

Fagan, Allison. 2016. "Translating in the Margins: Attending to Glossaries in Latina/o Literature." *Journal of Modern Literature* 39:57–75.

Fairclough, Marta. 2003. "El (denominado) Spangish en Estados Unidos: polémicas y realidades." *Revista Internacional de Lingüística Iberoamericana* 1:185–204.

Fanon, Frantz. 1963. *The Wretched of the Earth*. New York: Grove Press New York.

Fanon, Frantz. 2008. *Black Skin, White Masks*. New York: Grove Press.

Fear, A. T. 2000. "Prehistoric and Roman Spain." In *Spain: A History*, edited by Raymond Carr, 11–38. Oxford: Oxford University Press.

Fernández Aguerre, Tabaré, Angela Gonzalez Ríos, and Agustina Marques. 2016. "El lenguaje como factor de desigualdad en los aprendizajes en Pisa 2009: el caso de la frontera noreste de Uruguay con Brasil = Language as an Inequality Factor in

Learning in Pisa 2009: A Case Study at the Boundary between Uruguay and Brazil." *Civitas* 16 (1):119–35. doi: 10.15448/1984-7289.2016.1.24239.

Fernández García, María Jesús. 2006. "Portuñol y literatura." *Revista de estudios extremeños* 62 (2):555–76.

Fernández, María Jesús. 2009. "Áreas críticas de la traducción literaria portugués-español: bilingüismo y portuñol." In *Traducción y autotraducción en las literaturas ibéricas*, edited by Enric Gallén, Francisco Lafarga, and Luis Pegenaute, 77–91. Lausanne, Switzerland: Peter Lang.

Fernández, María Jesús. 2011. "Áreas críticas de la traducción literaria portugués-español: bilingüismo y portuñol." In *Traducción y autotraducción en las literaturas ibéricas*, edited by Enric Gallén, Francisco Lafarga, and Luis Pegenaute. Bern: Peter Lang.

Fish, Stanley. 2003. *Is There a Text in This Class?: The Authority of Interpretive Communities*. Cambridge: Harvard University Press.

Flavius, Josephus. 2017. *The Antiquities of the Jews*. Vol. 14: Project Gutenberg.

Flores-González, Nilda. 2017. *Citizens but Not Americans: Race & Belonging among Latino Millennials*, edited by Pierrette Hondagneu-Sotelo and Victor M. Rios, *Latina/o Sociology Series*. New York: New York University Press.

Flores, Juan, and George Yudice. 1990. "Living Borders/Buscando America: Languages of Latino Self-Formation." *Social Text* 24:57–84.

Flores, Nelson. 2014. "Let's Not Forget that Translanguaging is a Political Act." *The Educational Linguist* (Blog). https://educationallinguist.wordpress.com/2014/07/19/lets-not-forget-that-translanguaging-is-a-political-act/.

Flores, Nelson, and Jonathan Rosa. 2015. "Undoing Appropriateness: Raciolinguistic Ideologies and Language Diversity in Education." *Harvard Educational Review* 85 (2):149–71. doi: 10.17763/0017-8055.85.2.149.

Folkart, Barbara. 2007. "Authorship, Ownership, Translatorship." In *Second Finding. A Poetics of Translation*, 342–403. Ottawa: University of Ottawa Press.

Foster, David William. 1999. "Book Reviews. Yo-Yo Boing! by Giannina Braschi." *Review of Contemporary Fiction* 19:202.

Foucault, Michel, and Alan Sheridan. 1972. *The Archaeology of Knowledge*. 1st American ed., World of man. New York: Pantheon Books.

Foz, Clara. 1998. *Le Traducteur, l'église et le roi: Espagne, XIIe et XIIIe siècles*. Ottawa: University of Ottawa Press.

Franco Aixelá, Javier. 2004. "The Study of Technical and Scientific Translation: An Examination of Its Historical Development." *JoSTrans: The Journal of Specialized Translation* (1):24–49.

Fraser, Ryan. 2004. "Past Lives of Knives: On Borges, Translation, and Sticking Old Texts." *TTR: traduction, terminologie, rédaction* 17:55–80. doi: 10.7202/011973ar.

Gabai, Hyman. 2002. "Gematria of the Torah and the Prayer Book." In *Judaism, Mathematics, and the Hebrew Calendar*, 71–8, 117. Northvale: Jason Aronson.

Galván, Roberto A, and Richard V. Teschner. 1996. *The Dictionary of Chicano Spanish: El diccionario del español chicano*. Lincolnwood: NTC Publishing Group.

García, María Cristina. 2004. "Exiles, Immigrants, and Transnationals: The Cuban Communities of the United States." In *The Columbia History of Latinos in the United States since 1960*, edited by David G. Gutiérrez, 146–86. New York: Columbia University Press.

García, Ofelia. 2009. *Bilingual Education in the 21st Century: A Global Perspective*. Malden, MA: Wiley-Blackwell.

García Canclini, Néstor. 1995. *Hybrid Cultures: Strategies for Entering and Leaving Modernity*. Minneapolis, MN: University of Minnesota Press.

García de la Concha, Víctor. 2014. *La Real Academia Española: vida e historia*. Barcelona; Madrid: Espasa; Real Academia Española.

Garcini, Salvador. 1998. *Soñadoras*. Edited by Adrián Frutos and Juan Carlos Frutos. Mexico: Canal de las Estrellas.

Gasparini, Pablo. 2010. "Néstor Perlongher: Una extraterritorialidad en gozoso portuñol." *Revista Iberoamericana* 76 (232-233):757–75. doi: 10.5195/REVIBEROAMER.2010.6752.

Gauvin, Lise. 2000. *Langagement: L'écrivain et la langue au Québec*. Montreal: Éditions du Boréal.

Geller, Monica. 2012. *Contacto lingüístico, bilingüismo e ideología lingüística en el pueblo de Olivenza: ¿castellano o portugues?* Edited by Vicente Lledo-Guillem. Ann Arbor, MI: ProQuest Dissertations Publishing.

Gentzler, Edwin. 1993. *Contemporary Translation Theories*. London: Routledge.

Gentzler, Edwin. 2006. "Translation and Border Writing in the Americas: Fiction, Performance Art, and Film." In *Translating Voices, Translating Regions*, edited by Nigel Armstrong and Federico M. Federici, 365–84. Rome: ARACNE.

Gentzler, Edwin. 2008. *Translation and Identity in the Americas: New Directions in Translation Theory*. London: Routledge.

Gerber, Jane S. 1994. *The Jews of Spain: a History of the Sephardic Experience*. New York: Free Press.

Gesenius, Friedrich Heinrich Wilhelm, Emil Friedrich Kautzsch, and Arthur Ernest Cowley. 1910. *Hebrew Grammar as Edited and Enlarged by the Late E. Kautzsch*. 2nd English ed. Oxford: Claredon Press.

Giles, Howard, and Tania Ogay. 2007. "Communication Accommodation Theory." In *Explaining Communication: Contemporary Theories and Exemplars*, edited by B. Bryan and Wendy Samter Whaley, 325–44. Bahwah, NJ: Routledge.

Ginio, Alisa Meyuhas. 2010. "The History of the Me'am Lo'ez: A Ladino Commentary on the Bible." *European Judaism* 43 (2):117–25. doi: 10.3167/ej.2010.430211.

Ginio, Alisa Meyuhas. 2014. *Between Sepharad and Jerusalem: History, Identity and Memory of the Sephardim*. Leiden, Boston: Brill.

Ginio, Eyal. 2002. "'Learning the Beautiful Language of Homer:' Judeo-Spanish Speaking Jews and the Greek Language and Culture between the Wars." *Jewish History* 16:235–62.

Glenn, Evelyn Nakano. 2002. *Unequal Freedom: How Race and Gender Shaped American Citizenship and Labor*. Cambridge, MA: Harvard University Press.

Glick, Thomas F. 1979. *Islamic and Christian Spain in the Early Middle Ages*. Princeton: Princeton University Press.

Gold, David. 1977. "Dzhudezmo." *Language Sciences* 47:14–16.

Gold, David. 1983. "Planning Glottonyms for Jewish Languages (With Emphasis on Judezmo and Yahudic)." *Jewish Language Review* 3:71–95.

Gold, David. 1985a. "More on the Glottonym Judezmo." *Jewish Language Review* 5:151–3.

Gold, David. 1985b. "Proposed Latin-Letter Transliteration for Judezmo." *Jewish Language Review* 5:104–8.

Gold, David. 1987. "Review: Recent Studies in Jewish Languages." *Language in Society* 16:397–407. doi: 10.1017/S0047404500012471.

Gold, David L. 1980. "Modern Southeastern Judezmo /kor'jen/ ~ /kur'jen/ and Ladino / vin'jen/, /aladi'nan/ and /ma'nan/." *Sefarad* 40:415–17.

Gold, David L. 1985c. "Names for Jewish English and Some of Its Varieties." *American Speech* 60:185–7.

Gold, David L. 1986. "An Introduction to Jewish English." *Jewish Language Review* 6:94–120.

Gold, David L. 1991. "Some Notes on Yiddish and Judezmo as National Languages." *History of European Ideas* 13:41–9.

Gold, David L. 2003. "We Do Not Know Whether Jews in Sefarad Spoke or Wrote Basque." *Fontes linguae vasconum: studia et documenta* 35:537–40.

Goldberg, Harriet. 1993. "The Judeo-Spanish Proverb and Its Narrative Context." *PMLA* 108:106–20.

Gómez-Peña, Guillermo. 1992. "The New World (B)order: A Work in Progress." *Third Text* 6 (21):71–9. doi: 10.1080/09528829208576387.

Gonzalez, Juan. 2011. *Harvest of Empire: A History of Latinos in America*. Revised ed. New York: Penguin.

Graham, Joseph F. 1985. *Difference in Translation*. Ithaca, NY: Cornell University Press.

Grutman, R. 1990. "Literary Bilingualism as Intersystemic Relation." *Canadian Review of Comparative Literature* 17 (3–4):198–212.

Grutman, Rainier. 2006. "Refraction and Recognition: Literary Multilingualism in Translation." *Target: International Journal of Translation Studies* 18:17–47.

Gutiérrez Bottaro, Silvia Etel. 2014. "El portugués uruguayo y las marcas de la oralidad en la poesía del escritor uruguayo Agustín R. Bisio." *abehache* 4 (6):109–29.

Gutiérrez, David G. 2004. "Demography and the Shifting Boundaries of 'Community': Reflections on 'U.S. Latinos' and the Evolution of Latino Studies." In *The Columbia*

History of Latinos in the United States since 1960, edited by David G. Gutiérrez, 1–42. New York: Columbia University Press.

Haboucha, Reginetta. 1979. "Types and Motifs of Nine Folktales Collected by Cynthia Crews." *Estudios sefaríes* 2:39–70.

Haboucha, Reginetta. 1980. "Societal Values in the Judeo-Spanish Folktales." *Studies in Jewish Folklore*, 153–80. Cambridge, MA: The Association.

Haboucha, Reginetta. 1982a. "Collecting Sephardic Folktales in Israel." *Fabula* 23:221–34.

Haboucha, Reginetta. 1982b. "Women in Judeo-Spanish Folktales." *Sephardic Scholar* 4:32–47.

Haboucha, Reginetta. 1992. *Types and Motifs of the Judeo-Spanish Folktales*. New York: Garland.

Haboucha, Reginetta. 1993a. "Brides and Grooms: A Judeo-Spanish Version of Well-Known Literary Parallels." *Shofar: An Interdisciplinary Journal of Jewish Studies* 11:1–17.

Haboucha, Reginetta. 1993b. "Misogyny or Philogyny: The Case of a Judeo-Spanish Folktale." In *New Horizons in Sephardic Studies*, 239–51. Albany: State University of New York Press.

Haboucha, Reginetta. 2001. "The Lazy Wife: A Rare Jewish Version of an International Folktale Type." In *Jewish Culture and the Hispanic World: Essays in Memory of Joseph H. Silverman*, edited by Samuel G. Armistead, Mishael M. Caspi, Murray Baumgarten, and Karen L. Olson, 201–16. Newark, Delaware: Juan de la Cuesta.

Halberstam, Jack (Judith). 2011. *The Queer Art of Failure*. Durham, NC: Duke University Press.

Halio-Torres. 1980. "Writing the Spanish-Jewish Dialect." In *Studies in Sephardic Culture: The David N. Barocas Memorial Volume*, edited by Marc D. Angel, 95–106. New York: Sepher-Hermon.

Hall, Stuart. 1980. "Encoding/Decoding." In *Culture, Media, Language*, 117–27. London: Routledge.

Harris, Tracy. 1982. "Reasons for the Decline of Judeo-Spanish." *International Journal of the Sociology of Language* 1982:71–98. doi: 10.1515/ijsl.1982.37.71.

Harris, Tracy. 1993. "Judeo-Spanish in the Ottoman Empire." *Jewish Folklore and Ethnology Review* 15:112–17.

Harris, Tracy. 2006. "The Sociolinguistic Situation of Judeo-Spanish in the 20th Century in the United States and Israel." *Revista internacional de lingüística iberoamericana* 4:115–33.

Harris, Tracy. 2011. "The State of Ladino Today." *European Judaism* 44:51–61.

Hart, George. 1986. *A Dictionary of Egyptian Gods and Goddesses*. London: Routledge & Kegan Paul.

Hart, Ron Duncan. 2016. *Sephardic Jews: History, Religion and People*. Santa Fe, NM: Gaon Books.

Hassan, Iacob. 1978. "Transcripción normalizada de textos judeoespañoles." *Estudios Sefardíes* 1 (1):147–50.

Heilbron, Johan. 2010. "Towards a Sociology of Translation: Book Translations as a Cultural World System." In *Critical Readings in Translation Studies*, edited by Mona Baker, 304–16. London: Routledge.

Hensey, Frederick Gerald. 1972. *The Sociolinguistics of the Brazilian-Uruguayan Border*. The Haue: Mouton & Co.

Hidalgo, Margarita. 1986. "Language Contact, Language Loyalty, and Language Prejudice on the Mexican Border." *Language in Society* 15:193–220.

Hochschild, Arlie Russell. 2013. *So How's the Family? And Other Essays*. Berkeley, CA: University of California Press.

Holmes, James S. 2004. "The Name and Nature of Translation Studies." In *The Translation Studies Reader*, edited by Lawrence Venuti, 180–92. New York: Routledge.

Holtz, Barry W. 1984. *Back to the Sources: Reading the Classic Jewish Texts*. New York: Summit Books.

How, Laura. 2020. "Breaking Binaries: Rethinking Gendered Metaphors in Translation Theory." Master of Arts, Translation Studies, York University.

Ibargoyen Islas, Saúl. 1960. *Un lugar en la tierra*. Montevideo: Deslinde.

Ibargoyen Islas, Saúl. 2002a. *Cuento a cuento*. México, DF: Ediciones y Gráficos Eón.

Ibargoyen Islas, Saúl. 2002b. *Toda la tierra*. Tijuana: Ediciones y Gráficos Eón: Universidad de Tijuana.

Ibargoyen Islas, Saúl, and Eileen Zeitz. 1979. "Saul Ibargoyen Islas: El nosotros alla." *Chasqui* 9 (1):92–101. doi: 10.2307/29739593.

Jakobson, Roman. 2000. "On Linguistic Aspects of Translation." In *Translation Studies Reader*, edited by Lawrence Venuti, 113–18. New York: Routledge.

Jaksic, Iván. 2007. *The Hispanic World and American Intellectual Life, 1820–1880*. New York: Palgrave Macmillan.

Johnson, Paul. 1987. *A History of the Jews*. London: Weidenfeld and Nicolson.

Jordan, Shirley Ann. 2002. "Ethnographic Encounters: The Processes of Cultural Translation." *Language and Intercultural Communication* 2 (2):96–110. doi: 10.1080/14708470208668079.

Jusionyte, Ieva. 2014. "For Social Emergencies 'We Are 9-1-1': How Journalists Perform the State in an Argentine Border Town." *Anthropological Quarterly* 87 (1):151–81. doi: 10.1353/anq.2014.0004.

Kagan, Jeremy. 1981. *The Chosen*. 20th Century Fox, Analysis Film Releasing Corporation.

Kattan, Naim. 1986. "Adieu, Babylone: roman."

Keller, John E. 1950. "Elements of White Magic in Medieval Spanish Exempla." In *Romance Studies Presented to William Morton Day on the Occasion of His Seventieth Birthday by His Colleagues and Former Students*, edited by Urban T. Holmes, Alfred

G. Engstrom, and Sturgis E. Leavitt, 107–15. Chapel Hill: University of North Carolina Press.

Kerkhof, Erna. 2001. "The Myth of the Dumb Puerto Rican: Circular Migration and Language Struggle in Puerto Rico." *NWIG: New West Indian Guide/Nieuwe West-Indische Gids* 75:257–88.

Kevane, Bridget. 2001. "The Hispanic Absence in the North American Literary Canon." *Journal of American Studies* 35 (1):95–109. doi: 10.1017/S0021875801006545.

King, P. D. 1972. *Law and Society in the Visigothic Kingdom*. Edited by Walter Ullmann, *Cambridge Studies in Medieval Life and Thought*. Cambridge: Cambridge University Press.

Kingery, Sandra. 2019. "Translating Spanglish to Spanish: The Brief Wonderous Life of Oscar Wao." *Translation Review* 104 (1):8–29. doi: 10.1080/07374836.2019.1632764.

Koelb, Clayton. 2010. *Kafka: A Guide for the Perplexed*. 1st ed. London; New York: Continuum.

Koén-Sarano, Matilda. 1986. *Kuentos del folklor de la famiya djudeo-espanyola*. Yerusháláyim: Kanah.

Koén-Sarano, Matilda. 1991. *Djoha ke dize?: kuentos populares djudeo-espanyoles*. Yerushalayim: Kana.

Koén-Sarano, Matilda. 1993a. *Sipurei Eliyahu Ha-Navi mi-Moreshet Yehude Sefarad*. Jerusalem: Midrashiyat 'Amalyah.

Koén-Sarano, Matilda. 1993b. *Vini kantaremos: Koleksión de kantes djudeo-espanyoles*. Jerusalem: Old City Press Ltd.

Koén-Sarano, Matilda. 1994. *Konsejas i konsejikas del mundo djudeo-espanyol*. Yerusháláyim: Kana.

Koén-Sarano, Matilda. 1995. *De Saragosa a Yerusháláyim: Kuentos sefaradís*. Zaragoza, Spain: Edisión Ibercaja.

Koén-Sarano, Matilda. 1999. *Lejendas i kuentos morales de la tradisión djudeo-espanyola*. Yerusháláyim: Nur Afakot.

Koén-Sarano, Matilda. 2000. *Kuentos salados djudeo-espanyoles*. València: Edisiones Capitelum.

Koén-Sarano, Matilda. 2001. "Ensenyando el Djudeo-Espanyol (Ladino) en la Universidad Ben-Gurion." *Shofar: An Interdisciplinary Journal of Jewish Studies* 19:4–6.

Koén-Sarano, Matilda. 2002. *El Kurtijo Enkantado: Kuentos i konsejas del mundo djudeo-espanyol*. Yerusháláyim: Nur Afakot.

Koén-Sarano, Matilda. 2003. *Folktales of Joha, Jewish trickster*. Philadelphia: Jewish Publication Society.

Koén-Sarano, Matilda. 2006. *Por el plazer de kontar: kuentos de mi vida; seleksión*. Yerusháláyim: Nur Afakot.

Koén-Sarano, Matilda. 2010. *Diksionario Ebreo-Djudeo-Espanyol (Ladino)*. Jerusalem: Zak.

Koén-Sarano, Matilda. 2012. "Personal Interview – May 30, 2012."
Koén-Sarano, Matilda, and Reginetta Haboucha. 2004. *King Solomon and the Golden Fish: Tales from the Sephardic Tradition*. Detroit, MI: Wayne State University Press.
Kolatch, Alfred J. 1984. *Complete Dictionary of English and Hebrew First Names*. Revised ed. Middle Village: Jonathan David Publishers.
Kuhiwczak, Piotr, and Karin Littau. 2007. *A Companion to Translation Studies*. Clevedon: Multilingual Matters.
La Fountain-Stokes, Lawrence. 2006. "La política queer del espanglish." *Debate Feminista* 33:141–53.
Labov, William. 1972. "Sociolinguistic patterns."
Labov, William. 1990. "The Intersection of Sex and Social Class in the Course of Linguistic Change." *Language Variation and Change* 2 (2):205–54. doi: 10.1017/S0954394500000338.
Lane, Pia, James Costa, and Haley de Korne. 2018. *Standardizing Minority Languages: Competing Ideologies of Authority and Authenticity in the Global Periphery*. Edited by Marilyn Martin-Jones and Joan Pujolar Cos, *Routledge Critical Studies in Multilingualism*. Abingdon, UK: Routledge.
Laplantine, François. 1995. "L'ethnologue, le traducteur et l'écrivain." *Meta: Journal des traducteurs* 40:497–507. doi: 10.7202/003398ar.
Larkosh, Christopher. 2006. "'Writing in the Foreign': Migrant Sexuality and Translation of the Self in Manuel Puig's Later Work." *The Translator* 12 (2):279–99. doi: 10.1080/13556509.2006.10799219.
Larkosh, Christopher. 2011. "Translating South-South (and Other Lessons from the Future)." In *Literature, Geography, Translation: Studies in World Writing*, edited by Cecilia Alvstad, Stefan Helgesson, and David Watson, 28–39. Newcastle upon Tyne, UK: Cambridge Scholars Publishing.
Larkosh, Christopher. 2016. "Flows of Trans-Language: Translating Transgender in the Paraguayan Sea." *TSQ: Transgender Studies Quarterly* 3 (3–4):552–68.
Lauret, Maria. 2014. *Wanderwords: Language Migration in American Literature*. New York, London: Bloomsbury Academic.
Lazar, Moshe, and David Herman. 1972. *The Sephardic Tradition: Ladino and Spanish-Jewish Literature*. New York: W. W. Norton & Company.
Leap, William L, and Tom Boellstorff. 2004. *Speaking in Queer Tongues: Globalization and Gay Language*. Urbana, IL: University of Illinois Press.
Lears, T. J. Jackson. 1985. "The Concept of Cultural Hegemony: Problems and Possibilities." *American Historical Review* 90 (3):567–93.
Leeman, J. 2013. "Categorizing Latinos in the History of the US Census: The Official Racialization of Spanish." In *A Political History of Spanish: The Making of a Language*, edited by José Del Valle, 305–24. Cambridge: Cambridge University Press.

Lefevere, André. 1990. "Translation: Its Genealogy in the West." In *Translation, History, Culture*, edited by Susan Bassnett and André Lefevere, 14–28. London: Pinter.

Lefevere, André. 1992. *Translation History Culture*. London: Routledge.

Lefevere, André. 1999. "Composing the Other." In *Post-Colonial Translation: Theory and Practice*, edited by Susan Bassnett and Harish Trivedi, 75–94. London: Routledge.

Lehmann, Matthias B. 2005. *Ladino Rabbinic Literature & Ottoman Sephardic Culture*. Bloomington, IN: Indiana University Press.

Lehmann, Matthias B. 2016. "The Intended Reader of Ladino Rabbinic Literature and Judeo-Spanish Reading Culture of Ladino literature." *Jewish History* 16 (3):283–307.

Lemus Sarmiento, Aura. 2013. "Para muestra, un botón. La cuestión del Espanglish en la nueva (y no tan nueva) literatura hispanoamericana." *INTI* (77/78):289–97.

Levitt, Peggy. 2004. "Transnational Ties and Incorporation: The Case of Dominicans in the United States." In *The Columbia History of Latinos in the United States since 1960*, edited by David G. Gutiérrez, 229–56. New York: Columbia University Press.

Levy, Jiri. 2000. "Translation as a Decision Process." In *The Translation Studies Reader*, edited by Lawrence Venuti, 148–59. New York: Routledge.

Levy, Raphael. 1947. "The Background and the Significance of Judeo-French." *Modern Philology: A Journal Devoted to Research in Medieval and Modern Literature* 45:1–7.

Levy, Solly. 2012. "Presentación de la obra la vida en Haketía - para que no se pierda de Solly Levy." eSefarad. https://esefarad.com/?p=31534.

Lewis, M. Paul. 2009. Ladino. In *Ethnologue: Languages of the World*. SIL International.

Limão, Paula Cristina de Paiva. 2015. "O 'portunhol' da América Latina no ciberespaço: De interlíngua e língua de fronteira a língua de intercompreensão e língua literária sem fronteiras." De volta ao futuro da língua portuguesa. Atas do V SIMELP Simpósio Mundial de Estudos de Língua Portuguesa, Università del Salento.

Lippi-Green, Rosina. 2012. *English with an Accent: Language, Ideology and Discrimination in the United States*. 2nd ed. London: Routledge.

Lipski, John M. 1986. "The Construction pa(ra) atrás among Spanish-English Bilinguals: Parallel Structures and Universal Patterns." *Iberoamericana* 10:87–96.

Lipski, John M. 2006. "Too Close for Comfort? The Genesis of 'Portuñol/Portunhol.'" In *Selected Proceedings of the 8th Hispanic Linguistics Symposium*, edited by Timothy L. Face and Carol A. Klee, 1–22. Somerville, MA: Cascadilla Proceedings Project.

Lipski, John M. 2009. "Searching for the Origins of Uruguayan Fronterizo Dialects: Radical Code-Mixing as 'Fluent Dysfluency.'" *Journal of Portuguese Linguistics* 8 (1):3–44.

Lipski, John M. 2011. "Dialects and Borders: Face-to-Face and Back-to-Back in Latin American Spanish." *Southwest Journal of Linguistics* 30 (2):33.

Livia, Anna, and Kira Hall. 1997. *Queerly Phrased: Language, Gender, and Sexuality*. Oxford: Oxford University Press.

Locane, Jorge J. 2015. "Disquisiciones en torno al *Portunhol selvagem*. Del horror de los profes a una 'lengua pura.'" *Perífrasis. Revista de Literatura, Teoría y Crítica* 6 (12):36–48.

Lockhart, Darrell B. 2018. "The Semiotics of Djudeo-Espanyol in Recent Works by Myriam Moscona." *México Interdisciplinario* 7 (14):110–21.

López, Brenda V de. 1993. *Lenguaje fronterizo en obras de autores uruguayos*. 2nd ed. Montevideo: Editorial Nordan-Comunidad.

Lucas, Ian. 1997. "The Color of His Eyes: Polari and the Sisters of Perpetual Indulgence." In *Queerly Phrased: Language, Gender, and Sexuality*, edited by Anna and Kira Hall Livia, 85–94. Oxford: Oxford University Press.

Lynch, Andrew, and Kim Potowski. 2014. "La valoración del habla bilingüe en los Estados Unidos: Fundamentos sociolingüísticos y pedagógicos en 'Hablando bien se entiende la gente.'" *Hispania* 97:32–46.

Makoni, Sinfree, and Pennycook Alastair. 2006. *Disinventing and Reconstituting Languages, Bilingual Education and Bilingualism*. Clevedon, UK: Multilingual Matters. Book.

Mann, Paul. "Translating Zukofsky's Catullus." *Translation Review* 21–22:3–9. doi: http://dx.doi.org/10.1080/07374836.1986.10523383.

Marcus, Jacob Rader, and Marc Saperstein. 2015. *The Jews in Christian Europe: A Source Book, 315–1791*. Pittsburgh: Hebrew Union College Press.

Mariana Winikor, Wagner. 2016. "Living the Border: Social and Cultural Practices from the Sidelines." *Estudios Fronterizos* 17 (34):100–16. doi: 10.21670/ref.2016.34.a06.

Markova, Alla N. 2008. *Beginner's Ladino with 2 Audio CDs*. New York: Hippocrene Books.

McClure, Erica, and Montserrat Mir. 1995. "Spanish-English Codeswitching in the Mexican and Spanish Press." *Journal of Linguistic Anthropology* 5 (1):33–50.

McMorris, Mark. 2006. "Zukofsky's Bilingual Catullus: Theoretical Articulations upon the Translator's Method." *Paideuma* 35:217–49.

Melammed, Renee Levine. 2013. "An Ode to Salonika: The Ladino verses of Bouena Sarfatty."

Meléndez, Edgardo. 2017. *Sponsored Migration: The State and Puerto Rican Postwar Migration to the United States*, edited by Frederick Luis Aldama and Loudes Torres, *Global Latin/o Americas*. Columbus: Ohio State University Press.

Mena Segarra, Celiar Fernando Enrique. 2004. *Aparicio Saravia: Las últimas patriadas*. Montevideo: Ed. de la Banda Oriental.

Mendizabal, Amaya. 2015. "Miami Sound Machine Drove the Latin Beat." *Billboard*, 152.

Menocal, María Rosa. 2002. *The Ornament of the World: How Muslims, Jews, and Christians Created a Culture of Tolerance in Medieval Spain*. Boston: Little, Brown and Co.

Meylaerts, Reine. 2006. "Heterolingualism in/and Translation: How Legitimate Are the Other and His/Her Language? An Introduction." *Target* 18 (1):1–15. doi: 10.1075/target.18.1.02mey.

Miller, Royce W. 1993. "The Sephardim and Their Folk Literature." *Revue des études juives* 152:193–9.

Minervini, Laura. 2006. "El desarrollo histórico del judeoespañol." *Revista internacional de lingüística iberoamericana* 4 (2):13–34.

Minervini, Laura. 2008. "Formación de la lengua sefardí." In *Sefardíes: literatura y lengua de una nación dispersa: XV Curso de Cultura Hispanojudia y Sefardí*, edited by Ana Riaño, Iacob M. Hassán, Ricardo Izquierdo Benito, and Elena Romero, 25–49. Toledo: Universidad de Castilla-La Mancha.

Minervini, Laura. 2012. "La documentación judeo-aragonesa medieval: nuevas publicaciones y nuevas interpretaciones." *eHumanista* 20:204–14.

Minervini, Laura. 2013. "Los estudios del español sefardí (judeoespañol, ladino). Aportaciones, métodos y problemas actuales." *Estudis Romanics* 35:323–34. doi: 10.2436/20.2500.01.129.

Mirrer, Louise. "Reinterpreting an Ancient Legend: The Judeo-Spanish Version of the Rape of Lucretia." *Journal: Prooftexts* 6 (2):117–30.

Monegal, José. 1958. *Memorias de Juan Pedro Camargo*. Montevideo: Ediciones de la Banda Oriental.

Montalvo Arts Center. n.d. "Susana Chávez-Silverman." montalvoarts.org/participants/susana_chavez_silverman/.

Mora, G. Cristina. 2014. *Making Hispanics: How Activists, Bureaucrats & Media Constructed a New American*. Chicago & London: University of Chicago Press.

Morales, Manuel. 2018. "Nace la academia 'nasionala' del ladino en Israel." *El País*, February 20, 2018. https://elpais.com/cultura/2018/02/20/actualidad/1519127816_439498.html.

Morales, Manuel. 2019. "La Academia del ladino encalla antes de nacer." *El País*, 20 de marzo. https://elpais.com/cultura/2019/03/20/actualidad/1553106813_333945.html.

Morante, Elsa, and William Weaver. 1977. *History: A Novel*. London: A. Lane.

Moreno Fernández, Francisco. 2009. *La lengua española en su geografía*. Madrid: Arco Libros.

Motschenbacher, Heiko, and Martin Stegu. 2013. "Introduction: Queer Linguistic Approaches to discourse.(Special Issue: Queer Linguistics)." *Discourse & Society* 24 (5):519–35.

Moyna, María Irene, and Magdalena Coll. 2008. "A Tale of Two Borders: 19th Century Language Contact in Southern California and Northern Uruguay." *Studies in Hispanic and Lusophone Linguistics* 1 (1):105–38. doi: 10.1515/shll-2008-1007.

Museu da Língua Portuguesa. 2023. São Paulo.

Muysken, Pieter. 2000. *Bilingual Speech: A Typology of Code-Mixing*. Cambridge: Cambridge University Press.

Myers, David N. 2006. "Language and the Jews." *The Jewish Quarterly Review* 96:467–9. doi: 10.1080/01441640320000070891.

Nash, Rose. 1971. "Englañol: More Language Contact in Puerto Rico." *American Speech* 46 (1/2):106–22.

Navon, Yitzhak. 2011. "The Israeli National Authority for Ladino and Its Culture." *European Judaism* 44 (1):4–8.

Newman, David. 2010. "Interview: Susana Chávez-Silverman Speaks with David Newman." *New Delta Review*, 223–33.

Nida, Eugene. [1964] 2000. "Principles of Correspondence." In *Translation Studies Reader*, edited by Lawrence Venuti, 126–40. London: Routledge.

Nixon, Darren. 2009. "'I Can't Put a Smiley Face On': Working-Class Masculinity, Emotional Labour and Service Work in the 'New Economy'." *Gender, Work and Organization* 16 (3):300–22.

O'Grady, William D., and John Archibald. 2016. *Contemporary Linguistic Analysis: An Introduction*. 8th ed. Toronto: Pearson Canada.

Oboler, Suzanne. 2005. *Ethnic labels, Latino Lives: Identity and the Politics of (Re)presentation in the United States*. Minneapolis: University of Minnesota Press.

Olivas, Daniel A. 2010. "Interview with Susana Chávez-Silverman." *La Bloga*, April 19, 2010. labloga.blogspot.ca/2010/04/interview-with-susana-chavez-silverman.html.

Oscar Paredes, Pando. 1995. "Fronteras, cultura e integración en Madre de Dios." *Crónicas Urbanas* (4):15–20.

Osorio, Araceli. 2010. *The Role of Spanglish in the Social and Academic Lives of Second Generation Latino Students: Students' and Parents' Perspectives*. Edited by Sedique Popal. Ann Arbor, MI: ProQuest Dissertations Publishing.

Otheguy, Ricardo. 2009. "El llamado espanglish." In *Enciclopedia del español en los EEUU*, edited by Humberto López-Morales, 222–47. Madrid: Instituto Cervantes & Ed. Santillana.

Otheguy, Ricardo, and Nancy Stern. 2011. "On So-Called Spanglish." *International Journal of Bilingualism* 15 (1):85–100. doi: 10.1177/1367006910379298.

Otheguy, R., Ofelia García, and Wallis Reid. 2015. "Clarifying Translanguaging and Deconstructing Named Languages. A Perspective from Linguistics." *Applied Linguistics Review* 6 (3):281–307.

Owens, David James. 1993. "Spanish—Portuguese Territorial Rivalry in Colonial Río de la Plata." In *Yearbook (Conference of Latin Americanist Geographers)*, 15–24. Austin, TX: University of Texas Press.

Oxford University. 2017a. Polysemy. In *Oxford Dictionary*. Oxford: Oxford University Press.

Oxford University. 2017b. Syncretism. In *Oxford Dictionary*. Oxford: Oxford University Press.

Ozick, Cynthia. 1997. *The Puttermesser Papers*. New York: Knopf.

Pac, Teresa. 2012. "The English-Only Movement in the US and the World in the Twenty-First Century." *Perspectives on Global Development and Technology* 11:192–210. doi: 10.1163/156914912X620833.

Papastergiadis, Nikos. 2015. "Tracing Hybridity in Theory." In *Debating Cultural Hybridity: Multi-Cultural Identities and the Politics of Anti-Racism*, edited by Pnina Werbner and Tariq Modood, 257–81. London; New Jersey: Zed Books.

Pardo, Luis, and Juan Carlos Muñoz. 2004. *Rebelde*. Mexico: Canal de las Estrellas.

Payson, Alida. 2017. "Dirty Pretty Language: Translation and the Borders of English." *TranscUlturAl* 9 (2):13–31.

Penny, Ralph. 2002. *A History of the Spanish Language*. 2nd ed. Cambridge: Cambridge University Press.

Penny, Ralph. 2003. *Variation and Change in Spanish*. Cambridge: Cambridge University Press.

Pérez Firmat, Gustavo. 1995. *Bilingual Blues*. Tempe, Arizona: Bilingual Press/Editorial Bilingüe.

Pérez, Daniel Enrique. 2009. *Rethinking Chicana/o and Latina/o Popular Culture*. New York: Palgrave Macmillan.

Pérez, Joseph. 2007. *History of a Tragedy: The Expulsion of the Jews from Spain*. Edited by Anne J. Cruz, *Hispanisms*. Urbana, IL: University of Illinois Press.

Phaf-Rheinberger, Ineke. 2010. "La asimetría poblacional y el 'round-trip ticket': sobre el discurso de ser puertorriqueño." *Iberoamericana* 10 (39):267–81.

Polinsky, Maria, and Olga Kagan. 2007. "Heritage Languages: In the 'Wild' and in the Classroom." *Language and Linguistics Compass* 1 (5):368–95. doi: 10.1111/j.1749-818X.2007.00022.x.

Pomerleau, Marc. 2017. "La traduction comme instrument paradiplomatique: langues, publics cibles et discours indépendantiste en Catalogne." PhD, Département de linguistique et de traduction, Université de Montréal.

Pomona College. "Susana Chávez-Silverman." www.pomona.edu/directory/people/susana-ch%C3%A1vez-silverman.

Poplack, Shana. 1981. "Syntactic Structure and Social Function of Codeswitching." In *Latino Language and Communicative Behavior*, edited by Richard P. Durán, 169–84. Norwood: Ablex.

Potowski, Kim. 2015. "Ethnolinguistic Identities and Ideologies among Mexicans, Puerto Ricans, and 'MexiRicans' in Chicago." In *A Sociolinguistics of Diaspora: Latino Practices, Identities and Ideologies*, edited by Rosina Márquez Reiter and Luisa Martín Rojo, 13–30. New York: Routledge.

Potowski, Kim, and Naomi Shin. 2019. *Gramática española: Variación social*. Oxon: Routledge.

Poveda, José. 2011. Personal Correspondence. Gran Canaria.

Preciado, Paul. 2018. *Countersexual Manifesto*. Translated by Kevin Gerry Dunn. New York: Columbia University Press.

Puig, Claudia. 2018. "Latino Artists and Cultural Leaders Weigh in on How 'Coco' Got It Right." *Los Angeles Times*, February 22. http://www.latimes.com/entertainment/movies/la-ca-mn-coco-latino-culture-20180222-story.html.

Pym, Anthony. 2000. *Negotiating the Frontier: Translators and Intercultures in Hispanic History*. London: Routledge.

Pym, Anthony. 2009. *Exploring Translation Theories*. 2nd ed. London: Routledge.

Pym, Anthony. 2011a. "Translation Research Terms: A Tentative Glossary for Moments of Perplexity and Dispute." *Translation Research Projects* 3:75–99.

Pym, Anthony. 2011b. "The Translator as Non-Author, and I Am Sorry about That." In *The Translator as Author. Perspectives on Literary Translation*, edited by Claudia Buffagni, Beatrice Garzelli, and Serenella Zanotti, 31–44. Münster: LIT Verlag.

Pym, Anthony. 2012. *On Translator's Ethics. Principles for Mediation between Cultures*. Amsterdam: John Benjamins Publishing.

Quintana, Aldina. 2006. "Variación diatópica en judeoespañol." *Revista Internacional de Lingüística Iberoamericana* 4:77–97.

Rafael, Vicente L. 1988. *Contracting Colonialism: Translation and Christian Conversion in Tagalog Society under Early Spanish Rule*. Ithaca: Cornell University Press.

Raley, Rita. 2010. "Machine Translation and Global English." In *Critical Readings in Translation Studies*, edited by Mona Baker, 417–34. New York: Routledge.

Rangel, Natalie, Verónica Loureiro-Rodríguez, and María Irene Moyna. 2015. "'Is That What I Sound Like When I Speak?' Attitudes towards Spanish, English, and Code-Switching in Two Texas Border Towns*." *Spanish in Context* 12 (2):177–98.

Rawn, Jonathan David. 2008. *Discovering Gematria: Foundational Exegesis and Primary Dictionary*. 1st ed. Hixson: Gematria Publishing.

Reagan, Timothy. 2019. *Linguistic Legitimacy and Social Justice*. Cham, Switzerland: Palgrave Macmillan.

Redacción Clarín. 2005. "Cultura: el traductor es el poeta mendocino Carlos Levy: El Martín Fierro fue traducido al antiguo idioma judeoespañol [sic]." *Clarín*, 15 de agosto. https://www.clarin.com/ediciones-anteriores/martin-fierro-traducido-antiguo-idioma-judeospanol_0_SJgS8xOkRFl.html.

Reiss, Katharina. 2000. "Type, Kind and Individuality of Text: Decision Making in Translation." In *The Translation Studies Reader*, edited by Lawrence Venuti, 160–71. New York: Routledge.

Remeseira, Claudio Iván. 2009. "Is New York the New Center of Latin American Literary Culture ?" *Salmagundi* 162 (163):182–91.

Renard, Raymond. 1965. "Le système phonique du judéo-espagnol." *Revue de phonétique appliquée* 1:23–33.

Renard, Raymond. 1966. "L'influence du mode de transcription sur le système phonique du judéo-espagnol." *Revue de phonétique appliquée* 2:35–40.

Robinson, Douglas. 1997. *Translation and Empire*. Manchester: St-Jerome.

Robinson, Douglas. 2019. *Transgender, Translation, Translingual Address*. New York: Bloomsbury.

Robinson, Joanna. Nov., 16 2016. "How Pacific Islanders Helped Disney's *Moana* Find Its Way." *Vanity Fair*. https://www.vanityfair.com/hollywood/2016/11/moana-oceanic-trust-disney-controversy-pacific-islanders-polynesia.

Rodrigue, Aron. 1987. "The Alliance Israélite Universelle and the Attempt to Reform Jewish Religious and Rabbinical Instruction in Turkey." In *L'Alliance dans les communautés du bassin méditerranéen à la fin du 19ème siècle et son influence sur la situation sociale et culturelle: actes du deuxième Congrès International de recherche du patrimoine des juifs sépharades et d'Orient 1985, edited by Simon Schwarzfuchs, 53–70. Jerusalem: Misgav Yerushalayim.

Rodrigue, Aron. 2002. "The Rise and Fall of Ladino Literary Culture." In *Cultures of the Jews: A New History*, edited by David Biale, 141–63. New York: Schocken Books.

Rodrigue, Aron. 2005. "Jewish Enlightenment and Nationalism in the Ottoman Balkans: Barukh Mitrani in Edirne in the Second Half of the Nineteenth Century." *Princeton Papers* 12:127–43.

Rodrigue, Aron, Sarah Abrevaya Stein, and Isaac Jerusalmi. 2012. *A Jewish Voice from Ottoman Salonica: The Ladino Memoir of Sa'adi Besalel a-Levi*. Stanford: Stanford University Press.

Rodrigue, Aron, and Sarah Abrevaya Stein. 2012. *A Jewish Voice from Ottoman Salonica: The Ladino Memoir of Sa'adi Besalel a-Levi*. Stanford: Stanford University Press.

Rodríguez-González, Eva, and M. Carmen Parafita-Couto. 2012. "Calling for Interdisciplinary Approaches to the Study of 'Spanglish' and Its Linguistic Manifestations." *Hispania* 95 (3):461–80.

Rogers, Margaret. 2015. *Specialized Translation: Shedding the "Non-Literary" Tag*. London: Palgrave Macmillan.

Rojas Molina, Sandra Liliana. 2008. "Aproximacion al estudio de las actitudes linguisticas en un contexto de contacto de espanol y portugues en el area urbana trifronteriza Brasil-Colombia-Peru." *Forma y Funcion* (21):251.

Romero, Elena. 1993. "Relatos en lengua sefardí sobre el rey Salomón." In *Judentum-Ausblicke und Einsichten*, edited by Clemens Thoma and Kurt Schubert, 185–200. Frankfurt am Main: P Lang.

Rosa, Jonathan. 2015. "Nuevo Chicago? Language, Diaspora, and Latina/o Panethnic Formations." In *A Sociolinguistics of Diaspora: Latino Practices, Identities and Ideologies*, edited by Rosina Márquez Reiter and Luisa Martín Rojo, 31–47. New York: Routledge.

Rosa, Jonathan. 2019. *Looking like a Language, Sounding like a Race: Raciolinguistic Ideologies and the Learning of Latinidad*. Oxford: Oxford University Press.

Rosten, Leo, and Lawrence Bush. 2001. *The New Joys of Yiddish*. New York: Three Rivers Press.

Roth, Cecil. 1932. *A History of the Marranos*. Philadelphia: Jewish Publication Society of America.

Roth, Norman. 1976. "What Constitutes Sephardic Literature?" In *From Iberia to Diaspora: Studies in Sephardic History and Culture*, edited by Yedida Kalfon Stillman and Norman A. Stillman. Leiden: Brill.

Ruiz, Michelle. 2017. "Why *Coco* Just Might Be the Most Important Film of the Year." *Vogue*, November 27.

Ryan, Camille. 2011. Language Use in the United States: 2011. In *American Community Survey Reports*, edited by US Census Bureau. Washington, DC: US Government.

Sachar, Howard. 1998. *Farewell España*. New York: Random House.

Sadowski-Smith, Claudia. 2008. *Border Fictions: Globalization, Empire, and Writing at the Boundaries of the United States*. Charlottesville, VA: University of Virginia Press.

Said, Edward W. 1979. *Orientalism*. 25 Anniv. ed. New York: Random House.

Sailaja, Pingali. 2011. "Hinglish: Code-Switching in Indian English." *ELT Journal* 65 (4):473–80. doi: 10.1093/elt/ccr047.

Sánchez-Boudy, José. 1989. *Diccionario de cubanismos más usuales: (cómo habla el cubano)*. Miami: Universal.

Santacruz, Daniel. 2017. "Aki Yerushalayim, Oldest All-Ladino Magazine in the World Closes after 37 Years." eSefarad. https://esefarad.com/?p=76257.

Sarreal, Julia. 2011. "Disorder, Wild Cattle, and a New Role for the Missions: The Banda Oriental, 1776–1786." *The Americas* 67 (4):517–45. doi: doi.org/10.1353/tam.2011.0073.

Saul, Mahir. 1983. "The Mother Tongue of the Polyglot: Cosmopolitism and Nationalism among the Sephardim of Istanbul." *Anthropological Linguistics* 25 (3):326–58.

Sayer, Peter. 2008. "Demystifying Language Mixing: Spanglish in School." *Journal of Latinos and Education* 7 (2):94–112.

Schleiermacher, Friedrich. 2004. "On the Different Methods of Translating." In *The Translation Studies Reader*, edited by Lawrence Venuti, 43–63. London: Routledge.

Schroeter, Daniel. 2002. *The Sultan's Jew: Morocco and the Sephardi World*. Stanford, CA: Stanford University Press.

Schwarzwald, Ora R. 2004. "Judaeo-Spanish Studies." In *The Oxford Handbook of Jewish Studies*, edited by Martin Goodman, Jeremy Cohen, and David Sorkin, 572–600. Oxford; New York: Oxford University Press.

Seloni, Lisya, and Yusuf Sarfati. 2013. "(Trans)national Language Ideologies and Family Language Practices: A Life History Inquiry of Judeo-Spanish in Turkey." *Lang Policy* 12:7–26.

Sephiha, Haïm Vidal. 1981. "El ladino verdadero o judeoespañol calco, lengua litúrgica." In *Actas de las Jornadas de Estudios Sefardíes*, edited by Antonio Viudas Camarasa, 15–29. Cáceres, España: Universidad de Extremadura, Instituto de Ciencias de la Educación.

Sephiha, Haïm Vidal. 1986. "Le judeu-espagnol: un siècle de gallomanie." *CRISOL* 4:14–27.

Sephiha, Haïm Vidal. 2001a. "Ladino: Hebrew Dressed up in Spanish or Paradise Calqued." *Faits de langues* 18:191–200.

Sephiha, Haïm Vidal 1991. "Reponse a monsieur Paul Wexler." *Zeitschrift für romanische Philologie* 107 (1–2):167–72.

Sephiha, Haïm Vidal 2001b. "Le ladino: de l'hébrue habillé d'espagnol ou le paradis calqué." *Faits de langues* 18:191–200.

Sephiha, Haïm Vidal, and Bruce Mitchell. 2001. "The Instruction of Judeo-Spanish in Europe." *Shofar: An Interdisciplinary Journal of Jewish Studies* 19:58–70.

Severo, Fabián. 2010. *Noite nu norte. Poemas en Portuñol (first edition)*. Montevideo: Ediciones del Rincón.

Severo, Fabián. 2015. *Viralata*. Montevideo: Rumbo Editorial.
Severo, Fabián. 2017. *Noite nu norte (second edition)*. Montevideo: Rumbo Editorial.
Severo, Fabián. 2022. *Noite nu Norte (third edition)*. Montevideo: Estuario Editora.
Shakespeare, William, and Ilan Stavans. 2016. "Hamlet, Translated into Spanglish." Literary Hub. https://lithub.com/hamlet-translated-into-spanglish/.
Shandler, Jeffrey. 2004. "Postvernacular Yiddish: Language as Performance Art." *TDR (The Drama Review)* 48:19–43. doi: papers3://publication/uuid/5DF9E1F8-667D-4394-8982-61ADB45BE7B2.
Silva, Daniel do Nascimento e, and Adriana Carvalho Lopes. 2018. "'Yo hablo un perfeito portuñol': Indexicalidade, ideologia linguística e desafios da fronteira a políticas linguísticas uniformizadoras." *Revista da Abralin* 17 (2):144–81.
Simões Lopes Neto, João, and Leo Kades. 2015. *Lendas Do Sul*. Balneário Rincão: Grupo Oxigênio Ltda-ME.
Simon, Sherry. 1997. "Translation, Postcolonialism and Cultural Studies." *Meta: Journal des traducteurs* 42 (2):462–77. doi: 10.7202/1024517ar.
Simon, Sherry. 1999. Translating and Interlingual Creation in the Contact Zone: Border Writing in Quebec. In *Post-Colonial Translation: Theory and Practice*, edited by Susan (ed. and introd.) Bassnett and Harish (ed. and introd.) Trivedi. London, England: Routledge.
Smead, Robert N., and J. Halvor Clegg. English Calques in Chicano Spanish. In *Spanish in Contact: Issues in Bilingualism*, edited by Ana Roca and John B. Jensen. Somerville, MA: Cascadilla.
Snell-Hornby, Mary. 2006. *The Turns of Translation Studies*. Amsterdam: John Benjamins Publishing.
Soyer, François. 2008. "King Manuel I and the Expulsion of the Castilian *Conversos* and Muslims from Portugal in 1497: New Perspectives." *Cadernos de Estudos Sefarditas* 8:33–62.
Spivak, Gayatri. 1985. "Three Women's Texts and a Critique of Imperialism." *Critical Inquiry*. doi: 10.1086/448328.
Spivak, Gayatri. 1993. "The Politics of Translation." In *Outside in the Teaching Machine*. New York; London: Routledge.
Spivak, Gayatri. 2001. "From a Critique of Postcolonial Reason." In *The Norton Anthology of Theory and Criticism*, edited by Vincent B. Leitch, William E. Cain, Laurie Finke, Barbara Johnson, John McGowan, and Jeffrey J. Williams, 2197–11. New York: W.W. Norton & Co.
Spivak, Gayatri. 2005. "Translating into English." In *Nation, Language and the Ethics of Translation*, edited by Sandra Bermann and Michael Wood, 93–110. Princeton, NJ: Princeton University Press.
Spivak, Gayatri. 2010. "Translating in a World of Languages." *Profession* 2010 (1):35–43.

Spyra, Ania. "Language, Geography, Globalisation: Susana Chavez-Silverman's Rejection of Translation in Killer Crónicas: Bilingual Memories." In *Literature, Geography, Translation: Studies in World Writing*, edited by Cecilia Alvstad, Stefan Helgesson, and David Watson, 198–208. Cambridge: Cambridge Scholars.

Stavans, Ilan. 1996. "Introduction to the Hispanic Diaspora." *The Massachusetts Review* 37:317–22.

Stavans, Ilan. 2000a. "Life in the Hyphen." In *The Essential Ilan Stavans*, 3–25. New York; London: Routledge.

Stavans, Ilan. 2000b. "The Sounds of Spanglish." In *The Essential Ilan Stavans*, 26–40. New York; London: Routledge.

Stavans, Ilan. 2000c. "Tickling the Tongue." *World Literature Today* 74 (3):555–8.

Stavans, Ilan. 2003. *Spanglish: The Making of a New American Language*. New York: Harper Perennial.

Stavans, Ilan. 2004. "*Don Quijote* in Spanglish: Translation and Appropriation." *TTR: traduction, terminologie, rédaction* XVII (1):183–9.

Stavans, Ilan. 2008a. *Resurrecting Hebrew*. New York: Schocken.

Stavans, Ilan. 2008b. *Spanglish*. Westport, CT: Greenwood Press.

Stavans, Ilan, and Diana de Armas Wilson. 2016. "Translating Don Quixote: A Conversation." *Translation Review* 94:1–10. doi: 10.1080/07374836.2016.1151731.

Stein, Sarah Abrevaya. 2002. "Introduction 'Ladino in Print.'" *Jewish History* 16:225–33.

Stein, Sarah Abrevaya. 2006. "Asymmetric Fates: Secular Yiddish and Ladino Culture in Comparison." *Jewish Quarterly Review* 96:498–509. doi: 10.1353/jqr.2006.0049.

Stein, Sarah Abrevaya. 2016. *Extraterritorial Dreams: European Citizenship, Sephardi Jews, and the Ottoman Twentieth Century*. Chicago: University of Chicago Press.

Stillman, Norman A. 2005. "The Judeo-Arabic Heritage." In *Sephardic & Mizrahi Jewry: From the Golden Age of Spain to Modern Times*, edited by Zion Zohar, 40–54. New York: New York University Press.

Stoltz Chinchilla, Norma, and Nora Hamilton. 2004. "Central American Immigrants: Diverse Populations, Changing Communities." In *The Columbia History of Latinos in the United States since 1960*, edited by David G. Gutiérrez, 187–228. New York: Columbia University Press.

Sturge, Kate. 2007. *Representing Others: Translation, Ethnography and the Museum*. Edited by Theo Hermans, *Translation Theories Explored*. Manchester: St. Jerome.

Sturza, Eliana Rosa. 2004. "Fronteiras e práticas lingüísticas: um olhar sobre o portunhol." *Revista Internacional de Lingüística Iberoamericana* 2 (1 [3]):151–60.

Susam-Sarajeva, Sebnem. 2002. "A 'Multilingual' and 'International' Translation Studies?" In *Cross-Cultural Transgressions. Research Models in Translation Studies. Historical and Ideological Issues*, edited by Theo Hermans, 193–207. Manchester: St. Jerome.

Tagliamonte, Sali A., and Alexandra D'Arcy. 2009. "Peaks beyond Phonology: Adolescence, Incrementation, and Language Change." *Language* 85 (1):58–108.

Taylor, Brandon. 2020. *Real Life: A Novel*. New York: Riverhead Books.

Taylor, Nick, and Jeffery S. McQuillen. 2018. "Hispanic Consumers' Preference for Spanglish in Print and Television Advertisements." *International Journal of Innovative Research & Development* 7 (2):239–45.

Teyssier, Paul. 2005. *A língua de Gil Vicente*. Lisboa: Impresna Nacional - Casa da Moeda.

The National WWII Museum. 2017. "By the Numbers: The Holocaust." www.nationalww2museum.org/learn/education/for-students/ww2-history/ww2-by-the-numbers/holocaust.html.

Tolentino, Jia. 2018. "'Coco,' A Story about Borders and Love, Is a Definitive Movie for This Moment." *The New Yorker*.

Toribio Almeida, Jacqueline. 2002. "Code-Switching among US Latinos." *International Journal of the Sociology of Language* 158:530–52.

Toribio, Almeida Jacqueline, and Edward J. Rubin. 1996. "Code-Switching in Generative Grammar." In *Spanish in Contact: Issues in Bilingualism*, edited by Ana Roca and John B. Jensen, 203–26. Somerville: Cascadilla.

Torres-Padilla, José L. 2007. "When Hybridity Doesn't Resist: Giannina Braschi's Yo-Yo Boing!" In *Complicating Constructions: Race, Ethnicity and Hybridity in American Texts*, edited by David S. Goldstein and Audrey B. Thacker. Seattle: University of Washington Press.

Torres, Lourdes. 2005. "Don Quixote in Spanglish: traducttore, traditore?" *Romance Quarterly* 52 (4):328–34.

Torres, Lourdes. 2007. "In the Contact Zone: Code-Switching Strategies by Latino/a Writers." *MELUS* 32 (1):75–96.

Toury, Gideon. 1995. *Descriptive Translation Studies and Beyond*. Amsterdam, Philadelphia: John Benjamins Publishing Co.

Train, Robert W. 2013. "Becoming Bilingual, Becoming Ourselves: Archival Memories of Spanglish in Early Californian Epistolary Texts." *Hispania: A Journal Devoted to the Teaching of Spanish and Portuguese* 96 (3):438–9.

Trudell, Barbara. 2014. "The Multilingual Education (MLE) Network Phenomenon: Advocacy and Action for Minoritized Language Communities." *Multilingual Education* 4 (1):1–11. doi: 10.1186/s13616-014-0017-y.

Tymoczko, Maria. 1999a. "Post-Colonial Writing and Literary Translation." In *Post-Colonial Translation: Theory and Practice*, edited by Susan Bassnett and Harish Trivedi, 19–40. London: Routledge.

Tymoczko, Maria. 1999b. *Translation in a Postcolonial Context: Early Irish Literature in English Translation*. Manchester: St. Jerome.

Tymoczko, Maria. 2003. "Translation, Ideology, and Creativity." *Linguistica Antverpiensia* 2:27–45.

Tymoczko, Maria. 2010. *Translation, Resistance, Activism*. Amherst: University of Massachusetts Press.
Ugwunov, Reggie. 2017. "How Pixar Made Sure *Coco* Was Culturally Conscious." *The Independent*, November 29.
University of California (System) Academic Senate. 1989. "1989, University of California: In Memoriam." University Archives, The Bancroft Library, UC Berkeley.
Unkrich, Lee. 2017. Coco. Walt Disney Studios Motion Pictures.
Unkrich, Lee. 2018. Viva - A Vida é Uma Festa. Walt Disney Studios Motion Pictures.
Valdés, Guadalupe. 2000. "The Teaching of Heritage Languages: An Introduction for Slavic-Teaching Professionals." In *The Learning and Teaching of Slavic Languages and Cultures*, edited by Olga and Benjamin Rifkin Kagan, 375–403. Bloomington, IN: Slavica.
Valdez, Luis. 1994. *Early Works: Actos, Bernabé, Pensamiento Serpentino*. Houston: Arte Público Press.
Van Rooten, Luis d'Antin. 1993. *Mots d'heures: gousses, rames: the d'Antin manuscript*. London: Grafton.
Varsi de López, Brenda. 1967. *Lenguaje fronterizo en obras de autores uruguayos*. Montevideo: Comunidad del Sur.
Venuti, Lawrence. 1998. *The Scandals of Translation: Towards an Ethics of Difference*. London: Routledge.
Venuti, Lawrence. 2000a. *Translation Studies Reader*. Edited by Lawrence Venuti. 1st ed. London: Routledge.
Venuti, Lawrence. 2000b. "Translation, Community, Utopia." In *The Translation Studies Reader*, edited by Lawrence Venuti, 468–88. New York: Routledge.
Venuti, Lawrence. 2005. "Translation, History, Narrative." *Meta: Journal des traducteurs* 50 (3):800–16. doi: 10.7202/011597ar.
Venuti, Lawrence. 2008. *The Translator's Invisibility: A History of Translation*. London: Routledge.
Venuti, Lawrence. 2013. *Translation Changes Everything: Theory and Practice*. London: Routledge.
Vermeer, Hans J. 2000. "Skopos and Commission in Translational Action." In *Translation Studies Reader*, edited by Lawrence Venuti, 221–32. London: Routledge.
Vianna, Helio. 1972. *História do Brasil: Período colonial e monarquia, Vol 2*. São Paulo: Edições Melhoramentos.
Vieira, Else Riveiro Pires. 1999. "Liberating Calibans: Readings of Antropofagia and Haroldo de Campos' poetics of transcreation." In *Postcolonial Translation: Theory and Practice*, edited by Susan Bassnett and Harish Trivedi, 95–113. London: Routledge.
Villa, Laura. 2013. "The Officialization of Spanish in Mid-Nineteenth-Century Spain: The Academy's Authority." In *A Political History of Spanish: The Making of a Language*, edited by José Del Valle, 93–105. Cambridge: Cambridge University Press.

Villanueva, Alberto. 1991. "Poesía reciente en el Uruguay (1960–1990)." *Iberoromania* 1991 (34):131–48. https://doi.org/10.1515/iber.1991.1991.34.131.

Voellmer, Elena, and Patrick Zabalbeascoa. 2014. "How heterolingual can a dubbed film be? Language combinations and national traditions as determining factors." *Linguistica Antverpiensia* 13 (13):232–50.

von Flotow, Luise. 1997. *Translation and Gender: Translating in the "Era of Feminism"*. Ottawa: University of Ottawa Press and St-Jerome.

Waard, Jan de, Eugene Nida, and United Bible Societies. 1998. *From One Language to Another: Functional Equivalence in Bible Translating*. New York: United Bible Societies.

Wacks, David A. 2015. *Double Diaspora in Sephardic Literature: Jewish Cultural Prodcution before and after 1492*. Bloomington, IN: Indiana University Press.

Waltermire, Mark. 2012. "The Differential Use of Spanish and Portuguese along the Uruguayan-Brazilian Border." *International Journal of Bilingual Education and Bilingualism* 15 (5):509–31. doi: 10.1080/13670050.2011.637618.

Warner, Michael. 2000. *The Trouble with Normal: Sex, Politics, and the Ethics of Queer Life*. Cambridge, MA: Harvard University Press.

Wexler, Paul. 1977. "Ascertaining the Position of Judezmo within Ibero-Romance." *Vox Romanica* 36:162–95.

Wheeler, André. 2020. "'I Didn't Write This Book for the White Gaze': Black Queer Author Brandon Taylor on His Debut Novel." *The Guardian*, March 5, Culture. Accessed April 19, 2022. https://www.theguardian.com/books/2020/mar/05/brandon-taylor-author-real-life-interview.

Whigham, Thomas L. 2002. *The Paraguayan War*. Edited by Mark Maslowski and Peter Grimsley, *Studies in War, Society, and the Military*: *Vol. 1: Causes and Early Conduct*. Lincoln, NE: University of Nebraska Press.

Wirth-Nesher, Hana. 2006. *Call It English: The Languages of Jewish American Literature*. Princeton: Princeton University Press.

Wishnia, Kenneth. 1995. "'A Different Kind of Hell': Orality, Multilingualism, and American Yiddish in the Translation of Sholem Aleichem's 'Mister Boym in Klozet.'" *AJS Review* 20 (2):333–58.

Wolf, Michaela. 2002. "Culture as Translation – and Beyond: Ethnographic Models of Representation in Translation Studies." In *Crosscultural Transgressions: Research Models*, edited by Theo Hermans, 180–92. Manchester: St. Jerome.

Young, Vershawn Ashanti. 2009. "'Nah, We Straight': An Argument against Code Switching." *JAC* 29 (1–2):49–76.

Young, Vershawn Ashanti, Rusty Barrett, Y'Shanda Young-Rivera, Kim Brian Lovejoy, April Baker-Bell, and Victor Villanueva. 2014. *Other People's English: Code-Meshing, Code-Switching, and African American Literacy*. New York: Teachers College Press.

Zapf, Harald. 2006. "Ethnicity and Performance: Bilingualism in Spanglish Verse Culture." *Amerikastudien/American Studies* 51 (1), 13–27.

Zeitz, Eileen. 1978. *Mario Benedetti, novelista uruguayo: Crítica, crisis y acción*. Ann Arbor, MI: ProQuest Dissertations Publishing.

Zeller, Beatriz. 2000. "On Translation and Authorship." *Meta* 45 (1):134–9. doi: 10.7202/004640ar.

Zentella, Ana Cecilia. 1982. "Spanish and English in Contact in the United States: The Puerto Rican Experience." *Word* 33:41–57.

Zentella, Ana Cecilia. 2002. "Latin@ Languages and Identities." In *Latinos Remaking America*, edited by Marcelo M. Suárez-Orozco and Mariela Páez, 321–38. Berkley: University of California Press.

Zentella, Ana Cecilia. 2017. "Spanglish." In *Keywords for Latina/o Studies*, edited by Deborah R. Vargas, Nancy Raquel Mirabal, and Lawrence La Fountain-Stokes, 209–12. New York: New York University Press.

Zohar, Zion. 2005. *Sephardic and Mizrahi Jewry: From the Golden Age of Spain to Modern Times*. New York: New York University Press.

Zucker, George K. 2001. "Ladino, Judezmo, Spanyolit el Kasteyano Muestro." *Shofar: An Interdisciplinary Journal of Jewish Studies* 19 (4):4–14.

Zuckermann, Ghil'ad. 2003. "An Italo-Hebraic Bilingual Homophonous Poem." Digital Commons @ Butler University.

Index

Abruzzese language 102–3
African American Vernacular English (AAVE) 12, 15–16
Alliance Israelite Universelle (AIU) 65
Al-Andalus, Muslim rule in 62–3
Anzaldúa, Gloria 1, 3, 7–8, 18, 25, 29, 32–3, 35–6, 41–2, 41 n.11, 77, 80, 84, 91–2, 99, 108
Appiah, Kwame Anthony 103
Autoridad Nasionala del Ladino (ANL) 68

Bertolotti, Virginia 54
bilingualism 12, 26–7, 55, 55 n.7, 113
Border Commerce Portuñol 49–50
Borderlands/La Frontera: The New Mestiza (Anzaldúa) 35, 41, 91–2
Bourdieu, Pierre 5, 8–9
Bracero Program 30
Braschi, Giannini 39–40
Brown, Adrienne Maree 86–7
Bueno, Wilson 50–1, 85
Bunis, David M. 62
Butler, Judith 83

calques 25–6
Chavez-Silverman, Susana 7, 24, 39–43, 84, 92–3, 108, 110–11
Chicanx 34–5, 34 n.7, 41, 101
Chinese language 13
Coco (film) 100–1
code-switching 18, 24–5, 27, 42, 122–3
Coll, Magdalena 54
communicative accommodation theory (CAT) 49, 89–90, 120, 123
contact varieties 14–16, 46
costumbrismo 57, 80–2
Countersexual Manifesto (Preciado) 114
cross-over music 37–8
Cussel, Mattea 95

Dean, Tim 77
Deleuze, Gilles 106, 118

Démont, Marc 95, 101, 103
Derrick, Roshawnda A. 42–3
Diegues, Douglas 50–1
diglossia 15 n.5

emotional labor 3–5
Englañol 26–7
Englishes 102, 115
Estefan, Gloria 37
Etchemendi, Javier 59–60

Fanon, Frantz 80, 87
Fernández, María Jesús 7, 49

Garcia, Ofelia 112–13
Gauvin, Lise 6, 34, 105, 110–12, 118
gendered work 4
Great Migration 30
Greece 66–7
Grutman, R. 102–3
Guaraní language 51
Guattari, Félix 106, 118

Halberstam, Jack 83–4, 86, 96
Hebrew alphabet 65–6, 68
Heilbron, Johan 92–3
heritage language 69, 107–8
Hochschild, Arlie Russell 3–4
hybridity 1, 15, 121–2

Ibargoyen Islas, Saúl 57, 81, 85
Iberian language 63–4
immigration 23–4, 28, 31–2, 82

Judeo-Spanish 2, 9–10, 14–17, 61–4, 73–4, 90. *See also* Koén-Sarano, Matilda
  Alliance Israelite Universelle 65
  diaspora 63–4
  Hebrew alphabet 65–6, 68
  Ladino 64–5
  linguistic palliative care 69–73

Ottoman Empire and the Second
  World War Turkey 66–7
Sephardim 61–3, 65–7, 69
Visigoths 61–2
Western European colonization 65–6
Zionism 67–8

Kafka: Towards a Minor Literature
  (Deleuze and Guattari) 106–10
Kagan, Olga 107
Koén-Sarano, Matilda 6–7, 69, 73–4, 81,
  84–5, 96, 108, 110–11
  life and passion 70–3

Ladino 64–5
language 113 n.4, 119–21. *See also* Judeo-
  Spanish; Portuñol; Spanglish
  Abruzzese 102–3
  Chinese 13
  definitions for 119–20
  vs. dialect 10–13
  dominant 1, 3–4, 8, 19, 33–4, 36–7, 40,
    51, 57, 67, 82, 99, 102, 107, 109–11
  Guaraní 51
  Hebrew 65–6, 68
  heritage 69, 107–8
  Iberian 63–4
  and identity 41–2
  minoritized 1–4, 8, 81–2, 87, 90–1, 93,
    95–6, 103, 109, 111, 117
  mixing 14–17
  and self-identification 13–14
  Spanish 109
  Turkish 65–7
Larkosh, Christopher 96
lexicalizing language 120, 120 n.1
linguistic labor 2–5, 109. *See also*
  surconscience linguistique
  artificial 85–6
  emotional labor and gendered work
    3–6
  queer first wave 79–82
  to queerness 77–8, 86–7
  queer second wave 82–5
  translation of 90–104
Lipski, John M. 46, 48, 55
literary doulas 2–3, 8–10, 17, 92–3,
  109–11, 117

pleasure and 86–7
poststructuralism 78–9
queer second wave 84–5

Manifest Destiny 28–30
Manifesto of the Race *(Manifesto della
  razza)* 70
Mar paraguayo (Bueno) 51
Matilda. *See* Koén-Sarano, Matilda
minoritized language 1–4, 8, 81–2, 87,
  90–1, 93, 95–6, 103, 109, 111, 117
Montevideo 53–4, 58–9

Ottoman Sephardim. *See* Sephardim

Paraguayan Portuñol Salvaje 50–1
Pérez Firmat, Gustavo 36
performativity 83–4
*Pleasure Activism: The Politics of Feeling
  Good* (Brown) 86–7
Polinsky, Maria 107
Portuñol 2, 10, 45–7, 96, 108, 110
  Border Commerce Portuñol 49–50
  literature 59–60
  Paraguayan Portuñol Salvaje 50–1
  prose literature 57–8
  Spanish and 54–5
  Tourism Portuñol 47–9, 47 n.4
  Uruguayan 52–6
postcolonialism 78–81, 94, 121
poststructuralism 78–80, 82–3, 118
Preciado, Paul 84, 114

The Queer Art of Failure (Halberstam) 83
queer/queerness 51, 77–8
  liberation 78, 83–5, 96
  of linguistic labor 77–87
  of literary doulas 84–5
  women and 9–10, 92

raciolinguistic ideologies 11–12, 80
radical bilingualism 23–4, 39
Real Life (Taylor) 98–9
Rosa, Jonathan 25–7, 110, 113

self-identification 13–14
Sephardim 61–3, 65–7, 69
Severo, Fabián 6, 57–8, 60, 108, 110–11

sex/sexuality 77, 114
Shandler, Jeffrey 107
Shaul, Moshe 73
Spanglish 2, 23, 82
   and cross-over music 37–8
   English and 24–7
   english-spanish tension 32–3
   growth of 32–3
   history of 27–8
   linguistics of 23–7
   literary doulas and radical 41–3
   literature 33–4
   Manifest Destiny 28–30
   poetry 35–7
   postwar and cold war immigration 30–2
   prose in 38–41
   in theater 34–5
Spivak, Gayatri 87, 93
Stavans, Ilán 40, 85–6
surconscience linguistique 6–7, 58, 105, 108, 110–12, 115, 118
Susam-Sarajeva, Sebnem 103

Taylor, Brandon 98–9
thick translation (Appiah) 103
Torres, Lourdes 38–9, 38 n.8, 86
Tourism Portuñol 47–9, 47 n.4
translanguaging 18, 24, 46, 48–9, 105, 114, 123–4
translation, linguistic labor 90–104
translinguistics 18, 105, 112–16, 118
trans-prefix 113
Turkish language 65–7
Turkish Republic 66–7

Univision (broadcaster) 31
Uruguayan Portuñol 52–3, 81
   history of 53–6

Valdez, Luis 34–5, 81
Valens, Ritchie 34, 37
Visigoths 61–2

Zionism 67–8

www.ingramcontent.com/pod-product-compliance
Lightning Source LLC
LaVergne TN
LVHW020201230425
809262LV00003B/63